◆

SOME

GIRLS

◆

JILLIAN LAUREN

♦

SOME
GIRLS

♦

EBURY
PRESS

An Ebury Press book
Published by Random House Australia Pty Ltd
Level 3, 100 Pacific Highway, North Sydney NSW 2060
www.randomhouse.com.au

First published in the United States by Plume, a member of Penguin Group (USA) Inc.
in 2010.

First published in Australia by Ebury Press in 2010. This edition published in 2011.

Addresses for companies within the Random House Group can be found at
www.randomhouse.com.au/offices

National Library of Australia
Cataloguing-in-Publication Entry

Lauren, Jillian
Some girls: my life in a harem

ISBN 978 1 74275 036 1 (pbk).

Lauren, Jillian.
Actresses – United States – Biography.
Concubinage – Brunei.
Harems – Brunei.

791.43028092

Cover design by Christabella Designs
Cover photo courtesy Getty Images
Internal design by Catherine Leonardo; typeset in Cochin
Printed in Australia by Griffin Press, an accredited ISO AS/NZS 14001:2004
Environmental Management System printer

10 9 8 7 6 5 4 3 2 1

to Scott

love redeems all

acknowledgments

Special thanks to Becky Cole, Alexandra Machinist, Patti Smith, Jim Krusoe, Leonard Chang, Joe Gratziano, Anne Dailey, Colin Summers, Nell Scovell, Claire LaZebnik, the Writer's Sunget, Robert Morgan Fisher, Tammy Stoner, Ivan Sokolov, Suzanne Luke, Carol Allen, Catharine Dill, Amber Lasciak, R. P. Brink, the Wooster Group, Richard Foreman, Lindsay Davis, Sean Eden, Dr. Keely Kolmes, Julie Fogliano, Jennifer Erdagon, Jerry Stahl, Shawna Kenney, Bett Williams, Austin Young, Lily Burana, Lynnee Breedlove, Gabrielle Samuels, Sherri Carpenter, and, always, Scott Shriner.

Deepest gratitude to my family and to all who shared my story.

◆

SOME
GIRLS

◆

prologue

The Shah's wife was unfaithful to him, so he cut off her head and summarily declared all women to be evil and thereby deserving of punishment. Every night the Shah's grand vizier brought him a new virgin to marry and every morning the Shah had the woman executed. After too many of these bloody sunrises, the vizier's eldest and favorite daughter asked to be brought to the Shah as that night's offering. The grand vizier protested, but his daughter insisted, and this daughter was known throughout the kingdom for her powers of persuasion. At the end of the day, the Shah married the vizier's daughter while the vizier wept in his chambers, unable to watch.

At first, the daughter's wedding night was indistinguishable from the wedding nights of the other ill-fated virgins who had married the Shah before her, but as morning approached, the Shah's newest wife began to tell him a story. The story had not yet reached its conclusion when the pink light of dawn crept around the edges of the curtains. The Shah agreed to let the woman live for just one more day, because he couldn't bear to kill her before he learned the story's end.

The next night the woman finished that story, but before the sun rose over the dome of the palace mosque, she began another, equally as compelling as the last. The following one thousand and one nights each concluded with an unfinished story. By the end of this time, the Shah had fallen in love with the woman, and he spared her life, his heart mended and his faith in women restored.

This is, of course, the story of Scheherazade. It's the story of the storyteller. We lay our heads on the block and hope that you'll spare us, that you'll want another tale, that you'll love us in the end. We're looking for the story that will save our lives.

One thousand and one nights—nearly three years. That's about the span of this story. Will you listen? It's almost morning.

chapter 1

The day I left for Brunei I took the subway uptown to Beth Israel, schlepping behind me a
green flowered suitcase. The last time I had used the suitcase was when I left my room in NYU's Hayden Hall for
good, dragged all my crap out of the elevator and onto
the sidewalk, and cabbed it down to the Lower East Side,
where a friend of a friend had a room for rent. The time
before that, my mother had helped me unpack from it my
college-y fall clothes, labeled jammies, and ziplock bags
full of homemade chocolate-chip cookies. Each time I un-

zipped that suitcase it contained a whole different set of carefully folded plans. Each time I packed it back up I was on the run again.

I heaved the suitcase up three steps, rested, then heaved again until the rectangle of light at the top of the staircase opened out onto the bright buzz of Fourteenth Street. Underneath my winter overcoat the back of my shirt was damp with sweat. I hadn't thought I'd packed so much. I'd stood in front of my closet for hours wishing the perfect dress would magically materialize in a flurry of sparkles, would soar through the door, held aloft by a host of bluebirds. I was going to a royal ball, goddammit. I was traveling to meet a prince. Was my fairy godmother really going to leave me with such a lousy selection of clothes to choose from? Apparently she was.

In the end, I'd settled for packing two tailored skirt suits, three fifties prom dresses, an armful of vintage underwear-cum-outerwear, two hippie sundresses, a pair of leather hot pants, and some glittery leg warmers. All those not-quite-right clothes weighed too much. Or maybe it was the anvil of guilt I was carrying around for the act of desertion I was about to commit by abandoning my sick father in favor of an adventure in a foreign country. Either way, I'd yet to learn how to pack light. I pointed myself toward the hospital, merged into the stream of pedestrian traffic, and allowed the collective sense of purpose to pull me along.

My father was being operated on for a paraesophageal hiatal hernia, a condition in which part of the stomach squeezes through an opening in the diaphragm called the hiatus, landing it next to the esophagus. The danger is that the stomach can be strangled, cut off from its blood supply. Hiatal hernias occur most often in overweight people and people with extreme stress levels, both of which apply in my father's case. In 1991, the surgery for a hiatal hernia was dangerous and invasive, requiring a major incision that would travel from his sternum around to his back. I had originally told my mother I would be there to help out in any way that I could, but when the Brunei job came around, I changed my mind.

This compulsion of mine to be forever on the move may have been a genetic inevitability. My birth mother named me Mariah, after the song "They Call the Wind Mariah," from the Broadway musical *Paint Your Wagon*. Maybe she knew I'd soon sail away from her in the airborne cradle of a 747. The name didn't stick. My adoptive mother renamed me Jill Lauren after nothing at all; she just liked it. An amateur thespian herself, she thought Lauren could serve as a stage name if I ever needed one, and so it has.

I may have been named for the wind, but I am a triple fire sign, a child of heat and sun. I was born mid-August 1973 in Highland Park, Illinois. *Roe v. Wade* was decided on January 22, 1973, which would have placed my biological mother at nearly three months pregnant, still swaddled under the layers of down that insulated her from the Chicago winter. I don't know if she considered an abortion as her slim dancer's body morphed into something cumbersome and out of control, as her flighty boyfriend took their car and headed east one day and never came home again, as the wind off the water turned the slushy streets to sheets of ice and bit at any inch of exposed skin, made more raw and vulnerable with the pregnancy.

Seven hundred miles away, in the not-so-posh apartments across from Saint Barnabas Hospital in West Orange, New Jersey, a young stockbroker and his wife despaired of their childless state. It was a time rife with shady adoptions, sealed files, and what my father has referred to as "gray-market" transactions. My parents contacted a lawyer who knew of someone who knew of someone who knew of a pregnant girl in Chicago looking to give her baby up for adoption. That lawyer was later disbarred and imprisoned for his role in many such adoptions because you're not supposed to arrange for babies to be bought and sold.

Gray-market babies didn't come cheap. My parents were not yet wealthy, but they were desperate for a family. They ate inexpensive food and wore old shoes and waited. They waited as the neighbors filled their plastic kiddie pools. They waited while my mother graciously attended baby shower after baby shower, tossing the little candy-filled baby-bottle favors into the trash on her way home. My parents waited and avoided the subject, talking instead about the stock market, tennis, the neighbors, until the lawyer finally called them and told them to get on a plane because their daughter had been born. My mother was a social worker at the time and she swears that she was at home to hear the phone because she had called in sick that day with an unexplained stomachache, psychic labor pains.

We lived together in that crowded one-bedroom for two years, until my father's stockbroking business picked up and my parents were able to buy a house in a neighboring town with a desirable zip code and good public schools. I grew up in the kind of town in which orthodonture was mandatory and getting a nose job as a gift for your sweet sixteen was highly recommended.

Those very early years were a love affair of sorts between my father and me. My father was a man who was most pleased by good looks and accomplishments, so I worked at being precociously bright, athletic, musical—anything to impress him. And whenever I wasn't, I cheated or I faked it. My father was wild about his little sidekick and to me, he was the king of the world. I waited each day at the top of the steps to hear the rumble of the garage door so I could run to greet him when he emerged, so important in his shiny shoes and Brooks Brothers suits.

My parents told me only one thing about my birth mother. They told me that she was a ballerina. In my fantasy, my birth mother was a life-size version of the tiny dancer twirling inside my satin-lined music box. My plastic ballerina had the smallest brushstroke of red hair and limbs the width of toothpicks. She never lost her balance; she never had to let her arms down. I imagined my birth mother posed in a perpetual arabesque, swathed in white tulle, with a tiara of sparkling snowflakes in her hair.

I would wind the key tightly and the opening notes of *Swan Lake* would chime double time at first, then more slowly, until they would plink to a stop. But somewhere in between, the little plastic figurine would turn at just the right speed. That was when I would raise my arms in the air and twirl along with her. Somewhere between too fast and too slow, we would be in perfect sync.

In my memory of that time, my adoptive mother is a blur with long red fingernails. She is the hand applying zinc oxide to my nose, the bearer of pretzels and Twinkies, Sisyphus in the kitchen. This may be the fate of mothers in memory—to be relegated to the ordinary and therefore condemned to invisibility. I think of this now as I watch my friends chase down their kids poolside wielding bottles of chemical-free sunblock.

I'm sure it's not entirely the truth, but the way I remember it, it was my father who responded to the screams of my night terrors, who toweled the sweat off me and scratched my head until I fell back asleep. It was my father who avidly coached my soccer and softball teams. It was my father who took me to see *Swan Lake* at Lincoln Center and showed me a world in which girls floated along as bright as snowflakes.

I watched the ballerinas glow blue-white in the spotlights and ached to be where they were. I watched the ballerinas and imagined that I understood why my birth mother had given me up for adoption. You had to lose something to be that light. It was reason enough to give your baby away—you could always be that luminous, that free.

The crowd spat me out at the entrance of Beth Israel. If I didn't have a fairy godmother who gave me dazzling ball gowns, at least I had one who gave me courage. Ever since I was sixteen and I'd first heard *Easter* and decided that Patti Smith was the barometer of all things cool and right, when faced with tough decisions, I would ask myself, What would Patti Smith do? It was the yardstick by which I measured what was the authentic choice, the balls-out choice. When faced with the decision of taking the job in Brunei, I had weighed my options: Should I stay or should I go? What would Patti Smith do? She would go. She would board the plane to exotic lands and she would never once look back. As I walked through the hospital doors, in my mind I was already settling back in my airplane seat and watching the city recede beneath me.

The lobby was actually quite posh as far as hospitals go, but my eye was drawn to every sad detail—the forced cheeriness of the gift-shop daisies, the seam of elusive grime where the floor met the wall. In truth, I'd always had a walnut of trepidation in my gut, a pinch of anxiety between my shoulder blades, when going to see my father, even at his healthiest.

By the time I was twelve years old, my love affair with my father had, like most, ended in heartbreak. We spent my high school years and beyond locked in a constant battle for control that sometimes ended in violence. When I was in high school, my father ate and ate until he was an obese freight train of rage, and I, in turn, starved myself until I was the smallest possible target for his invectives. Years of therapy helped him to forgive himself, though he quit before he got to the part about not holding everyone else eternally accountable for his misery. In the great tradition of Jewish parents, his dearest belief is that when he's dead I'll spend the rest of my life regretting my callous behavior toward him. His emblematic song for this sentiment is "Something Wonderful," from *The King and I*.

He called me the night before his surgery.

"Hi, honey. I was just sitting here on the couch in front of the fire and watching *The King and I* and Lady Thiang was singing 'Something Wonderful' and it made me think of me."

My father may be the only man in the world who would call to tell you he heard a song that made him think of himself. I hated him for making those ridiculous phone calls, in which he foisted on me the sentiment he wished I had for him. "Something Wonderful" is a love ballad to an imperfect but charming king, and it's a risky song to hang your hopes on. Unless you own a country and can waltz like Yul Brynner, it's never a safe bet to count on your enduring charm to redeem you from acting like a big asshole. If my father most identified in that pivotal moment with "Something Wonderful," I suppose I would have picked "There Are Worse Things I Could Do" from *Grease*.

There were worse things than taking a job that required I leave for Brunei on the day of my father's surgery. The Southeast-Asian sultanate of Brunei was a country I had only recently even heard of. My job description was elusive at best, but I fantasized that I might arrive and find a wild adventure, a pile of money, and an employer who was no less than Prince Charming. This was my opportunity to shake off my bohemian mantle and reimagine myself as an enigmatic export, maybe a royal mistress or the heroine of a spy novel. More realistically, I suspected I had signed on to be an international quasi-prostitute. There are worse things I could do.

I had prepared my parents for the fact that I was leaving town that day. I told them that I had gotten an important acting role in a movie, but that it was shooting in Singapore and I had to leave right away. When they later asked about my big break, I planned to tell them that my role had been cut. I justified my lies to my parents by imagining that I would make them come true and they would no longer be lies. Okay, the fantasy movie in Singapore probably wouldn't happen, but my soon-to-be stardom would overshadow it and all of this would be rendered irrelevant.

My parents believed in my acting career and had stoically received the news that I was leaving. Before I even got on the plane that day, they had already begun the process of accepting my absence. I would become the prodigal daughter, always off on an exotic adventure that few in my parents' world could ever fathom. That day at Beth Israel, they began their wait for my repentant return.

I hung out with my mother and my aunt in the bucket seats of the waiting room outside the ICU, our coats draped over the backs of the chairs. My aunt is a wild-haired ex-hippie who spent the sixties in acid-soaked communes and sleeping on European rooftops—a prodigal daughter in her own right. When my aunt and I get together, it's usually a nonstop talking marathon, but that day we were unable to think of anything to say. We focused instead on the *Jeopardy* answers coming from the TV mounted in the corner near the ceiling. My relatives were all *Jeopardy* fiends. I loved *Jeopardy*'s Zen premise: All the answers are really questions. When she was dying of cancer, my grandmother could easily clear a board, even in her morphine haze. My aunt and I held hands and answered in unison.

"Who is Thomas Mann?"

"What is the Panama Canal?"

My brother, Johnny, was notably absent, off at yet another boarding school and probably engaged at that very moment in a scheme to grow his own psychedelic mushrooms or to break out of his dorm and hitchhike to the nearest Phish concert. My mother sat quietly reading. Her hair was styled into a tastefully highlighted wedge, her diamond earrings twinkling under the hospital fluorescents. My mother shines in a crisis—hospitals, funerals, support groups. She is the lady you want around when things go way south. This is not to say that she wasn't worried about my father; just that worried is her natural habitat. When my grandmother was dying, my mother taught me that you have to make yourself at home in hospitals, have to know where they keep the ice, have to keep track of your own medication schedule, have to make friends with the nurses. If you sit around and wait for someone else to bring you a glass of water, you're bound to get very thirsty.

The three of us went to eat sweaty lasagna in the

hospital cafeteria. We sat with poor posture, like the rest of the people there, who huddled in groups around their lukewarm food. Laughter cut through the room from a table of doctors in scrubs. I couldn't imagine having to eat in that place every day. My father's doctor, Dr. Foster, was standing next to the table where the doctors were laughing. He was a handsome, young guy with a shock of black hair and tortoiseshell glasses. He glanced around the room; his eyes rested on us for a second, then moved on without an acknowledgment. It is the unique province of doctors to be in the same room with the family of a man whose internal organs he was just handling and not even nod hello.

I watched Dr. Foster walk away. When we had talked after the surgery, I had noted a flirtatiousness to his manner. (I know, classy timing.) There had even been a vague but unmistakable suggestion that we should have a drink later in the week. At any moment in time, I imagined, a parallel-universe Jill could make a different choice, could turn a fraction of an inch to the left and step onto a different path.

That moment I imagined a parallel Jill stayed in New York and altered the course of her days not by seeking fame and fortune but rather by succumbing to the dictates of her upbringing. She takes Dr. Foster up on that drink. She winds up the wife of a doctor, with shapely calves, a standing tennis date, and a two-carat diamond on her finger. She finds fulfillment in her children and in volunteer work. She reads design magazines and gourmet magazines and she does things like making homemade pasta and then indulging in only a few bites. She week-ends in the Hamptons and takes two-week Caribbean va-cations every year.

My mother radiated the calm of a martyr marching to the stake. She had surrendered to her fate. I never once saw her try to get out of her marriage to a domineering man who persistently demeaned her. I wondered where her parallel selves lived. Did she scroll back to each cross-roads of her life and wonder, or did she feel that some-thing higher was guiding the needle of her compass, that she was fated to be living out her life exactly as it was?

When we returned from lunch, a slab of cheese con-gealing in my stomach, my father was waking up from the anesthesia. A nurse informed us that only one per-son could go into the ICU at a time, so my mother went first. She emerged after about fifteen minutes looking un-shaken, saying only that I should go next because he was asking for me.

My father hovered somewhere between conscious and unconscious. A hundred tubes and wires traveled in and out of him. He had lost more than fifty pounds and lost it so quickly that his skin had failed to shrink to his new body. It hung off him like excess fabric. He looked shriveled.

I have a picture of my father and me when I was a baby. He is lying on the bed and I am sleeping across his round belly. He was so big to me then, a mountain. I feel like I remember the moment. I know it's a trick of memory, a conflation of photographs and reality, because I was only an infant. But I could swear I remember what it was like to lay my head so close to his heart.

His bloodshot blue eyes scanned the room wildly.

"It hurts," he said, his voice small and labored.

"You're going to get better now."

"I didn't know it would hurt this much."

I stood next to him, holding his hand, conscious of my teeth in my mouth, my toes in my shoes, the watch on my wrist reading ten minutes past the time I needed to leave to make my plane. I talked about my impressive new movie job. It seemed to cheer him up.

"Look at you," he said.

I could have simply not shown up at the airport, could have stayed for that drink with Dr. Foster, but I wasn't going to. I was unsure of my destiny, but I could tell you with absolute certainty that it did not lie there. I told my father that I'd telephone from Singapore every day. Then I kissed his cheek and left.

My father called after me in a whisper, "Grab your star and ride it to the top, Jilly."

I was a liar. And I left. I cried in the elevator for my dad, for all that was lost between us, for my own alarming recklessness. But my eyes dried up the minute my ass hit the vinyl cab seat. All my regrets and reservations were overshadowed by the fact that it felt so good to be moving—green flowered suitcase in the trunk, thirty dollars to my name, car window open to the unseasonably warm winter day.

As he has mellowed and grown older, my father has rewritten our history together and, with it, his opinion of me. He tears up and greets every milestone, from my marriage to my master's degree, by saying, "My daughter took the road less traveled by, and that has made all the difference."

With one hackneyed phrase he manages both to praise me and to brand me forever the outsider. Read the poem for real, I want to tell him, and you'll see that the roads are about the same. The traveler only imagines that one is less trodden than the other.

Nevertheless, two roads diverged. I picked the one that seemed a tiny bit wilder. Because that was who I wanted to be.

chapter 2

With overnight stays in Los Angeles and Singapore, I spent three days en route to Brunei. The long hours in the air provided me an opportunity for reflection.

These days, my life has taken on a slower pace and it seems that the moon can wax and wane and wax again and the time has marked my life in only subtle ways—the slight deepening of the marionette lines around my mouth, the easing of a yoga posture, the straining of a friendship, perhaps, or the birth of a new one. I embark on endless attempts to break bad habits, to acquire new, healthier ones. I usually fail at both, but not to any major detriment. Not anymore. Sometimes I buy a plane ticket. There is a birth, a death, a celebration, a tragedy. But when I sat on that plane to Singapore, I had much to reflect on and even more to hope for. At the time, the barreling truck that was my life hopped the divider and changed directions every five minutes or so.

I listened to Talking Heads on my CD Walkman. *And you may ask yourself, well . . . how did I get here?*

You may ask the same question. You know—what's a nice girl like you doing on her way to a harem like this? Allow me to back up a few paces.

How I got there started with a headlong sprint across the beach, well past midnight on an icy November evening in East Hampton. I broke into a flat run over the spotlit dunes, terror pasted across my face. The ground gave beneath my Reeboks and slowed me down as if I was running in a dream. The sand in front of me was strewn with elongated shadows. The only thing the director had told me before he called action was to hit three marks along my trajectory, each indicated with a barely visible sandbag. I wore a tear-away yellow and blue cheerleading costume that fastened with Velcro up the sides, and my chestnut hair was pulled into tight pigtails, each secured with a yellow satin bow. The salty air seared my windpipe and raised goose bumps along my bare arms and legs. I had turned eighteen three months before; I could have been an actual cheerleader.

I hit the first sandbag at an awkward angle and my ankle twisted. As scripted, a ghostly hand reached out of the darkness and tore my shirt off. I let loose my best Janet Leigh scream and ran, topless now, toward my next mark, spears of pain shooting up my leg.

I was there. I was for real. I was Patti Smith in pigtails and I was screaming my heart out in front of a camera—finally, in front of a camera. Who gave a shit if it was some trashy vampire movie scheduled for video release in Florida? It was a movie. It was a start. It was a brief stone on the yellow-brick road to being all I ever wanted to be—a shining star of stage and screen. My plan was to be so wholly and incontrovertibly loved that I would never again be left clinging to the outer orbits of anything.

This movie, this low, low rung on my ladder to success, was called *Valerie*. *Valerie* was about a high school girl who was so obsessed with vampires that she magically turned into one and then proceeded to terrorize her school. Two weeks beforehand, I had responded to an ad in *Back Stage* that led me to the kind of brick townhouse in Newark where old Polish ladies live. This was different from most of my auditions, in which you wound up standing around a generic Midtown casting studio with a bunch of other girls who all face the wall and silently read the sides with their lips moving and their eyebrows going up and down.

I knew Newark a little bit. My family is one of those old Newark Jewish families whose octogenarians are sought out for interviews by ethnohistorians. My great-

great-grandfather and his siblings came on a boat from a shtetl in Poland and, washed in sepia tones, they started with a fruit cart and opened a grocery store that became a grocery chain. They started by delivering newspapers in exchange for pens and wound up writing prescriptions. They were doctors and dentists and business owners and real estate moguls. They helped to found the oldest synagogue in Newark, the same one where my brother and I were Bar and Bat Mitzvahed.

Ask my father and he'll tell you all about it: Our family helped build Newark. We love Newark. Long after he left home, his parents were the last white family living on their block for years. They moved only when my grandfather retired and he and my grandmother were too old to take care of the house anymore. Though my father lives in an affluent suburb about twenty minutes away now, he's quick to tell you that he's no fancy guy; he's just that same old kid from Newark. My father is a sentimental man and when I was a little girl he used to take me for rides in his white Cordoba and point out the old house on Lyons Avenue, Weequahic High School, the Jewish cemetery. He talked about it so much that the sidewalks of Newark felt like home, even though we never actually lived there or even really got out of the car.

So I felt like I almost recognized the townhouse when I arrived at the address that was written on a sheet of paper in my purse. I knocked on the door and the unctuous director of the movie, complete with thinning ponytail and high-waisted jeans, ushered me into a living room, where every surface was cobwebbed in lace doilies and every piece of furniture was ziplocked in plastic; probably his mother's house. The coffee table had been shoved to the side of the room and in its place was a tripod that held a video camera the size of a toaster.

I stood in front of the camera and gave an audition, the entirety of which consisted of taking my top off and screaming. The director and his assistant furrowed their brows and took notes on a clipboard while shifting on the squeaking couch covers. They called me two days later to tell me I had been cast as Victim One. The director also told me that Butch Patrick, the guy who had played Eddie Munster, was his cousin, so there was a lot of potential for the project.

They say there are no small parts, only small actors, and since I hadn't yet figured out that this aphorism isn't true, I took the job.

I headed for my second mark, where a hand reached into the frame and yanked the skirt from my waist. This scream was less hearty, more winded. I ran the last leg of the gauntlet in only panties, sneakers, and ankle socks. When I hit the final sandbag, Maria the actress playing Valerie, stepped in front of me and blocked my path.

Scream.

Cut.

Maria was a clearly anorexic, haunted-looking blonde. Bruise-colored circles that even the white cake makeup couldn't completely cover shadowed her bruise-colored eyes. Wearing a tatty nightgown and backlit by the bright lights of the set, she looked like an alien, with her sylphlike body somehow supporting a skull that seemed huge in comparison. Why was this girl the star while I was Victim One?

While we waited for them to set up the next shot, Maria and I wrapped ourselves in a comforter pilfered from a nearby beachfront house that belonged to someone's parents. We huddled together for warmth and I could feel the sharp edges of her hip bones pressing into me, no insulation at all between her and the world. The crew bustled around us, setting lights and preparing our next scene together. It was my final scene. My Big Moment.

The director came over to talk to us as his DP set the camera for the shot.

He addressed Maria first.

"This is your first kill. You've finally given in to the bloodlust you've been struggling against all this time. It's ecstatic. It's orgasmic—the power as you overtake her. Savor it. Take your time. Especially with the bite."

He turned to me and simply said, "Fight her."

A mousy art-department girl wearing a down vest, a ski hat, and rubber gloves to her elbows mixed a bucketful of fake blood. In the first shot, Maria was meant to rip off the last thin barrier between my torso and the night—a pair of my own panties that were to be sacrificed for the occasion—and then wrestle me to the ground. The second shot was the homoerotic kill, in which I would succumb to the vampire and end up doused in fake blood. The art-department girl stressed to us the necessity of nailing the scene in one take because there would be no way to clean me off again.

The fight scene was pitiful. Maria barely had enough strength in her hands to grip my wrists. I am shaped like a living replica of the fleshy cartoon girls drawn by R. Crumb, with their big asses, sturdy, round thighs, small waists, and pert B cups, which is to say that I could have reduced Marie's brittle bones to a pile of twigs with one shove. I wasn't about to let her frailty ruin my moment. Instead, I interlaced my fingers with hers and jerked her around like a Muppet, attempting to make it look like I was battling for my cheerleader life. Then I pitched myself backward and pulled her down on top of me. She looked shaken.

Scream.

Cut.

The next shot was the gore shot. The art-department girl had added a black rubber apron, completing her authentic butcher couture. The rest of the crew buried some clear tubing in the sand and arranged it to emerge from behind by neck. While they bustled around me, I lay back on the sand, closed my eyes, and tried not to hyperventilate. I drew back into myself and became strangely sleepy, my twisted ankle pulsing and hot. I wondered if I might be starting to freeze to death. Voices behind me discussed there being some concern about the blood flowing freely through the tubing because it had begun to thicken and form a Karo syrup ice floe. The script supervisor nudged the director and pointed to me on the ground.

He mobilized. "Okay. The kill. We gotta go now; we're losing our Victim. Places."

Maria positioned herself over me, her bloodshot eyes

sunk with deep exhaustion and hunger. She checked that her fangs were secure. The butcher girl came over with a Dixie cup and filled my mouth with a foul Karo slushie that I was meant to spit out at the moment I surrendered.

Quiet on the set.

Rolling.

Action.

Maria widened her eyes in her best Bela Lugosi and moved in for a slow, dramatic chomp. I couldn't squirm much due to the precariously placed blood tubing, so I tried to let my face convey the panic. I considered it to be the kind of challenge that separated the amateurs from the pros; I had nothing but disdain for amateurs. I let out one final and absolutely genuine scream when Maria lowered for the bite and a river of what felt like frozen snot shot out from the tube like a geyser and drenched us both. I heaved in death convulsions as she raised her face toward the moon, her eyes wild with the slaughter. I finally lay still and hung my head to the side, blood streaming out of the corner of my slack mouth, my eyes staring straight ahead.

Cut.

"That's a wrap for Victim One. Maria, go get cleaned up for the next shot."

The five or so people there gave an unenthusiastic round of applause and the butcher girl threw me a towel. I made a break for it, limping as fast as I could toward the house. A production assistant guarded the entrance to the porch.

"Outdoor shower," he said.

"I'm dying here."

"I'm serious."

I took off my now-pink shoes and socks and grimly headed toward what was sure to be the crowning torture of the evening. What I discovered was that in East Hampton, unlike at the Jersey shore, outdoor showers have hot water and showerheads the size of Frisbees. I stood on a patch of concrete and pulled my matted hair out of the pigtails while the hot water washed the slime and the cold away and all that was left of the last few hours was the star-strewn Long Island sky and the black, churning ocean in the distance. I shook off the wiggle of misgiving in my gut. It was all in good, campy fun, right? The next audition would be a real audition. The next role I got offered would be a real role.

Four buxom girls perched on towel-draped couches in the downstairs den of the house. The makeup girl attempted to apply their body makeup evenly with a sponge, but the white pancake kept getting away from her, too thick and cakey in some places, too thin and drippy in others. The girls ran lines with each other, preparing for their upcoming scenes as the vampire wives who initiate Valerie into their coven.

I changed into my sweats, pulled back my wet hair, and settled in, preparing to wait out the remainder of the long night. The room was all cherry wood, chintz pillows, and wide navy stripes. A table in the corner offered a liter of Diet Coke, a package of bottled water, a stack of soggy sub sandwiches, and some Cheetos. I circumvented that sad scenario and instead found the wet bar. Then I walked around with the Jameson as if I was the lady of the house, acting the gracious hostess and spiking everyone's sodas with whiskey.

The whiskey livened up the party. We got buzzed and talked strip clubs and boyfriends, Scientology and colonics, acting teachers and downtown restaurants. We pondered that great feminist question: Why are female vampires called "vampire wives" when male vampires aren't called "vampire husbands"? In spite of this injustice to our gender, the vampire wives eventually went to shoot their scenes and I curled into a chair and fell asleep, hugging a pillow with a needlepoint pug on it.

I woke when the vampire wives returned, freshly showered and wrapped in towels, with faint smudges of white still clinging to their hairlines. The sky had begun to brighten with the pale predawn and only Maria remained outside, still filming her final scenes. The assistant director brought in some of the footage shot earlier in the evening and hooked up a second camera to the TV. We all gathered around to watch. I was excited to see myself. I thought I had done a stellar job, considering the obvious limitations.

We watched what seemed like hundreds of scenes before mine, and every one of them was unbearable. It shouldn't have surprised me that when I finally appeared on the screen, the lighting was so poor that you could barely see me. I was a flash of yellow hair ribbon, a pair of bouncing white boobs in the darkness.

The close-up of my death throes was blurry and would clearly be edited out.

I drifted out to the porch to watch the sun rise, deciding I didn't need to see any more. It wasn't even good in an ironic way. It was just another night with little sleep and another "deferred" paycheck that would never come. At least I had the story. At the end of all of these surreal and pointless nights there was always the story.

One of the vampire wives, a girl named Taylor who was a dead ringer for Ellen Barkin, followed me out. She and I swaddled ourselves in overcoats and comforters and nestled together on the porch swing. Taylor wore a J.Crew turtleneck and seemed out of place among the low-budget-porn types who comprised the rest of *Valerie*'s cast. She had thick, strawberry blond hair and a fading sunburn across the bridge of her freckled nose.

We talked as we watched the sky over the ocean slide through the palest shades of sherbet—frosty lemon and petal pink and powder blue.

"So what do you do when you're not freezing your blood-splattered titties off for no pay, sugar?"

Taylor spoke with a slight Southern accent, which allowed her to call people things like "sugar" with impunity.

I told her I worked as an intern for the Wooster Group, a legendary downtown theater company. I spent long days at the Performing Garage, on the corner of Wooster and Grand, where I filed papers for Spalding Gray and fetched lattes for Willem Dafoe. I sat in on rehearsals while director Elizabeth LeCompte, like some kind of postmodern shaman, deconstructed, reconstructed, and midwifed into being their current iconoclastic masterpiece.

When Kate Valk or one of the other devastatingly chic Wooster Group veterans would take pity on their pet interns and treat us to a drink at the Lucky Strike around the corner, the wine would burn the paper cuts at the corners of my mouth. But my hours at the Performing Garage were my best hours. My intern friends there were going to be the main players in the next wave of New York experimental theater; we were convinced of it.

"They may be the best theater company in the world and I am right there licking their fund-raising envelopes," I told Taylor.

"And what do you do for money when you're not a slave to the arts?"

I usually lied when people asked me that question, but for some reason I told Taylor the truth. I told her that I split my time between a seedy but hip Canal Street topless bar called the Baby Doll lounge and a far more seedy and completely unhip peep show in Times Square called Peepland.

I started dancing after I dropped out of New York University's Tisch School of the Arts. I had been accepted at age sixteen through an early-admissions program and my parents had packed me off to a dorm room perched twelve floors above Washington Square Park before I even got my driver's license. When I quit school six months later, I cited my preference for the proverbial school of life, but my father wasn't buying it. Over shrimp and mushrooms at Jane Street Seafood, he promptly severed my financial umbilical cord.

"Six months ago it was, I don't need high school, I'm ready for college," he said, his face blowing up into a scarlet balloon of rage. "Now it's, I don't need college, I'm ready for life. Life costs money."

"So does college."

"Always with the smart mouth. You think it's funny, this road you're on? You get nothing. You see how that works out for you and then we'll see if you change your mind about college."

He was right. Life did cost money. And life in New York costs money and a kidney, and that was way more than I was making as a terrible cocktail waitress at the Red Lion on Bleecker Street. One of the other interns at the Wooster Group worked at the Kit Kat Club on Fifty-second and Broadway and she convinced me that they'd be way more tolerant of my lack of natural waitressing ability. I followed her to work one day and spent about forty minutes as a waitress before I shucked my duds and got up on the stage in a borrowed G-string.

To those who haven't profited financially from their sexuality, those of us who have often inspired an extreme range of emotions: Why would we take our clothes off for money? What makes us take that initial plunge? What makes one financially strapped girl into a stripper and another into a Denny's waitress and another into a med student? You want to connect the dots. You all want reassurance that it won't be your daughter up there on the pole. Shitty relationship with my father, low self-esteem, astrologically inevitable craving for adventure, dreams of stardom, history of depression and anxiety, tendency toward substance abuse—put it all in the cauldron and cook and the ideal sex worker emerges, dripping and gleaming and whole.

Just look at that checklist. Don't worry, that's not your little girl. She'll never turn out to be like me.

Dancing at Peepland and the Baby Doll made me enough to keep me in vegetarian stir-fries, nights out at Max Fish, and a shared Lower East Side tenement apartment, but I was hardly bathing in champagne.

"You work way too hard and you make shit money and you're gonna ruin your knees," Taylor told me. "You eighteen yet?"

I was, barely.

"Good, because Diane checks up on it. You can't hand her some phony ID like she's a half-drunk bouncer."

Taylor handed me a card that read "Crown Club" in gold embossed script, with a little crown over the *o* and a phone number underneath. She found a pen in her purse and wrote her own number down, too.

"Diane runs the escort agency I work for. It's the best in New York. You've been way underselling yourself. You come work with me and your whole life will change in a heartbeat."

An escort agency. It sounded so simple and classy. I imagined Diane as an elegant woman in a cream-colored pantsuit, sensible pumps, and diamond stud earrings. She would seem shrewd and cold but would have a secret maternal side to her, like Candice Bergen in *Mayflower*

Madam. She would be someone to admire, someone who could help me out. I would be less exhausted, have more time to pursue my performing career.

Taylor put her arm around me. We were new friends braced against the cold, staring out at the cloudless expanse of sky. The sun had risen; the crew had wrapped the equipment and was loading it into vans. The cast members trickled out onto the porch to wait for their rides back to the city.

The *Mayflower Madam* thing was a nice fantasy, but I knew I probably wouldn't call Diane. Escort work was one step too far. I pocketed the card anyway, just in case I changed my mind.

chapter 3

On Thanksgiving of 1991, I pulled the card Taylor had given me out of my wallet and called the number. When you find yourself doing things you never dreamed of, it often happens in stages. You take a tiny step over the line, and then you advance to the next line. You might find you're lonely one day. Or broke, or depressed, or just curious. Or sitting on the couch at your parents' house and slowly suffocating, an invisible pillow of memories pressed over your face. And you're already that kind of girl; you've already come this far—so what's one phone call more?

My boyfriend, Sean, and I were spending the holiday with my family. I had debated whether or not to bring him along, but my desire to have him with me won out over my hesitancy to bring anyone over to my parents' house. I thought that I was maybe in love with Sean, though I qualified that with the belief that romantic love was a conspiracy employed by the capitalist establishment as a marketing tool and by the media as a Cinderella soporific.

Before I met Sean, I had engaged in tryst after tryst, crush after crush, boy after boy (and one or two girls), never blinking at the rapid demise of the flame, never expecting anyone to stay. When I met him, I was still seventeen. I had already been a stripper for six months and had never had a real boyfriend, not even a high school boyfriend. Then Sean dropped by the Performing Garage one afternoon to visit friends.

Sean was thin and doe-eyed, with wiry, shoulder-length dark hair and gorgeous musician's fingers. He was a broke artist with a patrician pedigree, a talented actor and guitar player who shared a two-bedroom Rivington Street hovel across the street from Streit's Matzo Factory. I shared a one-bedroom Ludlow Street hovel around the corner.

We spent our first date eating egg rolls and drinking beer on my rooftop while above us the clouds hung heavy and low. A sudden clap of thunder startled us both to our feet and set off a symphony of car alarms from the parking lot below. Fat drops of rain pelted the tar roof and we stayed there until we were soaked, him bending to hold my head in his hands and kiss me—slow, beer-flavored kisses—while the remains of our Chinese food flooded. It was corny. It was great. It was the best date I had ever had and he was the best guy I had ever met, by far.

Sean didn't really care about my stripping. He even came to see me a few times. He liked the shoes and he found it all somewhat titillating. He regularly listened at length to my Fellini-esque adventures, even though he harbored a misgiving or two around the edges.

We ate our meals at El Sombrero or Two Boots pizza and we drank late at Max Fish with our friends from various bands and theater projects. We bought bad Avenue B coke and snorted it off his *Houses of the Holy* LP cover while we drank gin and tonics from coffee mugs and talked all night about art, about levels of disconnection, about media, about our desire for a "real" experience of life. After a while, I figured I was in love, but I kept my fingers crossed when I said it, in case I was wrong.

Sean and I arrived at my parents' house by the same bus I'd ridden a thousand times throughout high school when I traveled to the city for acting classes or dance classes or rock shows that I'd lied about and said I was sleeping at a friend's house. The trees had already shed most of their leaves but the lawn was still bright, poison green. The gray, bi-level 1970s house was a no-statement statement, a proud monument to the status quo. Every house on the street was a variation on the same theme, a different configuration of the same Legos.

My parents swept us in the door with overeager hugs. My father was thinner than I'd ever seen him, his hiatal hernia making it nearly impossible for him to eat. His cheek touched mine and it was damp with cool sweat. He was visibly sick and it shook me. What would I do if something happened to my father? He had always been a rock, one of those people who think doctors are for the weak and dentists are a waste of time.

He goosed me on my way up the stairs and I tripped, catching myself with my hands.

"Hey there, porky. Guess you decided to start eating again."

And to my boyfriend, he said, "Isn't she dainty? She used to dance around up here and we'd call her Katrinka."

The Powerful Katrinka is a character in a series of silent films. She was played by Wilna Hervey, a comedic actress who stood six feet three and weighed three hundred pounds. It was my father's pet name for me when he thought I was being a clod. My father was a rock. A rock tied to my ankle as I fell overboard. That quickly, I shifted from being concerned for his health to hoping he would starve to death right there at Thanksgiving dinner, with a banquet of food in front of him.

I escaped the ensuing Thanksgiving preparations and took a breather in the downstairs den. I sat on the sectional sofa underneath a recent family photo that I had reluctantly consented to. In it, my family stands stiffly on a patch of grass in the backyard. The white pool deck hovers behind us like a flying saucer and the harsh light of the sun flattens us into two-dimensional blocks of color. Incongruously spindly legs support my father's porcine torso. He squints into the sun, his crow's-feet an etching of dissatisfaction.

My mother's skin is shiny and stretched and still young looking but she stands like someone just poked her sharply in the sternum. My brother, Johnny, wears a gorgon's head of unkempt dreadlocks and I balance beside him with an innocuous white T-shirt and a strained smile, the same smile that appeared whenever I was in my parents' house, an involuntary reflex as dependable as a leg twitch following a rubber mallet to the kneecap.

Sean was with Johnny in his room listening to Pink Floyd. They hung their heads out the window and Johnny shared the joint that was usually glued to his bottom lip.

My parents adopted Johnny when I was four years old. I waited on tiptoe for his arrival, dangling my pigtails over the white iron railing that ran across the top of the staircase. My mother walked up the stairs holding a blanket-wrapped burrito of a baby with a prune face and black hair that swirled like cupcake icing. I loved this tiny, warm person immediately. He was a living doll for me, with his baby smell, his fat, soft arms, and his wide blue eyes. I liked to cradle him on the couch for what felt like hours, to tickle his ears and kiss his miniature nose.

Johnny wasn't an easy baby. He wasn't as quick or funny or eager to please as I was. Whether or not this was true initially, it's difficult to deviate from such a script once it's written for you. Johnny was troubled from the very start, my father says, the implication being that it's not his fault how Johnny turned out—the Obsessive

Compulsive episodes, the ruinous acid trips, the religious extremism.

For the first few years of his life, Johnny clung unceasingly to my mother's leg, while I slept in the T-shirts from my father's company softball team. We had chosen sides. I loved Johnny, but I loved being my father's favorite even more.

Now Johnny is Hasidic and lives in Jerusalem. He spends his days davening at the shul and occasionally works as a migrant olive picker or a seller of organic herbal tonics. He dreams of a small plot of land, a herd of goats, and some olive trees of his own. In his world, men and women eat in separate rooms. It is a world with its own logic, but it's not a world with much of a place for me. We still talk on the phone once in a while. When I can remember, I send his son birthday presents.

I like to blame Johnny for the distance between us. He's the one with the wide-brimmed black hat and the archaic belief system, not I. But the truth is that when things took a bad turn, I ran from our house and I left him. I promised him I would come back for him and I never did. That Thanksgiving, I went downstairs and sat by myself on the couch and didn't listen when he tried to tell me that my father had hit him over the head with the telephone the night before.

My mother bustled between the dining room and the kitchen, engaged in the mysterious arts of table setting and perfectly timed food preparation. In the living room, my father played his prized Steinway baby grand. He tirelessly progressed through a medley of show tunes played halfway through at three times their intended speed. He always played as if there were a more important song somewhere on a constantly receding horizon, which he never quite reached. It was to that same off-tempo music that I first started belting out the songs from *South Pacific* and twirling around the living room.

As I had twirled, my father had called me Katrinka, but I'd never heard of the Powerful Katrinka. I kept dancing. I was the Graceful Katrinka, the Talented Katrinka, born of a woman so ethereal she'd simply floated away.

After escaping to New York, crossing back over the border to New Jersey was like putting a plastic bag over my head. The longer I spent there, the less oxygen I had. I was running out of air, suffocated by the house itself and the music and the family portraits and the family in person and the boyfriend upstairs who had seen it all. Maybe that was why I made the decision to pull the card Taylor had given me out of my wallet. I was trying to poke a hole in the bag, trying to breathe. The Crown Club seemed like a pretty sharp tool and it was the best I could think of right then. The music was loud enough upstairs so that no one would hear me. I didn't think anyone would really answer the Crown Club phone on the afternoon of Thanksgiving, but, of course, someone did.

chapter 4

When I arrived for my interview at the Midtown brownstone, a petite, short-haired brunette in a sweat suit and bare feet answered the door with a smile.

"Diane's on the phone in the office. Come on in and wait a minute. I'm Julie."

I shook her hand and introduced myself. I assumed we were using real names for purposes of introductions. I'm not sure what made me think that. In strip clubs, I would use my stage name from the minute I walked in the door. Maybe it was the fact that the name Julie was so prosaic. Although you never know the logic behind another girl's working persona. Maybe Julie was working a small-town-girl angle but her real name was Jezebel.

I followed her down a short hallway to where Taylor and another girl sat in a living room decorated with a monochrome vanilla-ice-cream color scheme. The walls, carpets, couches, cushions, and Formica wall unit were all vanilla. The only splash of color was an orange Georgia O'Keeffe poppy poster that hung on the wall over the couch. My grandmother used to have a small, framed picture of the identical poppy in her hallway. Underneath the picture had been a quote from O'Keeffe: "Nobody sees a flower, really . . . to see takes time. Like to have a friend takes time." Georgia's poor poppies—rendered invisible yet again, mass-produced and hung on the walls of Midwestern doctor's offices and Midtown escort agencies.

Julie plopped down next to a lank-haired, model-thin girl with a vague Eastern European accent. The model introduced herself and then immediately returned to watching *The Golden Girls*. The room smelled like Chinese food, though none was in evidence. Taylor popped up from the chair she was sitting on, trotted over and embraced me.

"I'm so glad you came," she said, turning to the girls on the couch. "This is that girl I met on that movie I did."

They looked at her blankly. All three of the girls wore sweats, but their hair was coiffed and they wore makeup and jewelry. They reminded me of ice skaters waiting backstage.

Beyond the living room was a formal dining room that was set up as an office. A long table lined with multiple Rolodexes and phones was pushed against one wall. Along the other stood four off-white filing cabinets. At the far end was a window overlooking the city, a square of twinkling black velvet in a sea of otherwise relentless cream. Two rolling desk chairs faced the table. In one sat a pink-cheeked, round-faced woman wearing a plaid headband with a bow. A stuffed Christmas reindeer already decorated her workstation. She looked over at Taylor and me and waved, giving us the five-minutes sign. Next to her, facing the window and talking on the phone in a loud, irritated voice was what looked like a beige pantsuit crowned with a mushroom cap of brassy hair. The pantsuit sounded like it was from Queens. Diane, I presumed.

Taylor used the next few minutes to begin my initiation. She gathered me into a corner and chatted conspiratorially.

"Where are your clothes?"

I had worn a green crushed-velvet cap-sleeved minidress, which I estimated to be the classiest thing I owned, along with fishnets and a pair of two-inch pumps my parents had bought me years before to wear to temple. They were the only heels I owned that didn't have a platform the height of the *OED*. I still carried my black overcoat over my arm.

"I'm wearing them."

"Really? That's all you have?"

Taylor marched me to the closet and pulled out three neatly pressed suits, the skirts short but tasteful, the jackets tailored. I guessed it was the business attire of the ice skaters.

"You never want to look like a hooker when you're walking through a hotel lobby. Suit or dress, sexy but conservative, three-inch heels, thigh-high stockings, expensive underwear."

I owned none of these things.

"But you're not horrible," she said. "I've seen worse."

At this point Diane had ended her call and beckoned to me from the office. Diane's first glance at me contained a whole conversation. She was no Candice Bergen. Pugnacious and brusque, she baldly assessed me like the merchandise I was destined to become. After asking me a few initial questions, she fired off a description of me to the phone girl with the plaid headband, whom she introduced as Ellie. Ellie wrote down Diane's dictation on an index card.

"Hair: auburn. Eyes: hazel. Thirty-six, twenty-four, thirty . . . nine. Might as well play up the big ass. Eighteen-year-old, curvaceous theater student with a face like . . . Winona Ryder. What will you do?"

"What do you mean?"

"Will you do nurse fantasy?"

"Um, yeah."

With each answer, Ellie checked a box on her card.

"Dominatrix?"

"Sure."

"Girl on girl?"

"Yes."

"Maid?"

"I don't have to actually clean, right?"

To Ellie, she said, "That's a yes."

"Private dance?"

Diane turned to Ellie and talked over my final answer, saying, "Will do whatever."

Ellie nodded and checked a final box. Was there a box for whatever?

"Will do whatever" was pretty much accurate. In the peep shows and strip clubs I'd worked at, I had done more unseemly deeds for money before I turned eighteen than most women would ever contemplate in their whole lives. What was one more? But escort work was different, wasn't it? A tiny misgiving fluttered somewhere under my occipital bone. Call it whatever euphemism you chose; this was fucking for money we were talking about, right? I had been the embodiment of confidence until I stood in the middle of that room in my trashy dress while Ellie checked the "whatever" box. I was flooded by a cascade of anxieties. What if I got a disease? What if it was disgusting? What if I got raped? Got killed? What if this next step would create a fissure in the landscape of my heart that could never be repaired?

"You bring your ID and passport?"

I had been told that my interview would require two forms of ID. I handed them over.

Luckily, I had obtained a passport as a gift to myself for my eighteenth birthday a few months earlier. I had

been ensnared by tales of Paris in the twenties and it was
my dearest hope to get my ass there at all costs. I knew
the Paris of seventy years before was long gone. Nevertheless, the call of that city resonated in my bones. The name
alone could send me into hours of happy daydreams. I
wanted to drop down right in the center of Paris, where
I would drink wine and write poetry and let Paris infuse
my soul with continental urbanity and sophistication. I
had hoped to hand my passport to a customs official at
Charles De Gaulle International Airport. Instead I was
handing it to Diane at the Crown Club, but it was a mere
stopover, I told myself, a brief detour.

Diane gave me the same shtick about my clothing
that Taylor had and I vowed to go get myself some class
as soon as I could afford to. I was catapulted into the job
within a couple of hours. Taylor informed me that I was
lucky to get a call on my first night of work. I was going
to do well, she assured me, if for no other reason than my
age. I was the youngest girl there and have always had
the advantage of an innocent appearance. My most drastic attempts to be punk and hard never fooled anyone—I
am a nice girl to the bone. It has served me well in my
not-so-nice endeavors.

So that first night I got a call to go to the apartment
of a well-known talk radio host. Ellie, who was basically
a plump, cookie-baking, Laura Ashley–wearing assistant
pimp, taught me how to use my own little credit-card machine and gave me specific instructions about how and
when the transaction was to take place (immediately
upon arrival), as well as the rules for reporting in. Before

I left for my first "date," Taylor took me into the bedroom, sat me down on the bed, and gave me a few pointers. She had taken me under her wing.

"The whole trick is, how much can you get for how little you give, get it? You want to turn one hour into two into three and to make a blowjob seem better than sex."

Like Scheherazade, we looked for the story that was so irresistible they had to keep us around for another hour to hear the end.

"Some nights suck," she said. "Some nights we hang out here with no calls at all, but some nights are eight-hour limousine windfalls with coked-up, limp-dicked, out-of-town businessmen. It evens out. Always, always use a condom. Put it on with your mouth and he won't even notice."

For my escort name, I picked Elizabeth because it sounded real and because it had been, along with Janice and Eduardo among others, one of the aliases I had used when playing make-believe games as a kid. I had been Elizabeth the Queen of France, Elizabeth and the Three Bears, Elizabeth the seventh Brady kid, Elizabeth the French Resistance fighter.

Add to that résumé Elizabeth the call girl, Elizabeth the cheater. Sean and I didn't have the kind of relationship in which we checked in with each other every five minutes, so I hadn't exactly lied to him; I had just neglected to mention my whereabouts that evening. But if I stuck with the job some hard-core lying would definitely be called for. Taylor said that the girls sometimes told their boyfriends they had jobs as night temps. Waitressing was a risky lie, because your boyfriend could show up to surprise you at work and then you'd be screwed. I supposed that I could let Sean assume I was still dancing at the club. But though I had been a stripper, until that point I hadn't been much of a liar. To my parents, yes, but not to my friends. Not to my boyfriend, my kind boyfriend with the elegant hands.

Sean had introduced me to Elvis Costello. As I left that night for my first trick, the lyrics to "Almost Blue" played in my head. *There's a part of me that's always true. Always.* The rest of me—Elizabeth, eighteen-year-old curvaceous theater student with a face like Winona Ryder's, will do whatever—stepped into the street alone and hailed a cab to an uptown high-rise.

It felt like a movie with a good jazz soundtrack. Like a Woody Allen New York love song. One of the characters is a young, lost actress who finds herself in a cab headed uptown to turn a trick with a radio personality. Starring Mariel Hemingway. Starring me. The film was already rolling. I couldn't stop to reconsider.

I stepped out of the cab, my breath visible in the cold night, and plunged my hands into my pockets before walking past a doorman, who nodded politely. I rode the elevator to the almost-top floor and knocked on a door. Instantaneously, the radio host appeared in the doorway. I recognized his face from ads for his show that I had seen plastered on the insides of subway cars. He was holding a sweating, half-empty drink in his hand and his paisley robe hung open, the belt coming undone and revealing a pair of silk boxers underneath.

"You must be Elizabeth. Can I get you a drink, sweetheart?"

I readily accepted his offer for a drink, totally ignoring Taylor's suggestion to stay sober. I wanted to be classy and in control like her, but I'd have to work up to it. Nothing sounded better than the comforting burn of a drink. I followed him into his apartment, where he took my coat, threw it over the back of a chair, and indicated a black leather sofa. I sat while he freshened his vodka tonic and poured mine.

The apartment was a classic bachelor pad with an elaborate entertainment center, five tall CD towers, and a panoramic view of the city. His back still turned, the radio host fired questions at me. Habit, I guess. He asked me how old I was and what I did when I wasn't doing "this." I told him I was an eighteen-year-old theater student at NYU.

"You're older than eighteen, sweetheart. I can tell. It's my job to read people." His eyes sparkled with self-satisfaction as he sat down next to me and handed me my drink, his hand resting on my thigh. "You don't have to lie to me. Now, how old are you really?"

He seemed so pleased with his intuitive gifts that I thought it best not to argue.

"You're right. I'm twenty. I'm graduating next year."

It occurred to me as we chatted more that I was going to be good at this. I was discovering a new talent. I had spent all this time in my acting training trying to uncover the authenticity in every moment, trying to lay myself bare. Here, I was going for pure artifice, the exact opposite result, but I was using the same skills of listening and improvisation.

I had been a good stripper—a natural, everyone always told me. I was never the prettiest or the girl with the best body, but I had that something that made people want to look at me. More important, I had that something that makes people feel seen themselves. Lonely guys couldn't get enough of it. It was easy for me; it was acting, which was my thing, after all. And I suspected that I was going to be the same way as a call girl. A natural.

The radio host was very impressed that I was a theater student, which I had actually ceased to be six months before.

"I went to Yale drama," he told me. "You should consider it."

"Good idea. I'll definitely consider it."

"You like Sam Shepard?"

"I love Sam Shepard."

"I'm a close personal friend of Sam Shepard. I could get you an audition one day."

He gave me the tour of his hallway gallery, which consisted of black-and-white pictures of a younger him in Off-Broadway productions. All of them hung slightly crooked, as if someone had banged into the wall hard enough to shake it—maybe he himself, staggering from the bedroom to the bar.

He grabbed my hand and led me toward the bedroom.

"There's something really cool I want to show you in here."

Please don't let it be a bottle of chloroform and a set of antique surgical instruments, I thought. I started to ask for another drink, but he didn't give me a chance. With a flourish, he opened the door of one of his bedroom closets and yanked me inside. It was a walk-in, lined floor to ceiling with cowboy boots of all kinds.

"Wow. Cool."

"I'm famous for wearing cowboy boots," he said. "It's my trademark. Would you like to undress?"

I reached behind me for my zipper and a chill shot up the back of my legs, the kind you get when you're caught doing something wrong.

"No, in here," he said, and indicated the bedroom. The bedroom had gray walls and gray berber carpeting. A garnet-red bed was the only furnishing, and it faced a set of mirrored closet doors. He sat on the edge of it and watched as I took off my dress and stockings and folded them, dropping them in a pile in the corner. The fishnets had embossed a pink honeycomb pattern in the flesh of my thighs. I put my heels back on and left my thong in place, planning to hold on to it until the last possible moment.

I stood awkwardly in front of him while he looked at me for a brief moment with no notable reaction and then began fiddling in the drawer of his nightstand. It was one thing to be naked and half drunk on stage with music and rosy lights and a rowdy audience. It was another entirely to stand under track lighting in silence in a stranger's bedroom. My arms felt long and awkward. I didn't know where to put my hands. I opted for my hips, with my feet in beauty-contest position. It seemed a bit stagy, but it was the best I could come up with.

"Have you ever done Rush?" he asked. He found what he was looking for. It was a bottle of poppers.

"I'm not in the mood, but you go ahead."

I would have juggled chain saws for another drink right then, but I didn't want to be passing out on the job. It was the first time I had seen amyl nitrate outside the dance floor of a gay club. Maybe this guy was gay? I had learned enough from fantasies revealed to me by customers at the club to know that there are many shades of gay.

The radio host slithered out of his silk ensemble and matter-of-factly asked me to get on my hands and knees on the bed, facing the wall of mirrored closets. Until then, he had only touched my leg once and grabbed my hand a couple of times, but it became clear that he had an aversion to further skin-on-skin contact. This was so different from guys at the club, who always wanted to hold my hand like it was some kind of date. Sometimes they asked me to the movies. Not this guy. He knelt on the bed behind me, straddling the back of my legs, not touching me at all.

"Just put your ass up in the air for me so I can look at it."

I did what he asked, but he didn't even really look at my ass or anything else about me. Instead he looked at himself in the mirror while he jerked off. He ran his other hand through his feathered hair and flexed his pec muscles.

"Lick your lips for me. Push your tits together," he said, looking straight into his own eyes the whole time.

Just as he was about to come, he grabbed the Rush off the nightstand, inhaled deeply until his eyes rolled back, and then collapsed sideways in a heap. I only had to shift subtly so that he came on the bedspread and not on my back. I disentangled myself from his legs and took the precariously tilting bottle out of his hand, placing it on the nightstand so the toxic liquid inside wouldn't spill. He quickly regained consciousness and smiled as he wiped the drool from his chin.

"Beautiful. That was great."

He even gave me a nice tip on my way out the door. To help out with tuition.

I walked out past the doorman and found the sky swirling with an unusually early snow flurry that stirred something in my chest. I love the first few hours of snow in New York, before the days of winter wear on and the streets turn to a gray, sludgy mess. A New York winter's first snowstorm is a magical thing, in which for a moment the whole city is blanketed in quiet and clean.

chapter 5

A month later, Taylor and I walked into the lobby of the Ritz the way we always did— confident, conservative, purposeful. We were both exactly five feet nine in three-inch heels. Taylor wore a tan, tailored skirt suit hemmed extra short with a white camisole underneath and, as always, a pearl choker she got on her twelfth birthday as a gift from her grandmother. Her signature look was very little makeup and a bouncy, strawberry blond, blow-dried bob. I was her photonegative, with my black suit jacket nipped at the waist, shoulder-length, chestnut hair, and red lipstick. Red lipstick because above all there is no kissing. Yes, the *Pretty Woman* thing is true. The no-kissing part, at least; the rest is an insulting crock.

I had perfected the art of not looking anyone in the eye as we walked toward the elevators. It could trip me up sometimes, how people looked at me, the barb of disapproval followed by the self-satisfied smirk—always so impressed with their own street smarts because they had spotted the hooker in the fancy hotel.

Taylor had convinced me to trade dancing for escort work with promises of easier money and a swankier life in general. In the span of a month I had seen nearly every five-star hotel in New York without ever staying the night. When we walked into the Ritz that day, I was queasy and exhausted. I had spent the previous evening at the St. Regis with an aging Italian art dealer who had freebased cocaine until yellow film edged the corners of his mouth and stretched in long strings when he talked. He had smoked until he was impotent and then opted to watch hotel porn and poke his dry, twitchy fingers inside me for what felt like about nine hours but was really only two. I was definitely making more money than I had before, but it wasn't always as easy as Taylor had led me to believe.

It turned out that Taylor sometimes worked outside of the Crown Club. Occasionally she even engaged in the extremely risky practice of snaking the Crown Club's clients. Diane didn't scare me, exactly, but she wasn't the highest rung on the ladder. We never saw or heard from the unseen hand that ran high-class prostitutes in our neighborhood, but it was safe to assume that these were people you didn't want to steal from. But Taylor was a lionhearted free spirit, possibly a sociopath of sorts. She was someone I wanted to be near, whose love and approval I craved. I imagined I resembled Taylor. I, too, was that brave, in my dreams.

In spite of my outwardly bold existence, when I was alone I literally looked under the bed for monsters each night, consumed by irrational panic. I checked the locks on my doors and windows three times a night and insisted that my roommate, Penny, do the same. I often woke from night terrors, a constant in my life since childhood, in the early-morning hours and lay there frozen with fear, reminding myself to breathe, unable even to get up and go to the bathroom. But with Taylor I was fearless. I could breathe freely. I never once looked over my shoulder. So when she called me to go along with her on sketchy jobs—bachelor parties out in Westchester, a masochistic Columbia professor, a Japanese businessman who liked to talk about enemas while Taylor and I made out—I always said yes. It wasn't exactly the money that motivated me. I could have made similar money coloring inside the escort-agency lines, but my transgressions with Taylor gave me a feeling of free fall, a sense that anything could happen, and that was worth the risk.

Taylor didn't know much about the job we were interviewing for that day. All she knew was that a talent agent in L.A. had tipped her off to a meeting with a woman who was in New York looking for entertainers to amuse a rich businessman in Singapore. The money was meant to run into the tens of thousands.

"What if they peddle us to some third-world brothel?" I asked in the elevator.

"You're always so negative."

Taylor was taking a class in Dianetics. She was all about being positive and freeing herself of the limiting imprints left by her past (this lifetime and others) on the fabric of her existence. She believed that success was her birthright and was only a week or two away. It was an infectious faith.

When we reached the room a man in a suit opened the door. I couldn't place where he was from. He looked kind of Persian but also kind of Asian. Taylor stuck her hand out and he ignored it. He went back across the room to join his friend, and the two of them acted as silent observers for the rest of the afternoon.

We were the last girls to arrive. A woman stood and came to greet us, introducing herself as Arabelle Lyon. When working as an escort, I usually tried not to have expectations, not to make assumptions, but Ari was a genuine surprise. She shook our hands and shot me a whole-milk-white smile. She wore almost no makeup and her hair was the natural sunny color that most mousy brunettes had when they were five years old. The two lurkers in the corner were mysterious, but it was this Gidget look-alike with the French name that made me suspect. How could she be anything but shady, with a disguise like that?

I looked around the room. Among the seven or so girls lined up on the couches there were one or two obvious duds, one or two who could be tough competition, and an anomaly named Destiny.

"Jesse?" Ari asked, when Destiny introduced herself.

"No. Destiny. It's on my license."

Destiny's fried brassy extensions put Jon Bon Jovi to shame and her green contacts made her look like something out of *Cat People*. Her three-inch acrylic claws were painted with neon zebra stripes that matched those on her fingerless gloves. No classy suit for her. I couldn't stop staring. I was enthralled.

Ari sat across from us in a straight-backed chair. She could have been a kindergarten teacher getting ready to read us a story. She began by explaining that she worked for a rich businessman in Singapore who threw nightly parties for himself and a few friends. They were looking for a handful of American women to join the party as his guests for two weeks, and we could expect to receive a cash gift upon leaving. This cash gift would be somewhere in the neighborhood of twenty thousand dollars. She assured us of our safety and told us that we'd be treated with respect, even pampered.

I watched the reaction of one of the girls I had pegged as tough competition. She was a long blonde with crazy cheekbones. I could tell she thought she had it in the bag. My competitive spirit kicked in. I didn't know if I believed Ari or even if I wanted to go on this mysterious and potentially dangerous job, but I knew I wanted to be picked. Ari asked us questions.

"Have you traveled at all outside the country?"

"I've been to London and to Ibiza," bullshitted Taylor, "and I plan on touring Bali in the spring."

"No," replied Dud Number One.

"I went to Hawaii once," answered the blonde.

I thought it best to leave out my family trip to Israel. I told her that I had been to the Cayman Islands and that I was saving to go to Paris. It was the truth.

"Does the Bronx count?" asked Destiny. "Nah, I'm just messin' with ya."

Ari paused and tilted her head, contemplating Destiny as if she were an exotic animal. Then she snapped back into business mode and told us that the job would require maturity and respect for other cultures and that she was looking for girls with whom it would be easy for her employer to get along. I caught some of the Gidget spirit from Ari. Gidget Goes Geisha.

"I love traveling," I said. "I love experiencing other cultures and I'm a fun party guest and I'd be perfect for this job."

I felt like I was vying for a job in the Peace Corps, until we reached the second half of the audition and went into the next room for a photo shoot. The bed had been pushed aside in order to make room for the lighting setup. We lined up along the wall and waited for our turn in front of the camera. A too enthusiastic photographer took pictures of each of us in our underwear and handed us his card, in case at a later date we needed head shots at a good rate.

The whole thing seemed dubious and I soon forgot all about it. It was just another afternoon standing around another hotel room in my underwear. But less than a week later, I received a call from Ari telling me that I had been selected, along with Destiny. Destiny of the finger-less gloves. Not Taylor. I dreaded telling Taylor that I had been picked and she hadn't. I knew her well enough to know that our relationship was contingent on the power imbalance between us and I didn't want to lose her. She was the only girlfriend I had who understood what I did for work every night and liked me anyway. I loved Sean. I dug my friends from the theater and they were far more sophisticated than Taylor in matters artistic and intellectual. Still, they were forever on the other side of an invisible membrane, the barrier that separated me from most of the world, from anyone who wasn't a stripper or a hooker. Taylor stood firmly on my side of the wall and I didn't want to be left standing there alone.

Ari went on to explain that she didn't work for a Singaporean businessman at all, but rather for the royal family of Brunei. The money was better than she had intimated at first, though she couldn't be specific. The parties I was to be attending would be thrown by Prince Jefri, the youngest brother of the Sultan, and I would be his personal guest.

To which I responded, "The Prince of *where*?"

chapter 6

 ri said that she would need my passport Fed-
Exed in order to arrange for an immediate
visa. Fantasies of doing the dance of the seven veils in
a domed palace warred with fears of being forced into
white slavery on a bare mattress. Could I trust this
woman? I instinctively felt that I could. The story was too
farfetched to be a lie. But how could I know? I spontane-
ously decided to accept the invitation, figuring I could
change my mind at the last minute. Buzzing with the rush
of making such a daring move without instigation from

Taylor, I walked to the mailbox place on Houston Street and sealed my passport in an envelope headed for Los Angeles.

I hadn't told my roommate Penny yet. Penny was an aspiring director and in the hours she didn't work as an intern for the Wooster Group or as a waitress at an Italian restaurant uptown, she was constructing an ambitious theater piece, featuring a handful of our friends.

Penny and I rode the F train out to a friend's loft in Park Slope, which we were using as a rehearsal space. I meant to tell her about the Brunei job on the ride out there, but for some reason, I couldn't. I'd have to miss rehearsals for a couple of weeks, but that wasn't the primary cause of my reluctance. Penny was bright and ambitious and hardworking. I was all those things, too, but I was constantly in search of a way to ditch the hardworking part. Penny was completely nonjudgmental of my pager and my late-night cab rides, of my being the only girl trotting down Ludlow Street at two in the morning dressed in a business suit. But I looked at myself through her eyes and I judged me.

I went the whole rehearsal without telling her. We had divided the loft into four quadrants, with a separate drama being enacted in each one. My scene involved a blond drugstore wig, a basket of cosmetics, and a phone conversation with our friend Ed the Meat Poet (as opposed to Beat Poet), a performance artist who was pursuing his doctorate in German philosophy. We'd all gone to see him perform on my birthday and he'd presented me with a raw birthday steak (as opposed to cake) onstage.

Afterward, when we'd gone for drinks at Max Fish, he'd given me a wrapped gift. It was a franc.

"For when you get to Paris."

I'd have to get back to my dream to go to Paris. Maybe this new job would even finance it.

On the ride home, I stared out the dark subway window at nothing, at my own face reflected back at me. We sat in the comfortable silence of roommates for half the ride before I turned toward her and explained about the job in Brunei—what I knew about it, anyway.

She paused. "Are you joking?"

Once she'd established that I wasn't kidding, she knew me better than to try to stop me. She thought for a minute and then she launched right into elaborate emergency plans. Penny was a girl of action.

"How long do we have? I need a copy of your license and credit card and passport. We need to come up with a secret password that you can use to signal me if anything is wrong—if you can contact me somehow. What else can we do?"

After a beat, she continued, "We could go to the botanica."

Penny had a botanica she went to for cleansings and card readings and dressed candles. I neither believed nor disbelieved in her talismans, but there are times when I'll take whatever help I can get.

"For what?"

"Protection."

I agreed, though I knew that if this escapade went awry, it would take more than a coconut shell and a candle to save me. Still, we stopped on the way home to get a protection candle. On it was a picture of the archangel Michael, his torso itself a suit of armor, his hair a glowing helmet, his foot securely planted on Satan's head. I had wanted Mary, but the woman behind the counter insisted on Michael. I doubted a man, even an angel-man, would intervene in this case. Still, I burned the candle. But just to be safe, later that afternoon I headed uptown with my backpack over my shoulder. I thought I'd try to protect myself with the imperfect armor of information, too.

I walked past the incense sellers and the stone lions guarding the columned entrance of the public library. I was a pioneer in the position Ari offered, only the second group of American women to be invited to the parties of the Prince. There was no one I could talk to, no real way to ascertain the validity of Ari's job offer. So, as it was the Paleolithic, pre-Wikipedia age, I camped out at the library for the afternoon and researched the country of Brunei and its royal family.

I turned the pages of encyclopedias, glossy-paged photo books, and a small paperback tell-all (which didn't tell very much) titled *The Richest Man in the World: Sultan of Brunei*. The book was mostly an account of the Sultan's business dealings involving people with names like Kashogi and Fayed.

I learned Brunei is a Malay Muslim monarchy located on the north coast of the island of Borneo. Independent from England since 1984, Brunei still retains strong cultural and diplomatic ties with the Queen. At that time, the Sultan of Brunei was, thanks to oil and investments, the richest man on the planet, though he's since been blown out of the water by Bill Gates. He now comes in at number four, in between Microsoft's Paul Allen and Saudi Arabia's King Fahd.

I copied down the stats in a notebook. Brunei occupies approximately 2,228 square miles of the northern coast of Borneo, making it slightly smaller than the state of Delaware. Often called the Shellfare State, it has a population of 374,577 citizens, all of whom receive free education and health care on the Sultan's tab. The Sultan has three brothers: Mohammed, Sufri, and Jefri, who would be my host. Mohammed, I read, was the most religious of the three brothers, taking only one wife and often vocalizing his criticism of his liberal (and libertine) brothers.

I found picture after picture of the Sultan and his two wives and one picture of his brother Mohammed, but I couldn't find one of Jefri. The Sultan looked so official, with all his royal regalia and military badges. It was hard to imagine interacting with someone like that. The expectations of middle-class Jews from New Jersey don't include run-ins with royalty. Most of the girls with whom I had gone to high school left town to attend college in places like Michigan or Syracuse, then wore their sorority pins home a few years later and stayed to marry dentists or optometrists.

Finally, in the back of a yellowing paperback, I found a small photograph of Prince Jefri. In it, he wears a polo helmet and a blue uniform. He stands next to a horse with a coat so glossy it throws a glare. Jefri seemed kind of short, but confident and athletic and surprisingly handsome. I caught something cold in his eyes, a glimmer of meanness. This, combined with an Errol Flynn mustache, gave him the look of some raffish scoundrel from another era. He was a real live Prince Charming, with a dash of villainy mixed in. I was suddenly convinced that I was going to Brunei after all. There in the library, I prepared myself to fly off to this parallel universe of palaces and parties, imagining that my life in New York would remain intact, awaiting my return.

That night, I told Taylor. She acted true to form and demanded a commission from my earnings. I acted true to form and agreed to give it to her.

When I explained the situation to Sean, I got my first indication that my departure wasn't going to be as seamless as I had anticipated. There were going to be casualties. Previously, I had simply let Sean assume I was still dancing at the club, but the deception made me feel like shit. When I took the job in Brunei, I knew I had to come clean.

"I'm putting my foot down here," Sean said calmly. "You cannot do this."

We were standing in his narrow kitchen, with the yellowed paint peeling off the walls and the chrome legs rusting out from beneath the kitchen table.

"Are *you* going to give me twenty thousand dollars?"

"Not everything is about money. You make enough money at the club."

The fact that he was right made me angrier, made me fight harder. The fact that I had lied to him about working at the club made me feel guilty and that made me fight harder still. Plus, I kind of did believe that my work "relationships" and my relationship with Sean were unrelated. They were light years away in my emotional landscape. I thought that he should understand and, furthermore, that he should agree.

"I just want this money so I don't have to worry about money for a while."

"That's not how money works. More money gives you more to worry about, not less."

"This is a job, okay?" I explained deliberately, as if he had been struck stupid. "This has nothing at all to do with us."

Sean seemed to grow taller and broaden by a foot.

"Do you know that you're fucking insane?"

"I am not insane. You're a bourgeois, controlling asshole."

He looked like he wanted to hit me. I recognized the look; I had seen it in my father a thousand times. The difference was that Sean would never actually do it. My upbringing had led me to believe that this meant he didn't love me enough. I had no such hesitation and I threw a plate at his head to prove it. He ducked and it hit the wall behind him, shattering. I immediately felt like an idiot. It's so humiliating to clean up the shards of the dishware you've pitched across the kitchen. He looked around and sighed and I could tell he agreed with me; I should be ashamed of myself. He asked me to go.

I didn't understand why he insisted on standing between me and what I wanted. It was just an adventure, a stack of cash, a foreign prince. Couldn't we give each other a little freedom? Meanwhile, I was the one who had gone through his letters, listened to his answering machine, excavated his apartment looking for relics of old girlfriends. I suppose I knew my stance was hypocritical, but I stood by it anyway. Because in the end I was going to do what I wanted to do. No one was stopping me from getting on that plane.

I paused on the landing in the stairwell. Up a flight stood Sean in his doorway; down a flight was the door to Rivington Street. I really did love Sean. I just did it poorly.

"Don't leave me," I said.

"I'm not leaving. You are."

chapter 7

I spent my last thirty dollars on a cab from Beth Israel to Kennedy Airport. The international terminal was an erector set of beams and soaring ceilings that transformed me from a throbbing vein of guilt into an anonymous traveler adrift in the midday light. Walk through the doors of Kennedy and you're swept into a liminal state, not exactly here anymore but not there yet either.

I spotted my fellow traveler Destiny from behind as she waited on a long check-in queue. Her teased hair aspired to brush the skylights and she wore a spandex tube dress that shifted from neon pink to neon orange, like a tropical sunset. The top of the dress smooshed her boobs into one amorphous form. My mother says tops like that make your bust look like a loaf of challah. Destiny's loaf of challah would have fed a developing country. I gave her a quick hug and noted that she reeked of Aqua Net and Amarige. I was traveling with a superstripper. So much for anonymity, for mystery and the fluid identity that travel allows.

The plan was for Destiny and me to fly to L.A., where we would spend the night and then hook up the next day with Ari and a girl we hadn't met yet, named Serena. We'd travel on to Singapore, where we'd stay another night before a short flight the next day to Bandar Seri Begawan, the capital of Brunei. I dreaded the many hours that stretched out in front of me with Destiny as my traveling companion. What would we talk about? The surprising practicality of Lucite platforms?

As we walked to our gate, every eye looked up from its newspaper and stared at Destiny. The corridor became a catwalk. That quickly, my attitude toward Destiny shifted from repulsion to loyalty. I trained my eyes straight ahead. I was used to being stared at: I had been a teenager with fuchsia hair at a preppy private school, a club-goer dressed as Marie Antoinette on a Tuesday night in July, a drinking companion to drag queens on the stoops of the Lower East Side. Stares made me feel defiant, made me affect a greater degree of self-confidence than I truthfully possessed.

What would Patti Smith do when facing three days of international travel with a walking porno movie? She would straighten her spine and stare right back at the gawkers with a look that said, I see you. I see you, too, motherfucker.

While we taxied down the runway, I learned that Destiny made all her own clothes, did her own acrylics, enjoyed power-lifting, had posed for *Hustler*, loved Jesus, and was a collage artist. I relaxed some about the next few days. They might prove more interesting than I had anticipated. I also learned that Destiny had left her five-year-old daughter at home with her mother. I didn't think less of her for leaving her kid. You do what you have to do, right? Sometimes you have a daughter who gets left behind.

She put a little blue pill on her tongue and got teary as she flipped through wallet picture after wallet picture of her little girl while the jet engines revved beneath us. I couldn't summon a tear for anyone I was leaving behind, not even Sean. That, I imagined, was freedom.

Destiny and I awoke the next morning and ate breakfast on the balcony of our airport hotel. With only a couple of hours to spare before heading back to LAX, we decided to go to Venice Beach. Seduced by images from *Baywatch*, we wanted to dip our toes in the Pacific, wanted to see bikini-clad beach bunnies diving for volleyballs, wanted to be Surfin' USA for the day. We weren't disappointed. The wind kicked off the water and blew the sky clean, turning it the kind of blue that painters use to represent heaven. On a good day, the light in L.A. can make your heart hopeful; it can make even the grungy boardwalk look like a perfectly lit movie set. We squinted and shopped for sunglasses that shone on their racks like hard candy.

In my memories of my first time in Venice, there are cameos by characters I see today when I stroll the boardwalk. I'm almost positive that the tall man with the electric-guitar-and-amp rig whizzed by us on his roller skates playing "Purple Haze." But I can't be sure. I do know that the woman with the faux Gypsy getup and the cardboard sign offering psychic readings was there, because I remember she called out to me, "You're pregnant. It's a girl. You'll want to hear the rest."

I ignored her. I'm not above card readings from waterfront charlatans, but I thought it was a mean trick to try to lure women with what was often either their dearest wish or their greatest fear. I wasn't interested in a phantom pregnancy. Now, if she had said, "You're going to travel to exotic lands," or, "You're going to meet a handsome prince and fall madly in love," I'd have hit Destiny up for five dollars to hear more.

I helped Destiny pick out postcards and T-shirts for her daughter. We ate at a boardwalk café connected to a little bookstore and then played on the swings in the sand. I have a picture of me dressed in black jeans and big, dark glasses, laughing hysterically as I begin to swing backward, my hair flying in the wind. Destiny caught the exact moment that my forward momentum stopped and gravity pulled me back down.

❊   ❊   ❊

That evening Ari met us at the airport with a freshly scrubbed face and a monogrammed tote bag. California was not New York, I decided. In the New York sex industry, I had encountered neurotic, carefully coiffed, mercenary people in positions of authority. That or Hells Angels. Serena stood by Ari's side at the ticket counter. She was a platinum blonde, porcelain-skinned, poor-man's Marilyn with mean blue eyes. She had the kind of upturned nose that grandmother would have said could catch raindrops. I immediately didn't trust her.

Ari, I learned as we waited, hadn't started out as a procuress. She was a nice girl from Northern California, a rich girl, a girl with a close family who imported French wines and sold them to most of the upscale restaurants in the Bay Area. She had begun working for the royal family of Brunei as a property manager and personal assistant, whose duties included looking after one of their many palatial Bel Air estates and regularly traveling back and forth between the two countries to meet with the Prince.

On one of Ari's trips, the Prince casually suggested she bring a friend with her next time, preferably one who looked like Marilyn Monroe. I guess he thought that Marilyn Monroes were walking around all over the place in Los Angeles—surely everyone knew one. No one ever said no to the Prince, so Ari had scoured the city until she found Serena, a Marilyn look-alike with dreams of stardom, grudgingly working a retail job at the Beverly Center. The next time Ari returned to Brunei, she had Serena in tow.

So these were the women with whom I was traveling halfway around the world: a Jesus-loving *Hustler* centerfold, an evil shadow Marilyn, and a summer-camp counselor gone wrong. This was Serena's third trip to Brunei, but she wasn't exactly bubbling over with helpful hints. Even after a half hour of plying her with chardonnay at the airport bar, I was no wiser about what lay ahead of me. She enjoyed her seniority, blowing us off with a little wave over her shoulder as she passed through the first-class doorway with Ari while Destiny and I stayed in business class.

We stretched often, complained even more often, sucked down champagne, and requested extra cookies from the pretty flight attendants in long, dragon-pattern skirts. We watched *Beauty and the Beast* and eventually sort of slept. Business class was kind of like a flying hotel, but even a flying hotel wears on you after a while. I imagined my mother and my aunt at that moment, probably perched on plastic chairs at my father's bedside. Then I shoved the thought aside. No point in worrying about something I had no control over. No point in rehashing a decision I'd already made. We changed planes in Tokyo and did it all over again, for a total of about eighteen hours. Thus began my hard lesson of parking it and chilling—not easy for such a restless girl. If I had learned the lesson better, I'd have become a lot richer.

I rubbed my eyes and leaned my forehead against the window, watching the miles and miles of stormy blue slip by underneath us. By the time Singapore's narrow hem of coastal beach appeared, I was so exhausted that I was seeing halos around all the lights and starbursts every time I blinked. My tongue and my brain had both grown a coat of fur. I was grateful to have our den mother, Ari, to take charge and herd us through customs and into the cabs to the hotel. On the ride, Serena let it slip that the royal family actually owned the hotel and that the sixty-third floor, where we would be staying, was always reserved strictly for their guests.

The Westin Stamford Singapore is the tallest hotel in the world, a cylinder rising seventy-three floors above the harbor. When we got there, I didn't have the energy to explore even the rest of the hotel, much less the streets of the city. I ordered satay from room service and passed out with the lights still on. When I opened my eyes eight hours later, jet-lagged and wide awake, it was just before dawn. I got out of bed, hugging my own naked ribs, and pulled the heavy drapes to reveal a navy sky shifting to cobalt. One or two stars still shone out beyond the balcony. I walked out into the warm, soft air and watched the fishing skiffs glide out of the harbor. I was alone, exactly halfway around the world from where I had started, and I had an ocean of unknown possibilities in front of me.

I was sure that this was how I had been waiting to feel.

chapter 8

Two serious men dressed in matching white shirts, ties, and sunglasses greeted Ari, Serena, Destiny, and me at the airport in Bandar Seri Begawan. I thought it was funny how much they looked like secret-service agents. I was thrilled that they had received the memo about me starring in my own personal spy movie. In retrospect I realize, of course, that they *were* secret-service agents. It took me a while to catch on to the fact that I was the clandestine guest of the leaders of a foreign government—an extremely wealthy and therefore influential foreign government. There was a whole apparatus at work that facilitated our trips to Brunei, but we never saw the man behind the curtain. In Brunei, there were elaborate ciphers in the clothes people wore, the food they ate, their gestures, but it was a language I didn't speak.

A triad of huge photographs hung on the wall of the Bandar Seri Begawan airport. The same images decorated the walls of every restaurant, business, bank, and beauty shop in the country. The center picture was of Hassanal Bolkiah Mu'izzaddin Waddaulah, the Sultan of Brunei, a man I would come to know as Martin. In the photo, the Sultan wears a white military jacket laden with medals, a round hat, and a gold sash across his chest. Slightly lower and to either side of the Sultan hung pictures of his two wives: his formidable first wife, Saleha, and his scandalous second wife, Miriam, a former Royal Brunei Airlines flight attendant. The wives wear beauty-pageant makeup, elaborately beaded gowns, and enormous diamond tiaras.

Looking up at the pictures while we waited by the luggage carousel, I imagined children playing at being kings and queens: Two little girls fight over who gets to be the queen and someone's mother settles it by telling them there can be two queens. The mother cuts two crowns out of yellow construction paper to prove her point. The little girls are happy for a minute with their saw-toothed headgear, but somewhere they know that it's not the same as being the only queen. They learn that sometimes you take what you can get.

❊   ❊   ❊

The airport doors opened and the Southeast Asian humidity hit us like a wall. It soaked into my skin immediately, slowing me down. It soaked into my suitcase, making it feel ten times heavier. An irregularity in the pavement caught the toe of my shoe and I tripped, my suitcase falling to the ground and my arms pinwheeling like in a comedy gag. Like the Powerful Katrinka. I caught myself before I went for a tumble. Everyone in our little party turned to look and I did a little dance move.

"I meant to do that."

I try so hard to be graceful, but I've always been the girl with the bruised knees and the Band-Aids on her elbows. The stripper who wanted to be a ballerina. The circus clown who wanted to be an aerialist. Indeed, sometimes you take what you can get.

We piled into two black Mercedes with windows tinted nearly opaque and traveled the perimeter of the city before plunging into what seemed like a jungle. Brunei was green—sticky, overgrown, ancient green. Through openings in the trees I caught glimpses of a mishmash of modern office buildings, nondescript homes, and domed mosques.

As we drove along the water, I recognized the Kampung marsh villages from my research at the library. The villages comprised tilting shacks perched on stilts above murky marsh water. The shacks looked like they could slide off their precarious foundations at any moment. The plank walkways between them seemed no more secure to stand on than the lily pads beneath them.

"The Sultan offered the marsh people houses, but

they chose to stay where they were," said Serena, wrinkling her nose. "It's filthy out there. They don't even have plumbing."

This reminded me of a story I had heard once about the nomadic tribes in Persia. In the seventies, the Shah, obsessed with modernization and Western culture, forced the nomads to abandon their customary migrations and settle down in houses. The nomads put their goats and camels in the houses and slept in tents in their backyards. When the Shah was deposed during the revolution, the nomads picked up and resumed their former life; they were that sure of who they were. Their abandoned houses still stand on the Iranian hillsides.

As we drove, I caught only little slices of the sights through the trees and I wanted to see more. I asked Ari when we'd have time to do some sightseeing.

"You won't."

"You can sometimes go to the Yaohan if you request it in advance," said Serena. The Yaohan was the mall. "But you have to wear a baseball cap and long sleeves and people will still stare at you. I got flashed by a pervert once in the parking lot."

Serena was freer now that we were in Brunei. She had slid into a comfortable skin. She was the girl who knew more than we did, the tour guide. But I detected something else. She ran the nail of her middle finger back and forth on the pad of her thumb, a nervous tic. As she rattled off her knowledge about the country, I sensed it growing; Serena was definitely anxious about something.

❉ ❉ ❉

In about twenty minutes we reached a compound that appeared to be the size of a small city. High, off-white stucco walls surrounded the place, and above it we could see only treetops and a large blue dome in the distance. We pulled up next to a guardhouse, where a soldier stood wearing the kind of cap that an old-fashioned soda jerk would wear. I knew from a former Marine who liked to come into the Baby Doll and tell me his war stories that Marines call those caps piss-cutters. I had a mental file cabinet a mile deep where I kept those sorts of details.

The soldier opened the gate and as it rolled back it revealed a compound that looked something like a resort in Fort Lauderdale as envisioned by Aladdin. Eight four-bedroom guesthouses were arranged in a semicircle facing a palace on a hill. A road wound around the property, and we followed it to one of the houses, where five smiling Thai housekeepers in pink uniforms waved at us from the porch and rushed to the cars when we stopped, pulling our bags from the trunk while chirping, "Hello. How are you. Hello. How are you." They didn't wait for our replies.

Inside, the house itself was like a tacky mini-palace, decked with miles of Italian marble and plush carpets. The windows were smothered with yards of peach drapery and someone had stuffed huge silk flower arrangements into every possible niche. An odd detail caught my eye: There were at least three tissue boxes in every room, each with a decorative gold cover.

I stood on the back porch and looked out on the

property. Across acres and acres of lawn and partially obscured by a hill stood the palace. It was as big as a hotel. Up the road to the left I saw a glittering square of turquoise pool and beyond that some tennis courts. The light was beginning to wane and I realized I was starving. I took my shoes off before I walked across the freshly vacuumed tracks in the peach-colored carpeting and up the stairs to search out my room.

I found my suitcase stashed in a room, where Destiny was already unpacking. Ari had the master, Serena had a bedroom across the hall, and Destiny and I would be rooming together. I looked around. Our bedroom was a hall of mirrors with one king-size bed in the center of it, a vanity in the corner, and a wall of closets on one side. Destiny was underwhelmed.

"It looks like a rug dealer lives here."

She threw on a sweat jacket and the airbrushed words *Queen Bitch* bounced off every surface. There wasn't a spot in the room where each angle of us wasn't reflected on into infinity.

"That Serena seems like a snot," Destiny whispered as she began setting out piles of minuscule garments on the bed.

"No doubt."

When I opened my suitcase my heart sank. Against the backdrop of our lavish bedroom, I was clearly a shabby impostor. I didn't have two weeks of party clothes. I didn't really have two *days* of party clothes. I had never even been to a proper cocktail party. I had brought thrift-store duds, hooker suits, and clubwear and hoped I could accessorize and wing it. As I hung my clothes I felt like I was clinging to the edge of the boat and dragging along in the water while everyone else sipped champagne on the deck. I steeled myself. I knew I would pull it off. I always did.

We ate at a big, round marble table in the dining room downstairs. Serena wore a robe and had her hair already in curlers, her face dewy with moisturizer. Half ready and dressed in possibility, she looked beautiful. I still wore my travel clothes and felt covered with a film that I couldn't rinse from my face or my eyes.

The maids brought us a feast in large aluminum tins. It was twenty times the food we could possibly have eaten. There were delicious, oil-soaked Thai noodles and spicy chicken dishes and fruits and salads and a whole tray of tarts and pastries. The fruit tray smelled like filthy feet. Ari explained to me that the perpetrator was a fruit called durian. She began to fill us in on the protocol. We ordered our food for the next day the night before. Anything we desired would magically materialize and when we were done would just as quickly be taken away.

"Except papaya. You'll never see papaya here. Robin hates it," said Serena, scraping the sauce off a piece of chicken with a spoon.

"Who's Robin?"

Ari explained that with the exception of the devoutly religious Mohammed, each of the royal brothers—the Sultan, Prince Sufri, and Prince Jefri—had informal Western nicknames that we were to use at all times. We were to call Prince Jefri Robin. It sounded pretty, Sherwood Forest-y, almost feminine: Good Sir Robin. And I, his Maid Marian. I was such a dork.

"I called him Jefri once to tease him," added Serena.

"Don't try it," said Ari.

Day tumbled into night tumbled into party time. I could barely change my shoes fast enough to keep up. When we dressed for the party, I chose my best suit because it was sexy and was actually the most expensive item of clothing I owned. I hoped it might inspire some confidence.

Destiny, Serena, and I waited for Ari in the foyer. As I grew accustomed to it, the house was looking less like a palace and more like a banquet hall. I pictured a gaggle of bridesmaids posed on the staircase. But it was just the three of us, facing each other awkwardly, tallying up each other's flaws and assets as we waited for Ari's entrance. I figured that over Destiny and her acrylic claws, I had looks but not wildness. Over Serena and her china-doll eyes, I had smarts but not looks.

Serena leaned against a column opposite me. She was the blonde and I was the brunette. In the world of musical theater, she would be the soprano and I the alto. I was the one with the big ass who played her lines for laughs. Serena was the slender-waisted ingenue who got the guy in the end. I was Rizzo and she was Sandy. I was Ado Annie and she was what's-her-name in the surrey. We faced off until, with a subtle shift in posture, she dismissed me as not much of a threat. One thing Sandy always forgets is that Rizzo has the best song in the show.

The palace was too far to walk, so we drove the golf carts that were parked in our carport. Ari drove with Destiny and I hopped on with Serena, who silently steered through the winding, lit pathways, past the pools and tennis courts and palm trees. The air was humid and thick with the fragrance of tropical flowers. Not an hour out of the shower, I already felt sticky. My head raced with plans. I would make the best of my time here. I would improve my tennis game. I would get a tan. I would lose weight. And maybe I would even make a prince fall in love with me and my whole life would change in dazzling and unexpected ways. I longed for a magic pill to soothe the restlessness that prickled constantly under my skin. I'm not sure what made me think I'd find it in Brunei, but I wouldn't be the first person who hoped to step off a plane on the other side of the world and discover their true self standing there waiting for them.

Up close the palace reminded me of a picture I had seen once of Hearst Castle, on the California Coast. There were gold domes, columns, and twin marble staircases that curved like ribbons up to the main entrance.

"We normally go in the side because it's less of a hike, but I want you guys to see the entrance hall," said Ari. "I think you'll like it."

We were breathing hard when we reached the top of the stairs. We entered a cavernous cathedral of a room with a fountain at the center. I felt like I had walked onto the set of some 1930s MGM movie version of *Salome*. Surely a flock of harem-pants-clad showgirls was about to descend the stairs and launch into a Busby Berkeley dance number.

"It's all real," said Serena.

"Real what?"

"Like, the gold in the carpet is real gold. That ruby is a real ruby," she said, pointing at a ceramic tiger that stood near the fountain. The tiger held in its mouth a round, red stone the size of a tennis ball.

I spotted what looked like a Picasso directly across from the front door—also real, I assumed. We followed Ari around a corner and there, where a hallway bisected the main foyer, a Degas ballerina sculpture stood on a pedestal, a little girl cast in bronze. She clasped her arms behind her back and pushed her chest out defiantly, her foot thrust in front of her in third position. It looked exactly like the one that I had loved visiting as a child, when my father would take me to the Metropolitan Museum of Art on special Sundays to wander the wondrous galleries and then stuff ourselves with hot dogs on the steps. Each visit we chose a different gallery. We sat on a bench in front of a giant Jackson Pollock and looked for charging bulls and blooming irises and skywriters hiding in the paint splatter. We crossed our eyes and tried to reassemble the figures cut to pieces by Picasso. We stood washed in light next to the enormous wall of windows that faces the Temple of Dendur and told stories of time travel. But at the end of the day we always visited my Degas ballerinas, numinous and frozen in time, pinned like butterflies to the wall.

When she caught me staring at the sculpture, Ari told me that Robin was an avid art collector. He had countless walls to decorate. Robin owned other palaces where he lived, still others where his three wives lived, whole office buildings where he conducted business, and hotels and estates in Singapore, London, and Los Angeles. But Ari informed me that some of his favorite art was right here. We were standing in the palace where he unwound every night, his sunny pleasure dome.

"Come on," she said, with a hint of trepidation. "Let's go in."

We were so close I could have walked up and touched the Degas. In fact, I felt an overwhelming compulsion to do just that. I made a note to try to sneak back and do it sometime later. Like people touch the feet of Jesus on the Pietà and hope for a blessing, I would touch the feet of the dancer and hope for grace.

chapter 9

We entered a downstairs room, where beautiful women lounged on every inch of the upholstery. Scattered around the party were little seating areas where low chairs and couches surrounded glass-topped coffee tables with bases in the shape of silver and gold tigers. A tableau of Asian girls decorated each area, themselves looking like tigers draped over the rocks in their cage at the zoo. Shiny hair hung down their backs and they leaned shoulder-to-shoulder, as if propping each other up. They were set against a backdrop of deep blue upholstery, jade green drapes, a dark wood bar, and creamy carpets.

The women were of different nationalities: Thai, Filipino, Indonesian, Malaysian—maybe forty of them in all. At the far end of the room was a dance floor with a mirrored disco ball throwing lazy coins of light across the scene. Every gaze fixed on us when we walked into the room, except for those of a girl who, eyes closed, was lost in a moment of karaoke abandon. Behind her, a large screen played a video of a man and woman riding a carousel, with cryptic foreign words appearing along the bottom in yellow print.

A dowdy white woman with a wide forehead and wire glasses saw Ari and crossed from where she stood at the bar to meet us at the doorway. This was Madge, the Brunei equivalent of Julie, the cruise director from *The Love Boat*. Madge was a British woman who ran the parties, managed the affairs of the household, and made sure that Prince Jefri was happy at all times and that everything was going according to plan. She wore a cell phone, still an exotic sight at that time, clipped to one side of her belt, and a walkie-talkie clipped to the other.

Ari and Madge greeted each other with a warm hug and exchanged a few loaded pleasantries before Madge showed us to our little domain. We occupied the seats of honor, squarely in front of the door. Destiny and I followed the cues of Ari and Serena as we sank into the deep cushions of the chairs and ordered glasses of champagne from one of the army of servants who were standing by to take our order. Alcohol was illegal in public in Brunei, but it flowed at the Prince's parties. I sipped self-consciously. I could feel that the conversation in the room was all about us. The other women stared and murmured, their foreign words floating around and mixing with the cheesy synth sounds of Asian pop karaoke music.

Ari and Madge caught up about London and a bunch of people whose names I didn't know yet. Then Madge got a call and answered it out in the hall, while Ari took the opportunity to school us about the men we were about to meet, the royals and cabinet ministers and air-force generals and international financiers.

"The men with the Prince are his closest friends. Don't talk to them unless they talk to you. Don't show anyone the soles of your shoes; it's considered really rude in Muslim countries."

While being instructed on the best way to angle my feet in order to be respectful of Muslim customs, I thought with wry amusement of what Rabbi Kaplan would say if he could see me. Stodgy Rabbi Kaplan, the thin-lipped tortoise who had stood by my side while I confidently chanted my clear haftorah. I was that rarest and least cool of things—the girl who took her Bat Mitzvah seriously, the promising student of Hebrew.

It had been only five years earlier. I was a late bloomer and didn't even have to wear a bra under my dress. I could still remember the heft of the silver pointer we used to keep our place when reading from the Torah scroll, a treasure hand-lettered on parchment. The goat-skin parchment looked both powdery and oily, like the thinnest pie dough rolled out on the counter. When I stood on the bimah, the scroll seemed to glow in the light from the tall stained-glass window behind me. I wanted to smell the paper, to see if it smelled like an animal or like cooking oil or like silver or like the truth. For some reason, I thought it probably smelled like autumn, like damp leaves on the ground. But I couldn't say for sure because I was too self-conscious to lean my head down and sniff the Torah in front of the rabbi.

I believed that God was in that scroll somehow, in the gaps between the words. God lived in the negative space, in the hushed, vaulted hallways of the temple, between my roof and the clouds, between the branches of the trees. I had no question that God existed, because I felt him. God was a palpable presence, a warmth behind me. I talked to God all the time, except when I lay terrified in my bed at night. Because as certain as I was of God the rest of the time, I was equally sure God wasn't around then. When faced with my nightmares, I had to think quickly and start negotiating with the monsters instead. But those kind of negotiations—deals struck, promises made—dissolve with the sunrise.

I was twelve, not thirteen, when I was Bat Mitzvahed. The younger age is permitted for girls, particularly those who have their birthday over the summer and want to have their reception during the school year, when everyone is still around. In our town at the time, the popular thing was to have a theme party following your Bar or Bat Mitzvah ceremony—the more outrageous, the better. To celebrate this sacred coming-of-age ritual, this symbolic threshold crossing, classmates of mine had mini-carnivals, costume discos, and black-tie balls. One of the town's real estate magnates rented out Giants Stadium for his son's reception, which was attended by actual members of the Giants as well as Giants cheerleaders in uniform. We ate kosher hot dogs in the stadium restaurant while a marching band spelled out GREG, the name of the kid being Bar Mitzvahed, on the field.

The theme of my party was Broadway shows. Each table was crowned by a festive foam-and-fabric centerpiece representing a different show. My table was *A Chorus Line*. In the foyer of the catering hall was a picture station, where you could get your photo printed on your very own Playbill. To be accurate, it was called a Jill's Bill—very collectible now, I hear. A guy named RJ stood near the entrance of the catering hall eating fire and juggling. He had been in the original Broadway cast of *Barnum*, which, at the time, I thought was the coolest thing ever. I might have recognized the ominous portent if I had thought for a minute that performing at suburban Bat Mitzvahs probably didn't rank highly on RJ's list of dreams for himself.

My mother worked so hard to make my Bat Mitzvah all I could possibly have wanted, from my dress with matching purse and shoes (designed by me and featuring lots of fabric roses and pink Swarovski crystals) to the flowers, the balloon arch, the ice-cream-sundae buffet, and the fire-eating circus performer. But with my final bite of cake, I seemed also to swallow a worm of doubt that would make a home in my belly and grow in the coming months. If God had, in fact, scooped me up in his arms and carried me over the threshold that marked the entrance to womanhood, was this a disappointing room to find on the other side? A room filled with a bunch of spoiled preteens, most of whom weren't even my friends, wearing foam lobsters on their heads and dancing spastically to the B-52s?

Soon after, I began to question the wisdom of God altogether. It wasn't the Giants cheerleaders or the foam lobsters. It wasn't even the Holocaust or the famine in Africa that broke up God and me. It may have had something to do with the archery counselor I met that summer at sleepaway camp and fell in love with, the counselor who agreed with God about the Bat Mitzvah concept: He thought twelve-year-old girls were all grown up. It may have been the fact that when our little romance was exposed and we were dragged into a room to stand before the camp director and every other counselor in the camp, with my parents on the other end of the phone line, no one stepped forward to defend me. Not my father, not anyone.

Before that experience, I had often felt the kind of alone that comes from the suspicion that you are not only genetically different from those around you, but different in your very soul. I was a princess from another kingdom, abandoned on a doorstep by a mother who couldn't care for me because she'd been transmuted into a swan by the spell of an evil sorcerer. But after Nathan got fired, I was a different kind of alone. I was alone and ashamed of myself. It wasn't the fault of a sorcerer that I'd wound up unlovable, by my parents or God or anyone—anyone but a guy nine years my senior. It was no one's fault but mine.

It wasn't an exact cause and effect that led me to stop believing in God; more like an accumulation of evidence. First I stopped talking to God, then I kind of just forgot about him. Then I got to high school and discovered that a lot of people agreed with me about this no-God thing. I was so relieved.

So there I was in Brunei, not believing in the Jewish God, believing instead in the pernicious influence of all organized religion, and yet suddenly feeling very Jewish indeed.

"Don't have your head higher than Robin's. If you have to cross in front of him while he's sitting, bow," continued Ari.

"Bow like how?"

"You'll see."

I had a déjà vu from *The King and I.*

When I sit, you sit. When I kneel, you kneel. Etcetera, etcetera, etcetera.

"And watch what you say. When you think they can't hear you, they can. When you think they can't see you, they can."

What she meant was that there was surveillance everywhere in Brunei, even in the bathrooms; hence all the mirrors. It was a constant source of speculation and paranoia among the girls. Not exactly *The King and I* after all.

A bored-looking Filipino woman stood up from a couch across the room and crossed toward us, stopping to exchange a few words here and there with a handful of the women flanking her path. She seemed to be the only woman in the room who breached the invisible barricades that separated one seating area of girls from another. She was a bit older than the average age in the room and appeared almost matronly in a black, high-necked dress and diamond drop earrings. She introduced herself to us with a vague British accent.

"I'm Fiona. Welcome to Brunei."

Serena rose and kissed her on both cheeks. They looked thrilled to see each other, greeting each other like old sorority sisters and catching each other up on the latest gossip.

After Fiona left, Serena said, "I see she still hasn't shaved her mustache."

Fiona was Serena's archenemy and soon to be my closest ally.

Within half an hour I regretted my outfit choice. I had worn my little black suit and I felt stiff compared with Serena in her flirty, swingy dress and her Grace Kelly French twist. I shifted uncomfortably and braced my thigh muscles so that I wouldn't start to slide off the slippery upholstery.

Abruptly, the karaoke music stopped and the lights dimmed as the DJ changed hats and arranged himself in front of a keyboard. The languid couch decorations turned from slouching question marks into exclamation points. They prettily crossed their legs as a woman took her place beside the keyboard player. She began to sing Lisa Stansfield's "All Around the World."

I felt him coming before he entered the room. Prince Jefri walked in that night wearing shorts and a shiny Sergio Tacchini sweat jacket. He carried a squash racket, as if he'd just walked off the court. When he appeared, all the girls lit up with purpose. The pictures hadn't lied. In person he was handsome, in spite of his outdated, feathered porno hair and thin mustache. A wave of charisma swept the room in front of him. You could almost see it, like heat radiating off asphalt on a summer day. Behind him walked ten or so identically attired men. The whole entourage stopped when he paused to take a quick glance around.

His eyes rested on us, specifically on Serena. He made an expression of phony surprise and then strolled over to give both Serena and Ari a brief kiss on the cheek. Up close, the Prince appeared tightly wound, toned muscles curving around the bone, taut skin holding it all together. He smelled like too much expensive cologne. He half-sat on the arm of Ari's chair. What was it about Ari that seemed so out of place? *Plain* wasn't quite the word to describe her. She was like a real strawberry in a roomful of strawberry Pop-Tarts.

When Ari introduced us to Robin he welcomed us with a practiced smile, then ignored us and turned to Serena. She became a study in coy gestures and sexy glances—chin down, eyes turned up toward him, little giggles and tosses of the head, slight rearranging of the skirt, delicate hand signals. I was cooked. I was many things, but, alas, never delicate.

As they talked, the Prince watched Serena with

what seemed like fascination until something across the room caught his eye. I watched his gaze shift as his attention wavered. In that flicker of disinterest, I saw my window open. He nodded a few more times and gave her leg a familial pat before walking away.

After the Prince moved on to the next table, Eddie, the Prince's sycophantic right-hand man, seemed to teleport into the seat next to me. Eddie was sneaky like that; you never saw him coming. He was too accommodating for comfort, inquiring after our needs with bulging eyes that looked like they might pop right out of his head and land on Destiny's boob-shelf. Were we meant to "entertain" the Prince's friends? Was that the meaning of "entertainers"? I'm not sure why this was such a disappointment. I certainly wasn't this discerning when it came to Crown Club clients. Were they clean? Did they have money? Were they relatively sane or at least not homicidal? These were the criteria. But somewhere along the journey, in my mind I had become mistress to a prince.

But Eddie left pretty quickly. Two more men, named Dan and Winston, came over and said hello. They appeared to be friendly with Serena and Ari and they didn't give me the creeps like Eddie did but they, too, soon moved on.

There were three talented singers who changed off every few songs and sang a schlocky medley of Malay and American pop songs. The American songs were the kind played in grocery stores, the kind that can make you cry if you happen to be shopping for Cap'n Crunch and tampons at two a.m. on a lonely night.

By the end of the night I had to pinch the sides of my thighs to force my eyelids to stay open. I felt like I was in a math class in an overheated schoolroom, snapping a rubber band on my wrist so I wouldn't fall asleep. The Prince ended up seated in a chair by the wall next to Fiona. On the other side of him was an empty chair, and though plenty of people stooped to talk to him, no one sat down in it. The rest of the men socialized and drank with the Asian girls. A few of the men laid their arm across a girl's shoulder or held her hand. Other than the short visits at the beginning of the party, everyone ignored us. I wondered if I was supposed to be doing something more than sitting in a chair drinking champagne, but I was too tired to ask.

At some outrageously late hour, the lights dimmed even more and a dance hit from about two years before blasted from the speakers. The dance floor filled with girls immediately, while the men sat and watched. I had grown stiff with sitting and I felt like a barnacle on the chair, so when Destiny took my hand and led me to the dance floor, I didn't protest.

The only route to the dance floor was a narrow path that crossed right in front of the Prince's chair. All night I'd watched the bows of the women who passed in front of him. This was my chance to practice. I emulated the others, walking with a little shuffle and bending at the waist, with my head bowed. It made me want to giggle. I almost expected him to break out with a Yul Brynner–esque "'Tis a puzzlement!" Instead, he ignored us. But I felt his gaze hot on me as I passed him, and I flushed.

Was it the act of bowing itself that had made me suddenly shy?

Destiny kept her back defiantly straight and yanked me along.

"I'm a fucking American," she said when we were out of Robin's earshot. "Sorry, I don't bow."

When we hit the dance floor Destiny went nuts, which delighted the dancing girls and watching men alike. Across the sea of women, I could see through to where the Prince was watching, his head inclined toward Fiona as she whispered in his ear. All the eyes in the room were on Destiny except for Robin's. Robin was decidedly looking at me. I got the electrical surge that comes from being noticed, from being watched, the kind that makes your bulb glow a little brighter. The truly beautiful people of the world must live their lives buzzing with it. I looked away, but my feet were surer on the floor, my hips synced perfectly with the bass line.

After an hour of the disco, Robin stood. All the men preternaturally sensed this and darted up a millisecond later. He shook hands with a couple of them as he left the room with Eddie in tow. As soon as he was up the stairs and out of sight, the music shut off and the lights came up. All the party guests gathered in a group near the door, where Madge stood facing them, her hand on her walkie as if she was a gunslinger and it was her revolver. A few minutes later, a crackling, unintelligible voice came from her hip and she pulled the walkie off her belt and thanked whomever it was before standing aside. Everyone walked out looking tired. Even the men were like strippers matter-of-factly cashing out for the night, different people entirely than they had been a half hour before.

"What were we waiting for?" I asked Ari as we headed toward the golf carts.

"We wait until he's left the building, in case he changes his mind and wants to come back."

He never once came back. He just liked to know the party was always waiting.

chapter 10

The Prince was charming, dynamic, enigmatic, a polo player, a playboy, the minister of finance. The Prince was totally ignoring me. By the end of the first week, I was still on the fringes of the Brunei party microcosm. Serena was part of the inner circle in a way I didn't completely understand. Destiny was in a different tribe altogether and didn't give a shit. Ari was like one of those really great retail bosses who are fun and chummy, but are still management through and through and don't give any of the boss's secrets away.

I was nearly halfway through my time there and, contrary to my big plans, I hadn't gotten much of a tan, hadn't picked up a racket, hadn't fallen in love with a prince, and hadn't lost a pound. Time in Brunei was slippery. As soon as you tried to get a foothold in a day it was already gone. Some days I read for hours. When I did my nails, I felt a huge sense of accomplishment. The boxed set of French-language tapes I had brought along sat unopened on the shelf. Ari had helped me put a call through to my parents late one night so I could check on my father's health, which was steadily improving, though not so much that it didn't warrant a heavy dose of guilt. My father sounded like himself again, but slightly deflated. My mother's voice was worn. I kept it short, saying that I was needed on the set. You know—the set of the movie I was shooting in Singapore.

On Tuesdays, Thursdays, and Saturdays, the party lasted until four-thirty a.m. On the rest of the days it ended at three-thirty. We didn't get to bed until at least five in the morning, and the blackout drapes made it easy to sleep until one or two. Bleary, hungover, starving, we'd stumble to the kitchen in our robes, wolf down the lunch that was waiting for us in big tins lined up along the counters, then flop down in front of a laser disc in the upstairs den. Sometimes we'd go to the gym on the property or hang out by the pool to catch the last of the late-afternoon sun. Then we'd eat dinner and it would be time to get ready for the party again.

I was disappointed in Brunei and in myself. I hadn't made any kind of a splash at the party and the nights were melting away in a haze of small talk and champagne. The only good thing about my long nights of being passed over is that they gave me an opportunity to observe the subtle machinations that drove the social interactions around me. The parties were a petri dish, ideal conditions to breed fierce intimacies and fiercer resentments.

I had figured out that the tables were arranged by country: Malaysia, Thailand, the Philippines, Indonesia. There was a hierarchy of importance. I couldn't figure out the order exactly, but I knew the Filipino girls were on top and the Thai girls were on the bottom. The Filipino girls got their status from Fiona, who was the Prince's favorite girlfriend and the only one who sat next to him. Other girls in the room also counted themselves in the Prince's or one of his cronies' favor, and their rankings shifted from time to time, causing enmities and alliances to spring up within the various camps.

For instance, Winston had once had a girlfriend in the Indonesian camp, but he had given her the shaft in favor of a girl named Tootie, who made her home in what I called Little Thailand. So now the Thai girls and the Indonesian girls were practically in a gang war, which, of course, looked like nothing from the outside. Girls at war opt for a quieter cruelty than fistfights and drive-by shootings. Girls circumvent the corporeal and go straight for each other's souls. The bleeding is harder to stanch.

I knew, for instance, that the Thai girls enlisted the Thai servants to doctor the Indonesian girls' drinks. Some nights the drinks were too strong, some nights too weak. They did it to mess with their minds, so the Indonesian girls would get too drunk and make fools of themselves, so they wouldn't get drunk enough and would be too sharp, too present. This might shift in a period of a few days and some necessary alliance would make them all best friends again.

I got my insider information from a beautiful Thai girl named Yoya, with whom I had struck up a friendship. She fell somewhere on the Prince's list of favorites, though not even she was exactly sure where. Yoya was a curvy confection, with sparkling eyes, a chubby baby face, and a braid as thick as a horsetail that brushed her ass. She was bright and irreverent and eager to use her few words of English. I needed a break from the American girls, who had begun to bore me to the point of homicidal thoughts. Before the men showed up, when Serena had me yawning into my espresso with her improbable, name-droppy tales of Hollywood parties ("So this one time I was at a Halloween party and this guy was there in you know, whaddaya call it . . . in blackface, and he was trying to flirt with me all night long and I was like I recognize that voice I know I recognize that voice and guess who it was? No seriously try to guess. Okay it was Jack Nicholson. So I wasn't really into him or anything but I gave him my number and he would call once in a while and be like, 'Hi baby it's your daddy calling . . .'"), I would drift over to Little Thailand. Yoya's best friend, Lili, would hop on someone's lap in order to make a spot on the couch. They huddled up and pieced bizarre stories together for me. Yoya always referred to herself in the third person.

"Yesterday Yoya going to gym in the naked."

"Yes. Yes," agreed the other girls, leaning in and nodding.

"You went to work out naked? Ew. Why?"

"Someone watch somewhere," she whispered, looking around for dramatic effect. "Robin watch somewhere."

I was sure they were pulling my leg.

"You're shitting me."

"No shitting. Terrible going to gym that way. Stairmaster. Terrible."

"Oh, Yoya so shy," teased Lili.

"Yoya so shy," Yoya concurred. I couldn't tell if she was being sincere or sarcastic. Maybe both. Maybe she was truly shy in her heart, but under the present circumstances it was comical to say so.

I didn't need Yoya to tell me that the fulcrum of the room was Robin. Everything was a show put on for Robin, an audience of one. The men, even his closest friends, were his paid playfellows as much as the women were. But Robin didn't seem to have any interest in me, so I turned my thoughts to audiences I imagined would have a greater appreciation for my talents. I drank champagne and studied the crystal prisms of the chandelier while I schemed about my acting career. How would I get the killer audition? How would I meet the right people? How would I make meaningful art? Where was that asshole Sean and did he miss me uncontrollably? Would he take me back when this was all over and done with? What was going on over at the Performing Garage? How was Penny's show coming along? What would I wear while gracefully accepting my Academy Award even though I thought they were trite and gauche?

Eddie surprised me out of one such reverie by plunking himself down in the seat next to me and blurting out a question in the typically blunt Bruneian way.

"You will sing tomorrow night?"

It wasn't really a question. If Eddie was asking me to do something it was because he had been told to do so by Robin. I looked over at Robin and saw both him and Fiona nodding at me with encouragement. I decided the two of them were having a little joke, but I was happy to be singled out for anything that proved I wasn't just a piece of furniture.

"Of course. I'd love to."

Eddie acted overjoyed. People around the parties, even the sensible ones like Madge, always behaved as if every little thing was so life-and-death. It was as if my refusal would have been followed by a summary execution.

They didn't know that I was a singer of sorts. I'd grown up singing along with my father's piano repertoire every night of my life. I'll bet you a dollar I can sing any show tune you can name. And I can usually put on a show entertaining enough that you won't even notice I don't have a particularly good voice.

When I started out this grand singing career of mine, I was the One. Technically, there were two of us, but only technically. We stood in front of the other performers, making our own row. The rest of the seven-year-olds in group 5A wore top hats and carried canes that had been smeared with Elmer's glue and rolled in red glitter, but ours had been rolled in gold. Randy Klein and I got the gold hats and canes.

I suspect we were cast as the Ones simply because we already knew the words. I had the albums from *A Chorus Line*, *Cats*, and *Grease*, and I could sing each score by heart. Every song had an accompanying dance number rehearsed to perfection for an audience of attentive stuffed animals lined up on my bed. Whatever I lacked in talent, I made up for in dedication and enthusiasm. If you asked me what I wanted to be when I grew up, I responded that I wanted to be the white cat in *Cats*, the one with the spotlit dance solo at the top of the show.

As the camp talent show approached, a special period each day was designated for practice. Our counselor sat cross-legged in the corner of the basketball court and rewound a tape in a battered boom box again and again, chewing an enormous wad of Bubblicious while calling out the counts and the steps.

Canes out. And. Bounce up and down from the knees.

One. Singular sensation, every little step she takes.

And turn.

Dadadadadadada.

Bounce again.

I found the dance routine embarrassingly easy. We took a rest every five minutes, during which we drank apple juice from crumpled boxes and scratched our mosquito bites through our tights. I was annoyed with the constant breaks, with the lack of commitment. The other girls were bored and slow, watching the feet in front of them rather than learning the steps. Being the One made me bossy.

"Don't forget to smile. Smiling is the most important," I told the other girls.

I didn't care that they rolled their eyes. I didn't need them to like me. I needed for us to be good. I needed for everyone to love us when the day of the show came. Randy felt the same way. We practiced our side-by-side box step when we were on break. We insisted that we do a kick line for the last bars of the song, just the two of us.

My plan was for my parents to see me shine and change their minds about allowing me to go to Stagedoor Manor the next year. I wanted to go to the sleepaway theater camp, not the camp with the endless afternoons full of soccer games and lanyard making. Everyone knew that girls from Stagedoor Manor went on to be in the casts of *Annie* and *Really Rosie*. The kids in Broadway shows slept late and went to special schools and lived their nights floating between the orchestra and the scaffolding, the scenery and the audience, in that magical kingdom where conflict is resolved by big dance-number finales. That was the kingdom where I wanted citizenship.

In response to my ardent begging, my father said, "If you want to be an ice skater or a dancer or a gymnast or something special, you have to get up at four in the morning and practice every day before school and you have to have no friends and never do sports or eat ice cream or go to parties or have boyfriends. If you want to be like that blind girl in *Ice Castles*, you will never go to college and you'll ruin your feet and your back and your career will be over by the time you're thirty. It's okay for a hobby. Don't get out of hand about it."

He was just trying to be merciful, trying to spare me the heartbreak. I was too chubby for ballet; it was a waste of time. I was too uncoordinated for ice skating. I was too mediocre to really sing. "Don't try and you won't fail" was his motto. But I had seen *Ice Castles* and I knew that he had missed the point.

I knew that when my parents saw me as the One, my strong voice clearly leading all the others, my gold-glitter cane sparkling in the afternoon sun, I would convince them that I was tailor made for a life of singing and dancing, that I would happily ruin my feet. I didn't care if I had to wake up early. I didn't even like boys or ice cream that much anyway. They would see me shine and, even to my dad, my destiny would be undeniable.

On the day of the show, my parents were there, front and center. They snapped pictures and mouthed the words. I was adorable. They were delighted. They showered me with kisses and praise. But when I pushed again, I got the same response about the early mornings and the ice cream. In spite of my stunning debut as the One, I never did make it to Stagedoor Manor and was instead condemned to a purgatory of campouts and color war. But my father did indulge my thespian aspirations up to a point. After all, his hobby corresponded with mine.

Years later I stood next to his baby grand in the living room, rehearsing my song to audition for the school play.

"You're no fantastic singer," my father said. "So you've got to pick your song well and then you've got to sell it."

A successful stockbroker, he was an expert on selling nothing. Together, we chose "Tits and Ass" from *A Chorus Line* for that particular audition, perhaps a strange choice for a fourteen-year-old, but it did its job. It didn't get me the part—that went to my friend Alexis, who actually could sing—but I was the one who got the laughs, who got the attention. I was the one people talked about. So that's what I learned to do. I still can't ice-skate worth a damn, but I can sell it. Whatever it is, I can sell it.

I pulled aside Anthony, the keyboard player.

"What's Robin's favorite song?"

"Well, he likes a couple of Malay songs. American songs? I don't know. What can you sing?"

"I'll sing a Malay song."

"How long do you have?"

"Tomorrow night."

"Too hard. Can't do it."

Angelique, the queen singer and rumored to be the unrequited love interest of Prince Sufri, overheard us and interrupted.

"Sing 'Kasih.' It's his favorite. You can learn it. I'll help you."

Angelique took a sheet of blank paper out of one of Anthony's many three-ring binders. She found a pen behind the bar, wiped the counter in front of her, and began to write out the words phonetically. She had the bubbly handwriting of a junior-high girl.

"It's a love song. 'Kasih' means 'darling.'"

Then she went over every word with me, correcting my pronunciation. Anthony handed her a cassette tape and she wrapped it in the lyric sheet.

"Just sing it simply," she said. "You can do it."

I was touched by Angelique's encouragement. As she pressed the cassette into my hand, the thought flew through my mind that she'd make a good mother one day.

When I returned to our seating area, Serena narrowed her eyes at me.

"You're singing tomorrow?" she asked. "What are you singing?"

"'Kasih.'"

"Oh, God. Did Anthony tell you to sing that? Did he tell you Robin liked it or something? I hate those horrible pop songs. I'm singing tomorrow, too."

"What are you singing?"

"At home, I'm a jazz singer. That's what I do. I'm singing 'Fever.' He loves it when I sing 'Fever.' I used to sing it for him all the time."

Anthony and I arranged to rehearse the next day at four. That night I lay awake while Destiny slept next to me. Never troubled by insomnia, she would put on her cheetah-print eye mask and be asleep three seconds after she lay down. I envied her.

How was I going to learn a song in another language by the following night? I should have just picked a sexy little retro number like Serena had. I started out with confidence and wound up with a sour stomach that kept me awake.

I set my alarm early the next morning and quietly played the song over and over on the downstairs stereo, lying in front of the speakers and stumbling through the lyrics while my housemates slept upstairs. I pretty much kept at it all day until I went up to the main house to meet Anthony. I walked into the deserted palace by the front entrance. Daylight streamed in through the tall windows and flashed off the water in the fountain. The fake flowers, which usually looked real in the strategic evening lighting, showed their seams, their plastic dewdrops.

A door was open to the left that had been closed the first night I saw the entry hall. It was a ballroom, with a chandelier the size of a small car. A man waxed the floors with a machine. I thought of my grandmother's favorite joke for party entrances:

A ball! said the queen. If I had two, I'd be king.

I made my way through the carpeted corridors and downstairs to the party room. It was spotless and empty, waiting once again to fill with women. I've always liked rooms when the party hasn't started yet. Even more magical are theaters during the day, before the doors open, before the show begins, when the house lights are on and you can see the rafters and the scuffs on the floor. I love the feeling that anything could happen. After the party, when anything already has happened, there's usually the inevitable fact to face that anything wasn't all you'd hoped it would be.

Anthony accompanied me while I sang into the mike and smiled at Robin's vacant chair as I flattened the melody and fumbled the lyrics again and again. I could see Anthony was dubious.

"Do you know any other songs?"

"I can do it."

I sang it right once through and then wrong again.

"Okay, maybe I can't do it."

"Too late." Anthony looked at his watch. "You'll be fine. Just make it up if you forget it."

"Super. He'll love that."

On my way out I walked up to the ballerina sculpture. I remembered reading somewhere that the girl who had posed for this turned out to be a prostitute, and that prostitution was the fate of many failed dancers in the time of Degas.

I ran my finger along the edge of her bronze slipper, where it met her foot. If you are rich enough, you can own art like this. You can put it in a corner where no one will ever see it, except a passing girl—half a woman, even—who once wore the same shoes and imagined herself a swan.

Every time Serena sang the word *fever* she shot her palms out in front of her and did a little dip with her hip. I was happy to note that she was no jazz singer.

A new woman had joined us at our table. Her name was Leanne and she was a soap-opera actress from Hong Kong who was half Chinese, half English, and all smoky sex. She had sleepy eyes, loose, wavy hair, and a British accent attached to a voice that was thick with cigarettes—kind of Janis Joplin meets Princess Di. She wore a simple, floor-length Armani gown. It was not her first time in Brunei. Like Serena, she had a mysterious past there, but unlike Serena she was completely open about being in love with the Prince. She admitted as much to me within five seconds of meeting me. She slouched back on the couch, an arm on each armrest, a posture of elegant surrender.

"I gave up a movie role to come here but he doesn't know it. I can't stay away. Last time I left I swore it would be forever but I couldn't stand the broken heart."

There was something real but not real about Leanne. I instinctively believed she loved him but I also knew an actress when I heard one. We actresses write terrible dialogue for ourselves.

Leanne and Serena seemed close, conspiratorial, joined in common vitriol for Fiona. Earlier in the evening I had overheard them talking about her. Serena said that Fiona had been caught casting some Filipino voodoo spells in her bedroom. It was the only explanation: That cow had used witchcraft to ensnare the Prince. Did she get fatter as well as older? How old was she now, anyway? They were frightening, and so familiar—common as dirt, these mean, mean girls. And what was I? The opposite? Nice? No. What was the opposite of mean? Weak?

Eddie approached me.

"You will sing next?"

I had dressed in my best vintage ensemble and decorated my eyes with thick strokes of liquid liner. I imagined myself a slightly chubbier Audrey Hepburn from *Funny Face*. This was my chance to shine. And even if I blew it, at least I wasn't doing jazz hands and singing some tired Peggy Lee song.

When Anthony began the intro, my brain emptied. I forgot everything we had worked on. I was sure I was about to be the star of a living nightmare, the kind in which you wind up on stage with no memory of what you're supposed to be doing up there. I didn't panic; I had faith. I know something about performing. I know that when it seems like the avalanche is about to roll over you, you face into it and keep both arms swimming as hard as you can. You smile and you sell it.

"Kasih dengarlah hatiku berkata/Aku cinta kepada dirimu sayang . . ."

The Prince flashed an impenetrable smile at me as he tapped a finger on his leg. Next to him, Fiona smiled, too. What was her deal? She didn't seem to be the dragon lady that Serena and Leanne made her out to be.

I finished the song and the room broke into a round of applause. My Thai friends even cheered. The smile on Serena's face was that of the runner-up in the Miss America pageant who had been so sure she was just about to claim the crown. As I passed the Prince and bowed on my way back to my seat, he reached out and grabbed my arm. I stopped and faced him, still bent at the waist, my head inclined.

He took my hand between both of his, dry and soft and perfectly manicured, and said, "Beautiful." Then he let go.

"Yes, very lovely," said Fiona.

I was from New York. I worked around movie stars.

I was not unaccustomed to attention from almost-successful actors and the occasional after-party rock star. This touch, this crumb of approval should have meant nothing to me. But I must have been brainwashed during the course of a week, because one Midas touch from the Prince and I glowed all night.

After the lights dimmed and the disco started, I headed to the ladies' room for a lipstick touch-up. A painting caught my eye that every other night I had passed right by. It was a classic Orientalist portrayal of alabaster odalisques and their brown-skinned servants lounging by a harem bath. I had studied this kind of painting in art history, had analyzed each racist, imperialist brushstroke. And here was a romanticized, nineteenth-century Western portrayal of a harem hanging one hundred and fifty years later on the wall of—a harem. It was positively postmodern.

A harem. Why hadn't I realized it before? We were neither party guests nor prostitutes. We were harem girls.

chapter 11

Even locked away in a jewel box of a room on the island of Borneo, in my dream the gestapo was pounding on my door. Nazis had figured prominently in my nightmares ever since, at eight years old, I read *The Diary of Anne Frank*. In my dreams I was Anne, with my ear pressed to the floor, listening to the boots on the stairs as they marched up to take us away. In my dreams I was Anne and I was already dead but I was wandering through piles of shoes and fillings. I was looking for the suitcases. I knew mine was in there. I was trying to find it so I could leave.

As a child the night terrors had seeped into my waking life. Thoughts of the Holocaust obsessed me. Anne Frank's diary led me to other books that didn't leave one with a hopeful view of the human heart. I remember one book in particular from the town library, with a Star of David in flames on the front and a map of the camps printed on the inside cover. There were photographs inside. You know the ones—grainy black-and-white, the shadows between the ribs the blackest black, the naked skin on the piles of bodies the whitest white.

I was sure it was only a matter of time before the Holocaust happened again, and I wondered how my family would react when the Nazis came for us. How can you tell who you really are on the inside? We all like to believe that we'd be brave. We'd be the hero in the movie, the one who sacrifices himself to save others, the one who does the right thing when the world around him is wrong. In the movie, the right choice is clear. And we leave the theater feeling good about ourselves because we can say, Me, I'd do the right thing.

No one says, Me, I'd be the coward. Me, I'd rat out my neighbor to save myself. But that's what people do, mostly. Even at eight I knew this.

So who would I be when they came? Would I be brave? What about my parents? Would they try to hide us, try to escape? Would they kill us all rather than be taken, like the Israelites at Masada? Would they stand up and throw bricks, like the Jews in the Warsaw Ghetto? Or would they dutifully hand over their papers and then sing in the lines to the showers? I secretly suspected that my parents weren't the fighting kind. I knew it would be up to me to protect us, so I tried to be prepared. I detailed plans of how we were going to escape, and then how we were going to return to fight back. I knew that the plans to resist were probably futile, but I had resolved to fight anyway.

How could I ensure that I'd be the brave one, that I'd be the hero? I had to practice my moves, to go over and over the scenario in my head. I sacrificed my sleep in service of this mental rehearsal. I worried that caught off guard I'd act in ways that were less than estimable. I sensed that deep in my heart I wasn't Anne. I didn't have that kind of a soul—the kind possessed of a love so remarkable, so bright, that it was far more impermeable than her body.

In an attempt to help me sleep, my mother tried to convince me that we lived in different times, that the Nazis weren't going to show up at school one day and haul me away. But I was unconvinced. I found her naive. Didn't she understand that it was people who had done this thing? The same people who were all around us? Things were really not so different.

"It's not going to happen again," my mother carefully explained for the hundredth time. "That's why we remember it, so we won't let it happen again."

"Anne Frank's mom told her it wasn't going to happen, but it did."

My waking fixation on the Holocaust eventually wore off, but the dreams never quite did. So the dream in Brunei of the gestapo knocking on my door was no surprise.

But when I opened my eyes, the knocking didn't stop. It grew progressively more insistent. Destiny and I both sat up in bed and looked at each other, but neither of us went to answer it.

When we had arrived, Ari had taken our passports and handed them to a guard. She had said it was to update our visas or something. It had stayed with me like a hair you can't get out of your mouth. Is that what smart girls do? Go to Southeast Asia for some questionable employment and hand over their passports upon arrival?

The passport situation flashed through my mind as, blood pulsing in my skull and my chest, I opened the door a crack. Standing there was a guard in uniform. He wore a gray wool jacket with a Nehru collar, and one of those soda-jerk caps. I opened the door all the way and he looked at my nightie with alarm.

"You are not ready?"

"Ready for what?"

"You must get ready. Five minutes."

If he wasn't going to tell me what was going on, there was only one real question to ask. The answer to this question will reveal almost everything a girl needs to know to prepare herself for whatever trials lie ahead.

"What do I wear?"

"Wear a dress. Wear no tall shoes. No makeup. Five minutes you must get ready. We go."

I thought about running to Ari's room, but I remembered that she had left for the States early that morning to deal with some business and pick up a few new girls. She had assured me the night before that we would be fine there alone and that she would return before we left to make sure our departure went smoothly. I looked to Destiny, who shrugged, equally clueless and visibly relieved that it was me and not her.

Ten minutes later, in sandals and a black sundress with a print of pink cabbage roses on it and buttons up the front, I accompanied the guard out the front door and into yet another black Mercedes with tinted windows. It smelled of new car and warm leather.

"Where are we going?"

The guard pretended he didn't hear, picked up a cell phone, and made a call in Malay. These guards were inscrutable, and there seemed to be so many of them in on the secret. What did they think about chauffeuring the Prince's women around all day long?

I felt strangely calm; I settled back into the upholstery. I looked out the window and watched the world roll by. I wasn't really there. I was on a soundstage, sitting in a stationary convertible with fans blowing my hair and a screen behind me showing a winding road through the jungle. Then the scenery changed and we were in the city, whizzing down alley after alley. I had been behind a wall or a car window for my entire time in Brunei.

The car came to a stop at the back entrance of an office building, a tall, generic box of steel and glass. The driver handed me off to yet another guard, who took me wordlessly up in an elevator, down a hallway, and into a room. He gave me a glass of water and left me inside, locking the door behind him.

The interior of the room was incongruous with the businesslike exterior of the building. I had expected to see an office, but instead it was a sitting room stuffed with the same ornate furnishings as the palace, a skewed contemporary take on Louis XIV. It looked as if the Prince's decorator had multiple personalities. The surface of a massive mahogany desk was crowded with photographs of what I assumed were the Prince's wives and children. I looked at them, tried to look into them, to glean some insight into what their lives might be like.

The person who appeared most often in the photographs was a young man who looked like a huge, blown-up baby, often stuffed into a polo uniform. Was this Prince Hakeem, Robin's oldest son and heir? This giant couldn't possibly be the slight Prince's progeny. Hakeem reminded me of Francis in *Pee-wee's Big Adventure*. I imagined the smug, rotund teenager sitting in a bathtub the size of a swimming pool and playing with model battleships.

The women in the photographs were all gorgeous in a painted, glossy-lipped way. They were wrapped in brocaded gowns and wore gauzy scarves covering their hair. Were these his wives? There was a smiling little girl with pigtails. I wondered at what age she'd trade them for a head scarf. Was this his daughter? The Prince himself didn't appear in any of the pictures with the women, though he did stand next to Hakeem in one or two.

I didn't know exactly what I was waiting for, but I hoped that I was waiting for Robin. I suppose it should have seemed strange to me to be looking at pictures of Robin's multiple wives while I waited for him to show up, but I had become accustomed to the Prince's myriad of women after spending night after night at the palace. I arranged myself attractively on the divan and tried to look casual as the air-conditioning froze the room to a subarctic temperature that made me surprised I couldn't see my breath. According to a gold clock on a table across the room, ten minutes passed, then a half hour. I finally gave up on sitting properly and pulled my knees up under my dress, rubbing the goosepimply skin of my arms. I hugged myself into the tightest ball I could while still ready to uncurl and appear sexy at any indication of a turn of the doorknob. But the door stayed closed and locked.

An hour passed. There were no books, no magazines, no television. I walked in circles. I sat back down. I looked for a bathroom. I tried the door and it was locked. I tried a second door, also locked. I sat back down. Another hour. I was the star of a Sartre play with no audience. I considered peeing in a wastebasket. I was trembling from the cold, from hunger, from nerves. I tried to think through my searing caffeine-withdrawal headache. If they forgot about me would I just rot there like Antigone, entombed alive?

Worse yet, what if I wasn't waiting to be his highness's belle du jour? What if I was awaiting another fate? If I disappeared, who would look for me? My parents, certainly. But where would they start looking? An imaginary movie set in Singapore? Whom could they pin my disappearance on? I was aware that I could have vanished at that moment and there would have been no culpability.

But I was just being hysterical. And besides, there was nothing I could do. Was I somehow going to fashion a rope ladder from shreds of the white leather couch cushions and lower myself out the window onto the streets of Bandar Seri Begawan?

I closed my eyes and tried to warm up. I imagined myself somewhere sunny, on a beach, maybe. Too corny. Then I imagined myself in one of Robin's harem paintings, dipping my toes into the steaming bath. Too wet. Finally, I simply imagined I was in my bed at home, deep under the covers of my futon on the floor of my Ludlow Street hovel. I missed home. I was looking forward to going back there and being an intern at the theater again, to being just another girl on the subway again. I fell asleep on the divan with my knees pulled up under my chin.

I woke to the sound of the door opening and found myself staring up at Robin dressed in a gray uniform with medals on his lapel and a military cap. It was the first time I had seen him wearing something other than shorts and tennis shoes. He looked the part of a prince. I sat up too quickly, like a child caught napping when she was supposed to be doing her homework. I fell victim to Stockholm Syndrome—you can't help but fall in love with the guy who rescues you, even if it's the guy who locked you up for four freezing hours without a bathroom in the first place. I felt a profound sense of gratitude and a deep desire to be valued by this person standing in front of me. In extreme circumstances, this combination can look very much like love.

"You have been here long?" he asked, sitting beside

me and running his hand along the chilly skin of my arm.

"Yes."

He seemed to take some pleasure in this.

"And you're cold."

He placed his hand on the nape of my neck and drew me toward him for a soft kiss—not commanding, not confident, not what I had expected from this notorious playboy. I hadn't fallen straight from a crappy retail job into the arms of a prince. Girls like Serena pretended they had come strictly to gaze at the rainbow and that the pot of gold at the end was incidental.

I tried not to add self-delusion to my list of character flaws. I knew that we were prostitutes. Slant it any way you want, but when you're trapped at the same party every night and you wind up making out with the guy throwing the parties, and then you magically have a handful of cash when you leave to go home, you're a hooker. But every hooker has a little gold somewhere in her heart. Some hearts are just gilded, some are solid straight through, and some, like mine, are divided in two, one side shining and one side in shadows.

I knew I was a hooker, but somehow I felt like Cinderella as the Handsome Prince stood and led me by the hand to the second door in the room, which was now unlocked. I half-expected him to kneel and pull a glass slipper out of his pocket. Part of this was just me being a romantic ding-dong and part of it was him. He had something. Like many true great lovers of women, Robin looked at you a certain way and you were suddenly lovely.

Women will overlook all manner of philandering and cruelty, will crush their logic under a glass heel, if a man can make them feel they belong on a pedestal in the Louvre.

The coach turned into a pumpkin, however, when Cinderella got back from the bathroom and took a look at the room next door. It was a bedroom that looked like something Hugh Hefner could only fantasize about. The walls were draped in the same lustrous black silk as the sheets and the headboard. There were mirrors on the ceiling, mirrors on the closet doors, at least three visible video cameras, chinchilla bedspreads strewn about, and a TV screen mounted near the ceiling. Two black leather chairs faced a bejeweled gold-and-silver chess set. I thought of the comment Serena had made when we had entered the palace for the first time: It's all real. Really useless. Who was playing chess in there?

He trained a plain gaze on me. I stood and looked back at him.

"What do you do at home?" he asked me.

"I'm a student. And an actress."

"An actress," he said, nodding as if this was interesting. "And maybe some of this?" He waved his hand in a vague gesture at the bed.

I felt the heat rise to my face. Serena. That bitch. I had made the mistake of mentioning the escort agency during lunch one day when my guard was down and she was acting friendly. Of course she had gone and told him. I felt a sick little drop in my stomach. I didn't want to be seen as an escort right then, not just because it wasn't the role I was playing for Robin but also because it wasn't the fantasy I was living out in my own head. I stuffed the prickling of fury back down and plastered a look of innocence across my face. Now it was on. I was in the game. I would get her back.

"It's all right," he said. "I like actresses. I know lots of them. They have many feelings, I think. Very entertaining. Now, come here."

Robin reached over and pulled the strap of my sundress off my shoulder. I stepped closer to him and put his hands on my waist. He pulled me toward the bed and sat down in front of me. He folded his hands in his lap and looked at me expectantly, like someone who had never for a minute in his life worried about making someone else happy, who had never considered that it would take more than his mere presence to set someone at ease.

Mostly because I couldn't think of anything further to say, I dropped the other strap and stepped out of my dress, kneeling in front of him and laying my head in his lap. I ran my hands up the sides of his thighs, but he took my elbows and pulled me up. I sat on his lap and we made out for a minute before he stood up and I, who had many times mercilessly berated my mother for her mink coats, crawled under the fur blanket with a surge of gratitude, both for being covered and for being warm. I was so cold the beds of my fingernails were tinged with purple.

Robin took off his clothes like he was getting ready to step into a shower, draped them neatly on the chess chair, and joined me underneath the chinchilla. He smelled compulsively clean, like soap and cologne (Calvin Klein's Egoiste, I had learned from my trip to the bathroom). He was poreless, hairless, muscular. He had no scars, no leaky emotions, nothing notably human to speak of. He looked straight at me the whole time, his eyes obsidian, slightly sunken and weaselly. He was the kind of guy you'd swear was faking an orgasm if the physical evidence wasn't there. I did my finest porno-inspired blowjob, heavy on the eye contact, and he seemed almost bored. That was a first.

Robin wore some sort of talisman around his neck that looked like a mezuzah. When I was a little girl my father had worn one like it. I remember looking through the lacy silver filigree and trying to see the tiny parchment inside. I couldn't remember what was written inside a mezuzah. It was something like "Take these words which I command you this day to heart. Teach them faithfully to your children." I still loved the sound of those prayers even though I believed in signs and spirits and ghosts and muses and maybe in angels, but not in God at all.

My mind was doing what it did with club customers and agency clients and, honestly, with boyfriends, too. It got away from me. It spiraled up and out of the room so that half the time when I was done having sex, I couldn't remember it. It was kind of like riding the same subway that you've ridden a thousand times before: You space out and get to your stop and you've blanked out the stops in between. Sometimes you space out so completely that you snap back to awareness and find you've missed your stop and landed in Queens.

So that's what happened. I spaced out and woke up in Queens. I woke up and Robin was fucking me without a condom and I couldn't find my voice to stop him. This was the height of the AIDS epidemic and friends of mine from the theater were dying at home in medieval ways. But as fast as the panic rose in me I shoved it aside. My knees slipped on the fur, my hands pressing the cool silk of the headboard.

Afterward, he wrote something on my back with the edge of his necklace. It reminded me of the game we played as kids in summer camp. We would close our eyes and a friend would sit across from us holding our forearm. With the edge of a fingernail, the friend would write a word that we would then have to guess. It was almost impossible to guess from the actual sensation. It was really a test to see how well you knew your friend, to see if you could guess what word she'd picked to inscribe on you.

It also reminded me of a game I played later on when I lay naked with lovers and wrote my name on their backs with my fingertips, pretending I was just tickling them. I wrote "I love you" to Sean long before I said the words. I don't know what Robin wrote.

I lay on my stomach and Robin lay beside me for exactly three seconds before slapping my ass, kissing me on the cheek, and popping out of bed like he had hit the emergency eject button.

"That was very nice for me. I am late for a meeting."

I knew better than to say, Wait. Wait. Give me another chance and I'll make you want to stay. I knew better even than to feel it, but feel it I did. It was unlike me.

Was I actually taken with this guy (who was not only the least available guy on the planet but was also most likely some kind of sex addict who pencils a different girl in between every business meeting) or did I simply not want to be left alone again?

While Robin showered and dressed to leave, I used the ceiling mirror to arrange my hair on the pillow. I wanted to brand myself into his brain, wanted to make myself into a memory that would take him off guard while he sat in a meeting or rode in the back of his car or whatever princes did. When he left, he looked as sharp and creased as when he had come in.

I told myself I was a personal goodwill ambassador, single-handedly improving relations between Jews and Muslims the world over. I wasn't the first Jew in a sultan's bed. Hadassah changed her name to Esther to marry the Persian king. They made the holiday of Purim to celebrate Esther's story.

But there would hardly be a holiday commemorating my actions. I was no ambassador for anything other than my own wallet and my own desire to feel desired. I was barely hanging on to my own ass; I was saving no one. There had been countless women like me in the beds of kings but no one ever heard their stories, because who would care?

After I was sure Robin wasn't coming back, I went into the bathroom and showered. The glass wall and black marble of the shower were still streaked with water marks from Robin's shower. I stood there with the water on my back and thought back to the morning after the first night I spent at Sean's house. I hadn't wanted to walk home in my tight dress from the night before, so I had worn his old college sweatshirt and a pair of his jeans, the long legs cuffed and cuffed again. When I got home, I was exhausted and dirty and my hair reeked of smoke but I hadn't wanted to take a shower because I could still smell him on me. I had crawled into bed and taken a nap while still wearing his clothes.

Three hours passed before my suspicions that they had once again forgotten about me took over and I panicked.

"Hello. Help. I'm in here. Someone let me out."

I pounded on the door and hollered for a good fifteen minutes before someone came and turned the lock.

chapter 12

It was late in the afternoon when I walked back through the door of the house. I had hoped the girls would be at the pool, but instead they were lying on the couches in the upstairs den with their limbs layered over one another's while they watched *Henry & June*. Serena looked up and smiled. She reached across Leanne's thigh and plucked a strawberry from the bowl in the middle of the coffee table.

"We were worried about you," she lied.

I smiled back and looked at her straight on. "No need. Here I am."

"Are you okay?" she asked, her brow making a small fold of concern as she nibbled on the edge of the strawberry. Serena barely ate. Under her syrupy fakeness I saw in the corners of her eyes right then something that wasn't cruelty. It was hunger. Hunger I could relate to. It made me miss a beat. But I recovered quickly. I wasn't going to tip my cards first just because we were both starving.

"How's the movie?"

"I'm a big Henry Miller fan."

"Really. What's your favorite book of his?"

"*Henry and June*. This movie is based on it."

"I'll have to read that. Maybe you can lend it to me."

I decided that Serena pretending she'd read a non-existent Henry Miller book actually made her worthy of compassion. The thought put a smug little spring in my step as I crossed in front of her on my way to my room. I resolved not to let anything she said bother me ever again. While I was turning the doorknob, she said to my back, "Don't worry. He probably won't call again. He usually doesn't."

My resolve had lasted exactly thirteen seconds.

That night I curled my hair and pressed my last dress, an emerald-colored vintage number from the fifties with a sweetheart neckline and a bell skirt. It was the kind of dress that made me wish my shoes matched my bag and that I was going out with someone who knew how to jitterbug.

On the nightstand next to my side of the bed was a photograph of my grandmother as a young woman, all dressed up to go out and wearing almost the same dress. On her hands are white gloves with a pearl button at the wrist. Before she married and settled down in Newark, my grandmother traveled the world. She studied with the famous psychologist Alfred Adler in Vienna while renting a room in a fairy-tale flat from a bankrupt countess. She, too, had been a restless soul. If she were alive, I could have told her the truth about Brunei.

Behind me Destiny slipped her brown feet, tanned to the color and texture of a baseball mitt, into her Lucite platforms. Her nightstand also held a single framed photo. It was a picture of her daughter, sun-kissed and smiling in front of a backdrop of ocean.

The pictures we carry, the frames we gladly add to the weight of our luggage, are of the people we trust to love us no matter what.

That night at the party Yoya and Lili did a rousing karaoke version of "Paradise by the Dashboard Light." They had obviously been rehearsing, because they had a few little choreographed dance moves, most notably a shoulder shimmy to the part about being barely seventeen and barely dressed, a genius lyric, made more poignant by the fact that it was actually true for most of us in the room.

I thought what I always think when I hear that song: There are lots of songs about being seventeen. A long-haired man, wiry and handsome and looking like some kind of Cuban revolutionary, pointed this out to me once, after he found me separated from my friends, confused and tripping my face off at a Grateful Dead show when I was actually fourteen. But it's never a good idea to say you're fourteen. So I said seventeen. Then I told him I was lost.

"Lots of songs about seventeen," he said. "You're not lost; you're just misplaced."

I followed that guy back into the city, to his artist loft on Fourteenth Street. He smelled like turpentine and body odor and he had multicolored brushstrokes across the right thigh of his jeans. I had sex with him or, more specifically, he had sex with me—my first time—while I watched cartoon hallucinations dance in the darkness behind his head. I guessed that it was worth it not to be left alone in the middle of the night somewhere out on Long Island. In the morning, I stole thirty dollars out of his pants to get home. I walked with my shoes in my hands down the five flights of stairs, so as not to wake him, then put them on and ran the two blocks to the subway station.

I told my parents I had spent the night at my friend Julie's. Later, when I told Julie the story, I remember we laughed and laughed when I got to the "lots of songs about seventeen" part.

I sat up straight and acted giggly as the servants refilled our bottomless glasses of champagne. My back was facing the door, but I felt Robin walk in behind me and my body reflexively responded as if I'd just tossed back three shots of espresso. I nervously smoothed my skirt; I brushed aside a curl that kept falling over my eye. A few minutes later, when Robin drifted into my sight line, he gave me a brief hello while looking over my head. Then he didn't speak to me for the rest of the evening. He pulled Leanne out of her chair and had an involved conversation with her at the bar before taking his usual seat next to Fiona.

Leanne sat back down next to Serena and they acted particularly animated and interested in me. Nausea pushed up against my throat and I shoved it back down. I wanted to crawl over the table, grab Serena by her fucking French twist, and bring her pert little face down onto the glass tabletop. Instead I joined the conversation about astrological compatibility.

Robin, Leanne informed us, was a Scorpio, hence the charisma, the confidence, the power, the rampant sex drive.

Serena was a Taurus, Leanne a Pisces. Destiny told them she was a Christian, that's all, and they could shove it.

"Scorpio is a water sign," said Leanne. "Like Pisces. So Robin and I flow together but it's often way too emotional. For both of us."

I had a hard time imagining Robin getting too emotional.

"What sign are you?" she asked me.

"I'm a Leo."

"Fire," she responded, followed by a pause of quiet triumph.

Every evening Robin would disappear from the party for about a half hour sometime around midnight. While he was gone, we would look around and try to determine which girl was also missing. That night, Leanne's chair sat empty directly across from me. I drained my champagne glass faster than usual. I might have wound up truly plastered—ugly plastered—had Robin not left early with Fiona on his arm and cut the night short.

I chided myself for the stab I felt. When I went to the bathroom to retouch my lipstick, I recognized the tight smile on my face as the same one I had seen on Serena and Leanne. The girls at the other tables, the Asian girls, didn't seem to care too much where Robin was or whom he was with. Of course, Leanne and Fiona were Asian, too, but they had escaped exile to the lower-ranked seating areas based on celebrity status and the ability to speak perfect English.

If Robin was still absent when the disco started, we top-rung-ers often sat in snits with our arms crossed over our chests while the rest of the tables got up and danced anyway. The lucky ones slow-danced at the end of the night like it was a prom, resting their heads on their boyfriends' shoulders. We Western girls weren't required to have boyfriends in the Prince's entourage. Instead, we competed with each other for the Prince.

Another night passed the same way. I didn't bother to pretend to smile while I watched the heels of his sneakers as he climbed the long staircase to the exit.

One morning, Serena woke us early and told us she had received special permission (from whom was a mystery) for us to go to the Yaohan. She had fistfuls of Bruneian money to hand out. It was the first time I'd seen any money since we'd entered the country. I had been living for nearly two weeks free of commerce. Well, sort of.

I looked at the money she doled out like a Monopoly dealer, and there he was again: the Sultan, bearded and looking dignified, floating on the orange, green, and blue notes.

"What's the exchange rate?"

"I don't know. Who cares? We have plenty. Cover your hair. You're not blond so it's not as big a deal, but cover it anyway."

We piled into a waiting Mercedes and Serena sat up front chatting with the driver. She had penetrated this world and I hadn't. In three days I would go home and would have seen little, understood even less, and been sampled and passed over like the orange cream in a box of assorted chocolates. What was it about me? Why did I always come so close to getting what I wanted, only to get shut out at the last minute? Usually I took it upon myself to quit before I got rejected, but this time I didn't really have the option.

When faced with such despair, a girl can always shop. We hit the Yaohan with travel goggles on, the kind that make every little thing look irresistible because it's exotic and the money makes no sense and you feel like you're in a video game with tinny Asian pop songs and smiling wide-faced shop girls who speak to you in rhymes and giggle at your strangeness. In this video game you gain strength by acquiring snacks and T-shirts and little stuffed animals and sweet-smelling soaps and brightly colored lip gloss.

The women in Brunei, I noticed, did not generally cover their hair, as was the custom in some other Muslim countries, though they did dress modestly. They were miles away from the striking, stylish women I had spied during my brief stay in Singapore.

Leanne and I paired off, all rivalries from the night before discarded as she led me to the Shu Uemura makeup counter. The counter girls pantomimed lessons and suggestions for us. Leanne sat me down on a stool and charitably showed me how to do my eye makeup so I didn't constantly look like I was auditioning for *Gentlemen Prefer Blondes*.

"Beautiful skin," Leanne said, blending some blush into the apples of my cheeks. "Like Snow White. Where are you from?"

"New Jersey."

"No, I mean, what are you?"

That question always seemed weird to me. What are you? Are you a good witch or a bad witch? I'm just Dorothy Gail from Kansas.

"Russian. Polish."

"I thought something else."

"I was adopted," I said.

She paused in her ministrations and looked at me with something like interest mixed with something like sympathy.

"Do you know your real parents?"

"My adoptive parents are my real parents."

It's the kind of question you're trained to answer as an adoptee, a question you hear a million times. You hear it so often you don't even hear it anymore.

"Still," she said.

I let the conversation drop. I wasn't about to get into it with her. In order to get beyond my stance of defending my family, I needed to be talking to someone who could digest a little more complexity. But the truth was, she was right. The truth was, I wondered. My family was my family, but still. Still I wondered if somewhere in my DNA I would find an explanation for my restlessness, if somewhere in my biology lay the arrow pointing me in the direction I was meant to go.

Leanne turned me toward the mirror, and my makeup was subtle and lovely. I bought it all. It was the first makeup I had ever owned that hadn't come from a Rite Aid and the first grooming tips I had received that hadn't come from a drag queen or a stripper. Leanne and I each walked away with a hefty bag full of paints and potions. I was coming up in the world—quite a lady, with my eyeshadow palette and my mystery money. I also bought some diet tea and a new pair of sweatpants and promised myself that I'd work out the next morning. I planned yet again in my life to force myself into a thinner and more desirable body. Fuck biology. I could construct myself in whatever image I wanted. That was the freedom of not knowing the origin of your eye color. Audrey Hepburn, move over. Even if this Prince Charming had tossed me aside, there would be another and the next one wouldn't. I would make sure of it.

I ate only salad and a bit of chicken for dinner. I needed nothing, I reminded myself. Almost nothing. There were monks who lived on a grain of rice a day. Need was an illusion. There was only wanting, and the strong could live with wanting and not having. No one else was volunteering for the job, so I'd have to be my own cheerleader. Be strong. Go team.

I felt renewed, resolved, until I sat down to use my new makeup and looked in the mirror to find myself facing the truth. My cheerleader role peeled off as quickly as had that Victim One costume with the Velcro closures. My stomach gave a hollow growl. In spite of my pep talks, I knew I'd never starve myself into being beautiful. And I could read every book in the library and still not walk out brilliant. That was the truth.

Not cute enough, not smart enough, not popular enough, not talented enough, not special enough. I was just an average hustler who could sometimes talk my way into getting what I wanted. New eyeshadow or not, I loathed myself in the mirror exactly as much as before. Sighing, I picked up a makeup brush and went to work.

That night, Eddie, bug-eyed, nervous, and lecherous as always, sat on an ottoman between Serena and me. The men generally sat on these wide ottomans rather than the low armchairs, probably because they usually didn't stay in one place for long. The girls, on the other hand, sat parked in the same chairs all night, gradually sinking, turning into discarded marionettes, until the Prince entered and everybody sat straight up as if someone had just pulled the string rising from the center of their heads.

Eddie turned to Serena first.

"You will sing tonight?"

Of course she would sing. She had been right in her initial assessment of me. I was no threat to her icy, sassy blondeness. One thing you can be sure of, the soprano will get the guy.

Then he turned to my chair, where I felt myself receding further into obscurity every minute.

"And you will sing?"

Or maybe not. Serena crackled with annoyance.

"You will sing now."

I trembled slightly with the adrenaline that was injected into my bloodstream as I crossed to the microphone. I was unprepared. It had been three nights since I had miraculously pulled off "Kasih" and I was sure the gods would not weigh in on my side a second time. But I was wrong about a lot of things. I sang "Kasih" again just fine and drew approving smiles all around, including from the Prince.

When Serena got up and sang "Someone to Watch Over Me" she was cringe-worthily flat. I listened with genuine pleasure. She wasn't the Sandy she thought she was. During the first chorus, Fiona caught my attention and called me over to where she sat next to Robin. When I reached their hub of power, the three chairs against the wall, Robin turned toward me.

"Sit here," he said, patting the chair to his left. Fiona always sat to his right.

This was the coveted chair of the second-favorite girlfriend. I sat there the rest of the night, minding my manners, pressing my knees together, and speaking when spoken to. Sitting next to Robin kept me tense and alert. Robin mostly talked to Fiona, but occasionally turned and asked me disjointed questions.

"Do you like horses?"

"I love horses. I hear you play polo." I don't really love horses. I like horses just fine, but I'm more of a doggy/kitty kind of girl. I prefer animals that can watch TV with you on the couch. And I had never even seen a game of polo.

"I do."

"Polo is so dangerous." I was strictly guessing. "You must be really brave. I'd like to watch you play."

"You will, I think. How do you like my country?"

Our conversation proceeded along those lines. The dancing music started and we watched the girls dance together to "Things That Make You Go Hmmmm . . ." and "Like a Prayer." Everyone on the dance floor sang along with the hooks, though most of them didn't know what they were saying. When the girls got drunk, West and East alike could really get crazy out there—spinning around, lifting their skirts, grinding in a conga line. It was a release from the boredom. The skull-crushing boredom.

But at that instant I wasn't bored. At the Prince's parties, the ministers and the mistresses alike lived by their ranking, and mine had just soared. It was a delicate equation that shifted nightly. I had passed my first test: I had been ignored and had reacted accordingly. I had been upset but not too upset, jealous but not too jealous. If it was a game of Chutes and Ladders, I had just landed on that huge ladder that climbs to the top of the board and skips all of the spaces in between. I was about to become extremely unpopular.

Fiona leaned over and looked at me over Robin, as if confirming something they had been talking about.

He said, half to her but loud enough for me to hear, "I think my brother would really like her, don't you?"

She agreed.

Now, what the hell was that supposed to mean?

chapter 13

The sun bouncing off the fiberglass flanks of the yacht was so bright I saw sun spots when I turned away. The boat dwarfed me. It was so large that it looked like a cruise ship rather than a private vessel. Twelve crew members stood on deck to greet me.

The sticky heat immediately drew pearls of sweat to my upper lip and my bra line. I regretted my choice of pedal pushers and Destiny's little bolero jacket. When the knock came that morning, I had expected to be shut in another porno icebox, but instead they had driven me to the harbor. I wished I had a bikini, a wide-brimmed hat, and shiny, lacquered red fingernails wrapped around a glass of champagne. Wasn't that how you dressed for a cruise on a yacht with a prince? Proper duds or not, I was feeling pretty self-satisfied about the prospect of a pleasure cruise with a dozen crew members at my disposal.

This was me all over. Yachts and champagne. International femme fatale slinking up the gangplank.

But when I boarded the boat and stood facing the sharply dressed and uniformed crew, they looked confused. Their eyeballs shifted from side to side, each checking out their neighbor to see who was going to make the first move. The captain, a young, sunburned Australian, greeted me and promptly left me in the hands of two perky girls while the rest of the crew drifted off to their regular duties.

The one with wide teeth, the bigger one, a brunette, said, "I think you're about my size then."

They tossed sing-songy questions at me as they led me around the side of the deck and into the crew quarters below.

"Do you usually crew another of the family's boats?"

"No."

"Will you be staying with us then? It won't take us a minute to get Allison's old bunk ready for you. Allison left about three weeks ago but we thought we were just going to sail a man short."

They opened a closet filled with uniforms that matched their own, each hanging neatly in plastic, each hanger spaced the same distance apart. They held items up to my body, eyeballed the sizes, and put together an outfit, which they hung on a peg. I've always suspected that people who hang clothing in an orderly way are better people than I, with cleaner souls.

"Did Leslie just hire you?"

"Nope."

"Really? Is someone else doing the hiring now?"

"They never tell us anything," added the blond one.

They waited for some explanation. I stood my ground and waited right back. The Australian sailor girls were so scrubbed and healthy it almost hurt to look at them. I got the feeling that the close quarters of the ship allowed for no mess, no secrets. What would it be like to live a life you didn't have to lie about?

"How long have you been a stewardess?"

"I'm not, really."

"Huh." They were baffled. They looked at each other and then looked back at me.

"Not to be rude," said the blonde, "but what are you doing here?"

One of the most useful skills I had learned in Brunei was not to offer too much information. I learned always to hang back until I was absolutely sure what was going on. You never want to be the one who gives the game away.

"What did they tell you?" I asked.

"Nothing," said the brunette.

"They just told us to come on deck to greet the new stewardess."

"So if you're not a stewardess . . ."

"You see why we're confused."

"Well, let's just say I am a stewardess."

That satisfied them. We found a uniform that pretty much fit me. The starched polyester pants pulled a bit at the ledge where my ass hit my thighs, but pants usually did on me. As soon as I was dressed identical to the two girls, the conversation got friendlier. Together we decided that I'd simply do what they did. They'd have to give me a crash course, because in an hour the Sultan and his family would be coming aboard for a day cruise. Afterward, they'd give me the more detailed, proper job training. I was confident that would never happen, but I thanked them anyway. The Prince, I was realizing, liked to put his people in bizarre situations just to see what they'd do. We were his little lab rats. I wondered if there was something wrong with him, a sadistic streak or a touch of Borderline Personality Disorder. Or maybe it was just a symptom of having too much money and power.

The girls broke out three Diet Cokes for us and they told me about the job while we sipped from the cans. They were yacht stewardesses, hired out of Australia with the same crew they always worked with. The job on the Sultan's yacht was the easiest job either of them had ever had. They had been in the employ of the Sultan for about six months and he had yet to go on the boat for more than a day trip.

Being a yacht stewardess didn't sound too bad. I'd spend my nights rocking in a bunk and listening to the waves slap the hull. I'd spend my days striding purposefully across the deck with a tray full of drinks. On nights off, I'd drink merlot under a starry sky and flirt with the captain. Maybe I should consider it. Maybe I could stay on and no one in authority would even notice that I wasn't supposed to be there. Maybe I could get out from under the Prince's thumb now, before I became as miserable as Serena and Leanne.

They went on to give me the job description. We took drink and food orders. We cleared glasses and dishes, never letting an empty glass sit. We stood at the door of a room, on the ready for any and all requests. We were present and invisible at the same time. We passed appetizers. We straightened the room immediately after anyone left, so that if they returned it would be back in impeccable condition.

They took me to the bathroom in order to demonstrate the most important trick: how to fold the edge of the toilet paper back into a perfect point after anyone used the toilet.

"They love it when you do that. It makes them feel that you're on them like white on rice."

On second thought, maybe yacht stewardess wasn't it for me after all. I took a break from my toilet-paper tutorial and stood on the deck, letting the sun warm my back through the stiff white shirt. The sea air smelled of brine and the slight rot of low tide and was less oppressive than the tropical rainforest farther inland. I recalled the Jersey Shore.

Every summer our family would travel to Beach Haven, on Long Beach Island. There, Johnny and I would meet up with a marauding band of wild kids. A gang of us would run from the ocean to the Engleside Motel pool and back again, diving into the churning surf and then racing through the white-hot sand to cannonball into the deep end of the pool. Back and forth, all day long, breaking only briefly for Creamsicles from the ice-cream truck.

At the end of the day, sunburned and with sand still crusted in our hair, Johnny and I would go with our parents to the bay side of the island to eat fried-clam sandwiches at Morrison's restaurant. After dinner we'd walk out onto the pier and watch the sailboats returning to the harbor.

This, the smell of low tide rising from the harbor, was how the nights in Beach Haven smelled. But how Beach Haven felt was something else. I remember that it seemed I breached the borders of my skin. The lights of the carnival and the taste of the hot, cinnamon-sugary morning doughnuts and the tickle of the sand crabs weren't just something I felt from the outside in; they were a part of my body. They always had been. Brunei was the opposite. Every day I was further from my body. I was more disconnected all the time from the world around me. I noted the loss with some sadness but also with a kind of satisfaction. Not being able to feel your body was its own kind of safe harbor, its own kind of freedom.

From where I stood, I watched a caravan of the ubiquitous black Mercedes pull up. I retreated back to the cabin as both plainclothes security and uniformed guards emerged from the cars and came aboard, fanning out and securing the boat.

The security protocol was subtle. Once they were on board, the men made themselves unobtrusive. If you weren't looking carefully, you could miss how well protected the royal family was, how closely we all were being observed. Things were carefully orchestrated to preserve the illusion of a regular life for the Sultan, his brothers, and their families—or, rather, some rarefied bell-jar version of a regular life, in which every need or want was fulfilled practically before they even knew they had it. They probably thought the toilet paper just magically formed itself back into a perfect triangle after every time they wiped their asses. It was stifling. No wonder the Prince wanted to fuck and fuck.

The plainclothes guards were men dressed in sharp suits, who walked around and delegated, switching back and forth effortlessly from Malay to British-accented English. One of them talked to the blond stewardess for a while. They spoke in low voices across the room and at one point the conversation turned to me. I knew because the guard looked me over and then paused to think before continuing. He didn't know what the hell I was doing there either, but he knew more than the boat crew. He knew enough.

The blond stewardess changed her tone to a polite flatline when she told me I would simply be standing in the Sultan's cabin and taking drink orders. No cleaning bathrooms after all. I'm not sure what was said during that conversation, but whatever it was built an invisible wall between them and me. The toothy one stationed me by the door of a large sitting room that was lined in polished dark wood and surrounded by windows. They left me standing there and for the rest of the day the only person who talked to me was the bartender when he was filling my drink orders.

I didn't have to stand there doing nothing for long. Soon, there was a commotion as a gaggle of nannies and kids tumbled past me and into the lounge. It must have been more than just the immediate family, because it seemed like there were a lot of them. The Sultan and the Queen followed close behind. The Sultan looked less imposing in person than he did on the money. The Queen was twice his size and wore a shapeless traditional outfit with lots of sparkles. As we sailed, I watched her sit there quietly all day and smile graciously at what people said to her. She seemed to enjoy watching the kids play, but never left her seat to join them.

All day I brought the family sodas and then cleared their glasses when they were done. I passed around trays of appetizers. The Queen smiled at me and looked me in the eye, and she even seemed apologetic when she caught my attention to ask for a refill. As if I was busy doing something else. Man, I felt like a twat. My best guess was that I was there serving Coke to the guy's kids so he could get a good look at my ass.

The Sultan was handsome in a different way than Robin, slightly older, more serious. His mustache was more Magnum, P.I., and less Errol Flynn. He disregarded me. I began to suspect that maybe there had been an error in communication. Someone had thought to send me to the boat but hadn't told anyone what I was doing there—not even the Sultan. But at the end of the trip, when the Sultan and the Queen left the room, he looked me in the eye for the first time, gave me a knowing smile, and actually winked. I attempted to give him a look that portrayed utter irresistibility. He was the Sultan, after all, and if I was being passed along I was going to make the best of it.

My survival instinct had kicked in. I didn't have any reason to believe that if I was unwanted, was deemed uninteresting and undesirable, I would be thrown off a cliff or stoned to death in a public square or shoved in the trunk of a car, never to be seen again. Yet I was ready to fight with all I had to stay on the tightrope of royal favor. Maybe there didn't need to be a threat of corporeal danger; maybe the threat of being unlovable was enough. Looking back, it was good that the fight was growing in me, because I was about to need it.

When we docked, no one was there to pick me up, but the specter of being forgotten no longer worried me.

I returned the uniform and napped on a bench in the ship's galley until finally the bartender shook my shoulder and told me a driver had come to get me. Another of the more useful skills I picked up in Brunei is my ability to sleep almost anywhere with almost anything going on around me. I can curl up on a bench in a mall, a hotel bathtub, an airport floor and be asleep in seconds. When it is dark and I'm alone in my own bed, I have a harder time. For some reason, there's little danger of nightmares when sleeping on a bench.

By the time I returned to the compound everyone else had already left for the party. I took off my clothes as I walked through the room, plopped myself into the tub, and calculated that I had exactly half an hour to get to the party if I wanted to be there before the Prince showed up. It was understood that we had better be dying of malaria if we missed the party; otherwise we risked having to retreat ten paces, land on a chute, and be punished, ignored. I powdered the tender skin of my nose, which was already turning pink from my brief moment on the ship's deck, then threw my hair up and hopped into a golf cart.

It was after ten when I arrived and I hadn't made it in time. Robin was already in the room, leaning on the edge of a couch and talking to Yoya. Yoya was wide-eyed and gesticulating; she looked like a little girl telling her father about a particularly egregious event that had happened that day on the school playground. Robin was listening with his arms crossed and an indulgent half smile on his face. I saw something in his expression that distracted me to the point of catching the toe of my shoe on the carpet and stumbling a bit. He looked soft, unstudied. He looked like he loved her. Not a passionate love—more of a paternal one. It could have been a trick of the low lighting, a trick of my brain, but it gave me pause.

Though they pointedly didn't even glance in my direction, there was a treacherous energy around Serena and Leanne, a storm threatening to break and pour down on my head. It unsettled me. I steadied myself and walked toward my chair, toward the heavy storm clouds, but Eddie headed me off at the pass and yanked me right back outside. He had been waiting for me to show up.

It was Eddie who cued the girl chosen by the Prince to slip out of the party on any given night. That night I was the one. He led me down a staircase to a room I hadn't been in before. It was a huge, round room, its perimeter lined with doors. It looked like a game show. Behind door number three is a new refrigerator, behind door number six is a tiger, behind door number seven is . . . a bedroom, where Eddie deposited me and turned the lock from the outside. It seemed all the rooms in the palace locked from the outside. Robin arrived fifteen minutes later.

"Tell me all about your day. What happened? Did you meet him?"

I sensed that it was important to Robin that his brother had approved of me. I told him some of the choice details of my day. I thought it best not to mention the wife. The wives floated around like family secrets everyone pretends not to know about—always present, never mentioned.

"What did you think of my brother?"

"He winked. He smiled. He was nice."

"He winked?"

Robin seemed pleased and pulled out a digital camera. I had never seen one before. Was he now taking pictures of me to send to the Sultan?

"For us," he said, in answer to my psychic question.

There was an us? I was relieved. I didn't want to be passed off. It would make me feel like Robin had tagged my ear and put me up for auction. Even if I was a piece of property, I wanted to be more highly valued than that.

Any set of circumstances can become the normal shape of your days if you let it. The same girl who only weeks before had emphatically advised a sobbing friend to dump her cheating cad of a boyfriend could, without skipping a beat, sit on the edge of a bed hoping for love from a man with not one but probably forty or so other girlfriends, who were all sitting fifty feet away—and that wasn't even counting his *wives*. I had morphed from Patti Smith to Patty Hearst. What would Patty Hearst do? She'd fall for Robin, if only to save herself from boredom and disgust, from becoming sick of herself and everyone else. It was a setup.

Robin had been educated at England's finest schools, was powerful in the realms of both finance and politics, was a pathological narcissist, a professional manipulator, a sex addict, and a master collector of women. I didn't have a chance. I thought that surely he'd never met anyone like me before. Maybe I'd be different. Maybe I'd be the one to make him happy. Maybe I'd be happy myself in return.

He plugged the camera into a monitor on an occasional table in the corner of the room and began to snap pictures of me. I could see the monitor from where I lay on the bed. There I was on the screen, a pornographic parody, a round-faced, plump-assed little girl with only thigh-highs on.

"Look at you. You are perfect," he said later as he scrolled though the shots. "You must not change."

I was perfect. Throw me that snazzy little beret, Patty. I'll take it from here on out.

When we were dressed and ready to go back to the party, Robin handed me a box. In it was a gold chain with a diamond heart charm. It was the first piece of jewelry he gave me and much less extravagant than my later diamond-faced Rolexes and Bulgari sets, but it was far more intimate, my most personal gift from him. My chest flushed. I had become one of those girls who got to open jewelry boxes and discover what surprise sparkled out at her, one of those girls who lifted her hair while a necklace was fastened around her neck.

The necklace sealed the deal. When I returned to my seat wearing it, Serena and Leanne didn't even look at me. They talked sotto voce and I distinctly heard the word *fat*. Then I heard the word *hooker*. I was exhausted, sunburned, my skin worn thin; tears sprung to my eyes. It wasn't just Serena and Leanne. It was the years of spending lunchtime in the art room, hiding out from the same brand of cruelty, from the bared teeth that had changed only in that they were no longer fenced in by braces. You'd have thought I'd have been immune to it by then, but I never quite got used to the sting. I berated myself for my weakness—never let them see you cry.

Over the music, Fiona called to me. I turned and she waved me over. I walked and sat in the spot next to her, an empty chair in between us because Robin was making his rounds. My face was hot and I willed my eyes to absorb my tears. I didn't want anyone to see me wipe them, so I let one just roll down my face and brushed it from my chin when I brought my drink to my lips.

Fiona didn't acknowledge my tears or the fact that

she had just rescued me. She was a marvel. I never saw her play a sloppy hand. Me, I'm sloppy by nature. As soon as I sew up one seam another busts.

I needed an ally and Fiona was it. I didn't exactly trust her, but I was beginning to see her strategy. It was most useful to her to be friends with the girl on Robin's left. That's why she'd been giving my back a scratch here and there. I assumed she intended for me to scratch her back by not trying to unseat her. If so, that was fine with me. If this was what it was like to be the second favorite, I didn't want to know what it would be like to be Fiona.

chapter 14

For the next two nights I was the girl missing from the party.

At a cue from Eddie, I snuck out and waited in that same bedroom for Robin. As I sat there I remembered a middle-school birthday party for a girl I couldn't stand but who was so popular I couldn't turn down the invite, a girl so popular that my mother had insisted on a new dress and a new hairstyle. A girl from a family so rich and so ridiculous that one of the party activities involved a tall glass box that blew dollar bills around while you tried to grab as many as you could in thirty seconds. I had snuck out of that party, too.

I had stolen away to meet a boy who was also way more popular than I was. He was broad in the shoulders before the other boys, but there was also something dark around his edges. There was a tiredness under his eyes, a slight jaundice to his olive skin. There was a packet of insulin needles in his backpack. There were plastic bears full of honey in the desks of all his teachers in case of a dangerous drop in blood sugar.

I don't know what made Danny choose me out of all the girls at the party that night. He cued me with a nod of his head and we met on the putting green, then walked side by side across the grass. I took off my pink satin shoes with the tiny rose clips and then I took off my white stockings in order to feel the grass under my feet. The lawn glowed fluorescent green and the night was soft. I lay on his suit jacket and we kissed in the deep shadows of the trees and it was a new kind of sweet, getting something as unlikely as a kiss from Danny Rosen while looking up at a full spring moon.

Sneaking out of the Prince's party was hardly as new or as sweet, but it had a similar aftertaste. Being wanted and being somewhere so strange was almost magical.

Almost, but not quite. I still had a plane ticket to leave for home the next day. Ari was slated to return from Los Angeles the next morning to see Destiny and me off. The new crop of party girls traveling with Ari would replace us. I had retrieved my suitcase from the downstairs closet and was already mostly packed.

Even after Robin came to meet me that night, he didn't mention my plane ticket. I was disappointed that he was letting me go so easily, but I tried to console myself, telling myself that overall it had been a good experience. No need to get too dramatic; I knew that I'd get over Robin and that my time in Brunei would eventually make for an entertaining story. After everything, at least there is the story.

And I would be glad to get my money. Rumor had it they handed you an envelope, a "gift." You put it in your bag and looked at it later. The girls all assured me that it would be way more than we had been promised. The Prince hadn't fallen in love with me after all. My tiara-crowned fantasies were all but extinguished. But a big part of me was glad to be going home to the things I cared about: my friends, the theater, the grand love affair that is New York itself, my life that was only just starting.

I was in my chair and Fiona was in hers while Robin made his usual lazy stroll around the room with his vodka tonic in one hand and his invisible scepter in the other. Fiona was happy to chat as we sat there, and just as happy to stay quiet. She wasn't as phony as the other girls. Either that or her phoniness was so sophisticated as to be undetectable.

I tried to memorize the faces of the girls, the corners where the wall met the ceiling, what Robin looked like with his back turned. I sealed the details in a mental photo album that I could take out and show people when nights at Max Fish approached closing time.

I watched Eddie lead Destiny out of the room to give

her the notorious envelope. She gave me a wink when she walked back in. I watched as she gave her good-bye hugs to the party girls, the men and the servants she had gotten to know. Everyone was fond of her. She had been truly entertaining, with her giant boobs and outrageous outfits and frank talk.

"She was very popular," Fiona remarked. "Unfortunately for her, popular and successful aren't the same thing."

I braced myself for my summons from Eddie, but none came. I expressed my increasing anxiety to Fiona.

"Oh, you're not leaving. Just relax."

This was the first I had heard of the possibility that I would not be leaving. I decided I didn't believe her. She didn't run things around here. She didn't know everything. Before I had time to tell her that I thought she was wrong, Robin sat down. The night wore on and Eddie never came over, never said a word—nor did Madge or anyone else. A low buzz of panic started in my chest. Why were they not paying me? Had I done something wrong? Fiona finally brought it up, with an exasperated eye roll.

"She's all upset because she thinks she has to go home."

He gave me the fake-surprise act.

"You want to leave?"

"No, of course I don't want to leave. But my ticket is for tomorrow."

"You will stay, of course."

He turned to Fiona. "You should tell her things."

"I did tell her."

That was that. I sat back and rearranged my brain. I would be staying. For how long? I didn't have any more clothes, had already worn everything three times at least. I had things to do at home. I had . . . what? I ran through my list. My friends would still be there. New York wasn't going anywhere. Sean was beyond sick of me. My family and I had been through worse; we'd get through this, too.

As for my career, my protests collapsed right there. I had an internship with some very cool people, which did not mean that I was cool myself. I had a résumé that included Penny's work in progress, three student plays, two student films, and quite possibly the worst performance in the worst vampire movie ever made. Objectively, I had nothing, really. Nothing but big plans. Those could wait. I felt both ends of the spectrum of emotion at once: I felt elated and I felt sick. I was winning and I was sinking.

chapter 15

The days wore past the two- and then the three-week mark and a new set of shiny and clueless American girls now sat around the table. Taylor sat next to me. Of course she had found her way to Brunei. She had bullied and cajoled and otherwise hypnotized Ari into sending her a ticket. Taylor would not be denied. I was wary of her at first, but her ire had worn thin in the face of all the other competition and we were fast friends again.

The American and European girls now spilled over

from house five to house six. Most of the Asian girls, with the exception of Leanne and Fiona, stayed at another location, which was more like a dorm. Taylor and I shared a room in guesthouse six. Leanne had the room across the hall and Serena had the master. Ari took over the master in guesthouse five. The minor characters, the bit parts, the day players (don't get too attached; they change fast) were a blond Amazon volleyball player named Kimmee, an L.A. rock groupie named Brittany, who wore a promise ring that was supposedly from Vince Neil, and an anti-Semite named Suzy, who treated me to my first experience of hearing the word *Jew* used as a verb, as in, "I Jewed him down on the price of these earrings."

The Prince was allowed four wives and he had only three. So the subtext for all the vindictive vying between the girls in Brunei was that the prize might be a crown. The game was this: Transcend all assumptions, transcend all invisible hierarchies, inspire the love that conquers all and you can turn from stepdaughter of the world—Thai teenage hooker, aging Playmate, flailing actress, retail slave, delusional rock slut—to princess. From duck to swan with a nod of his head.

Some girls came and went, just interchangeable faces in the joke snapshots we took around the house when we were drunk and too amped up to get to sleep (snapshots that would embarrass me later when one of the girls sold hers to *E! True Hollywood Story*). Some girls stayed for long periods of time and hung out under the radar as pretty couch decorations. Some girls got off the bench and really got in the game with everything they had. All the girls changed during their time in Brunei. All the girls were transformed in some way by the pressure, the paranoia, the insidious insecurity that creeps in when you size yourself up against a roomful of other girls every night.

Who would you be? Would you shine or would you buckle? Would you stay and slug it out or would you run?

One of the favorite topics of discussion between the girls was what we told parents, boyfriends, and husbands. When a porn star first appears in a movie, hair pinned up and eyeglasses on, before she crawls onto the office desk, you always wonder, How did she tell her parents?

Serena said that she told her parents she was dating her employer. She told the guy she lived with (the redhead who had dropped her at the airport, who had moved with her to L.A. from Kansas, *not* her boyfriend, she insisted) that she was a nanny. Taylor didn't have parents as far as I could tell. She never talked about them and she never made a call. When we had first met she had told me a bogus story about a peach plantation, so I never asked again. I thought I'd spare her the lie.

I had put it off for too long and it was time to tell my parents something if I didn't want to cause an international incident. They were growing audibly suspicious of my rushed calls from the set of the eternal Singapore movie shoot. I sat in my kitty-print pj's by the phone table in the marble entranceway, picked up the receiver, and dialed their number.

The conversation was awkward, with the painful

pause of the international phone lines serving as a reminder of the distance between us. I told them that while shooting that mythical movie in Singapore I had met a man, that I was working as his assistant, that he was the Prince of Brunei.

"Where?" asked my father.

"Brunei."

"What the fuck is Brunei?"

I could have made up something less revealing, something without such an easily breakable code as "assistant." But you have to couch your lies in truth or they tighten around you like a Chinese finger trap.

It was harder than I thought. My parents sounded confused. They sounded worried and powerless, my father stuttering with anger and handing over the phone, my mother trying to figure out what the hell was going on while still staying on everyone's good side—ever the diplomat, whatever the cost. I pictured her with her fingers wrapped around the back of one of the kitchen chairs, her knuckles white; pictured a pot of tomato sauce bubbling on the electric burner behind her.

"When are you coming home?"

"I'm not sure. Two weeks. Three. Maybe longer."

I felt the noose of guilt tighten. I could taste the acid at the back of my throat. It made me physically sick, all the lying. Sorry I'm not a different daughter, I wanted to say. Sorry you weren't different parents. Sorry for hurting you. Sorry for this whole mess. Sorry and I'm doing it anyway. After everything between us, I still felt the constant compulsion to say I was sorry.

✤   ✤   ✤

When I had made my decision to leave home for good, I had been sixteen. I know it was a Saturday because I'd been babysitting. I pressed the code on the garage door and entered through the downstairs. My mother stood over the ironing board wearing jeans and a BeDazzled sweatshirt. She was backlit by the bare bulb in the laundry room, her mouth set and her shoulders squared. The house smelled like steamed cotton. I was thinking about my reading for school, about Holden Caulfield hiding his imaginary bullet wound, about April being the cruelest month—big, important things. I walked right past her.

"You could at least say hello."

"Hello." I kept walking. I didn't have time for my mother, but my father and I had endless time for each other. Every day called for a new maneuver in our permanent state of war. But my mother got passed over. I think she smarted from my dismissal.

"Look at me." She demanded some attention. "What have you been doing?"

"Drunk-driving."

"Don't talk to me like that."

"Like what?"

My father was halfway down the stairs; I could gauge his heavy footfalls above us. My mother left her ironing and stood confrontationally in my path. I tried to walk around her, but she grabbed my wrist.

"Don't you walk away from me. Look at me. Are you on drugs?"

This was her favorite question. She was on all kinds

of committees: drug education in the schools, date-rape awareness, silent auction for the school fair. The drug-education committee had made her paranoid. The truth was that I wasn't on drugs all that often and I definitely wasn't on drugs that night, if you didn't count the fact that I had sucked the nitrous out of the Cohens' whipped cream.

"Get off me." I pulled my arm away.

By this time my father was on the landing of the staircase. When I yanked my wrist out of my mother's hand it looked to him like I was about to hit her.

My father could move at incredible speeds. He was a short, Humpty Dumpty–shaped guy, but he defied physics with the momentum of his anger. His eyes were bulging and bloodshot. The veins along the side of his neck grew unnaturally large and the visible capillaries along his nose and cheeks darkened with effort as they struggled to accommodate the rush of blood to his face. He was so fast that I hardly saw him coming.

"Don't you ever raise a hand to your mother."

His hand clutched my throat and he swept me backward until I hit the wall.

"Shameful. Fucking disgusting. Ungrateful little bitch."

With every punctuation mark my father pulled me forward by my throat and then slammed my head back again. When he let go, I crumpled to the floor and pulled my knees to my chest. I called it my civil-disobedience trick. I closed my eyes and made myself into the tiniest ball. I showed no soft bits.

"Look at me when I talk to you."

He paced in front of me, clenching and unclenching his fists. The hitting was easy compared to the words. The hitting happened only infrequently but the words happened every day. I knew he was wrong, knew he was inexcusable. But still, the words were the worst part. He stammered as they tumbled out of him. He spoke in tongues, literally foaming at the mouth.

"You're a pig you dress like a fucking slob and you make yourself ugly you look like an ugly dyke and you think you'll meet nice people that way you won't you think you'll meet a nice boy that way you won't we are ashamed of you you're nothing but a fucking disappointment a waste a fucking waste of a person what happened what happened to you what did I do to deserve this this this piece-of-shit life these fucking kids you're a joke this is a fucking joke on me."

I knew my father's rages and I knew how to stop them. I knew it would get worse for a minute, but it would be over soon. I instigated him.

"Is that the best you can do?"

"What did you say to me in my house?"

He grabbed my hair and pulled me away from the wall.

"Are you on drugs?"

I flicked the off switch. I went limp in all my limbs and dead in the eyes. He straddled my chest and hit me in the face repeatedly, alternating his open palm with his nastier backhand. Every time his hand made contact, he asked me again, "Are you on drugs?"

My ears rang and the ringing was a thread. I took

the edge of the thread and pulled myself, light as air, to the top of the room and out into the deep green suburban night with the cut-grass smell and the crickets, the lights on behind curtains, the TVs flickering in their living rooms. I sailed past West Orange and Newark and along the Parkway and over the Hudson and never once looked down until I saw New York, the Emerald City, its spires shining in the moonlight. I knew something about New York. I knew I wouldn't be ugly when I got there.

My mother stood with her arms at her sides by the foot of the stairway across the room. She looked like someone in a movie who had been frozen in time while the other characters kept moving. The spell lifted just long enough for her to call out.

"Enough. Please. Enough."

I wasn't sure if she was talking to my father or me or God.

My father stood up and backed off, looking confused and lost. I imagined I knew what he was thinking right then: that his life was so very far from anything he had hoped for, had tried for, had dreamed of when he dreamed of a family. That he was so very far from the man he'd thought he was. I felt sorry for him.

"My children are a curse from God," he said, as he turned and walked out the door to the garage.

When my father snapped like this, hours later—or in the worst cases the next day—an entirely different person would sheepishly knock on my door and ask if I wanted to come downstairs and listen to music in front of the fire, or if I wanted to go for ice cream at Baskin-Robbins and rent a movie.

"I have a bad temper," he likes to say about himself. "But it's over fast." As if a quick beating is preferable to a big, long talk.

After that night, I told my mother I was leaving home. My mother—sender of award-worthy care packages to summer camp, cheerful carpooler, PTA president, tireless volunteer, meticulous writer of thank-you notes, thrower of flawless dinner parties, dedicated caretaker of any sick family and friends—thought it was a good idea. She suggested that I get my GED and apply for college a year early.

I got into NYU and my mother took me to Loehmann's to buy me some new clothes for college. Whenever we went shopping, my mother was generous to a fault. She often suffered the consequences later, when the bill came back and my father ranted about her carelessness, her uselessness. She couldn't even clean the house, he said. All she was good for was shopping. These reckonings happened every time a bill came back, but still she shopped.

"You have to understand men," she told me. "You let them say what they need to say and then you do what you want anyway."

My mother wanted to go to Loehmann's and I wanted to go to the only punk clothing store in all of North Jersey, so we compromised. I was terrified by what I had dubbed the "Hadassah thighs" on the old Jewish ladies in the Loehmann's communal dressing rooms and she was

appalled by the swastikas tattooed on either side of the
punk store clerk's Mohawk, but we were gentle with each
other that day.

"She shouldn't have a haircut like that with such a
fat face," was all that my mother said about the clerk.

We had lunch together and I can't remember what
we talked about. There was a sweetness to the ritual, the
final shopping trip before I left home for good. It was as if
I was any girl leaving home to go to college. And in some
ways it was true. Both realities existed simultaneously. I
was a half-broken anorexic teen hiding behind my purple
hair and running for my life and I was a precocious girl
with theatrical aspirations, an early admission to a good
school and a numbered list of dreams and plans that took
up ten pages of my diary.

And both mothers existed simultaneously: My mother
whose eyes went cloudy, who stared into space and stood
with her hands limp at her sides while her husband berated her kids; my mother who sewed labels onto every
last sheet before I left for college. I could hear both mothers on the other end of the phone line that day.

"Ask her if she's still going to come to the Caymans with
us this year," my dad said in the background.

"Honey, are you going to make it home in time to
come to the Caymans with us? We'd really like it if you'd
come," my mother translated.

"No, Mom, I don't think so."

"What did she say?" my dad asked my mother.

"No. She said no. She can't come this year."

"What? I'm stuck with just her brother? Tell her she's ruining my whole vacation."

My mother didn't translate this last comment. Instead she said, "Are you really all right?"

"I'm great. This is a great job. I can't pass it up."

By the time I hung up, I was relieved that they knew the sort-of truth and I was also relieved that I didn't have to see them for a while. No one was waiting for the phone, so I called Sean. I called Sean and wept. I missed him. I was homesick. I turned around and watched myself in the mirror as my face turned dough-pale and splotchy. I secretly liked watching myself cry. It was like watching someone else's face. It proved to me I was feeling something. Sometimes I spent so much time acting the part that I forgot how I was really feeling, forgot if I ever even had any real feelings.

"Then come home, Jill. Just come home," he said, sounding tired. Tired of me. Later he told me he wasn't tired of me, he was sad for me, for what I was becoming, for his inability to change my course.

"I can't."

"I can't help you."

I called Penny and she told me the show was proceeding without me, but assured me there would always be a place for me. We'd write in something new when I got back. Except I didn't know when I was coming back. I regretted not assuaging my mother's worry, not returning to Sean, not being there while Penny was writing our show, but I was compelled to stay in a way I couldn't explain to any of them. I couldn't just walk

away. I couldn't leave and let Serena win. I didn't want
to be the quitter.

At the parties I sparkled with laughter, but back at the
house I was grim and homesick. Serena was relentless.
She sent back the food before I got downstairs in the
morning. She organized mimosa parties out by the pool
and forgot to invite me. She blasted movies in the den,
next to my room, when I tried to nap. She told the other
girls that I smelled, that I was a hooker with herpes, that
I was a drunk, that I was a fat, bulimic slob. Everything
she said was overheard by the powers that lurk, that sur-
veil, so that after the herpes comment I was taken on a
surprise trip to the doctor.

I knew about Serena's treachery from Taylor, who
kept me in the loop because she hated Serena, too, and
because I was maybe her only friend in Brunei or New
York or anywhere, even though she still tried to charge
me commission on the money I made. Taylor and I lay in
bed together and looked up at the lights in the stepped
ceiling. It was kind of like a sunken living room in
reverse.

Taylor whispered in my ear with the music on loud
so no one could overhear us. She tried to get me to take
revenge on Serena.

"You have to retaliate."

"Nobody listens to me; they listen to her."

"Robin listens to you. Why do you think she's doing
this?"

I was beginning to believe that I somehow inspired

an ancient tribal instinct to cast out the one who was different.

"It's not because you're different, sweet pea," said Taylor. "Stop being so married to that whole self-concept. It's because you're better. It's because he prefers you. But that bitch may change his mind unless you get in there and defend what's yours."

But I couldn't remember ever having taken revenge on anyone. Instead, I would sink deeper into myself; I would run away. I clung to my dreams of stardom and knew that therein lay my revenge. Taylor had something much more immediate in mind, and under her tutelage, I was beginning to consider it. I was beginning to think I owed it to myself.

After all, isn't that what you do when you suddenly find yourself a member of a royal court? You plot. You scheme. You jockey for position. You take revenge. Isn't that the person you want to be? Or do you want to be the girl with the steadfast, good heart, the girl who gets stepped on, the girl you inevitably wish had less screen time because everyone else is so much more interesting?

"You have to stand up for yourself. You could tell him something about her that would get her sent home," suggested Taylor, twirling a lock of my hair absentmindedly around her finger.

"He's too smart. He would know what I was doing."

"Not necessarily. Not if you're smart, too. Smarter. You can be, you know. He has a weakness. He's blinded by his ego."

Taylor's visit to Brunei ended quickly, much to my

disappointment, putting a stop to our schemes. She was sent home after three weeks and wasn't asked back. Taylor and Robin didn't gel. Taylor may have been brilliant in her way, but she was too calculating, didn't have enough soft spots. She was just like him and he recognized it immediately. He preferred girls he could charm, girls he could hurt. Taylor was a good actress, but she had her limitations. She couldn't do vulnerable. But she had stayed long enough to plant a hard, cold seed in me.

The seed that Taylor planted, Fiona watered. After Taylor left, I would escape to Fiona's house in the afternoons to smoke and eat her chocolates. Fiona was the only girl on the property who got her own house. She slept in the master and used the other two bedrooms—the entire rooms—as closets. She had the beds removed and she rolled in wardrobe racks instead. Her suits and gowns and tennis attire and loungewear and even her pajamas were arranged first by genre and then by color. She didn't do it herself; she delegated with a grandiose sense of entitlement.

Fiona had twice as many servants in her guesthouse as we did in ours and they were always running around doing one task or another. Fiona spoke to them almost exclusively in Thai and they actually seemed to like her. I was always apologetic with the servants. I had so much to learn.

Fiona had been a popular television actress in the Philippines. She told me that Robin had fallen in love with her while watching her show and had sought her out and invited her for a visit. Initially she was intrigued, then she was repulsed, then he won her over. On her first night in Brunei, she had walked into the party and then walked straight back out. Robin had answered her consternation with diamonds. She pulled the necklace out of a drawer crammed with jewelry boxes and tried it on for me. It was in the shape of a diamond cougar that clasped to its own tail. It curled around her neck like something captured, declawed. She had been in Brunei six months already.

We drank tea in Fiona's living room as she reclined on the couch and chain-smoked. There was no smoking allowed anywhere; Robin loathed it. Fiona did it anyway.

I had a good, snotty cry and complained to her. The other girls were so cruel. Taylor had gone home. I missed New York. I missed Sean. I had mounting anxiety, had too many hangovers, woke every morning with a dark cloud over my head I couldn't shake.

"I can't take those mean bitches. I can't take this anymore."

"Stop being stupid. Are you here to make friends?" she asked. "That's a mistake. I'm not your friend. Robin is not your friend. Those morons are certainly not your friends. The money is your only friend."

I wanted to be like Fiona. I had considered myself all grown up when I was about fifteen, but I was changing my mind.

"Besides, you'll get back at them. I have my own ideas about retribution," she said. "Most of them include shopping."

❀   ❀   ❀

One morning soon after, I received the by-then familiar knock on my door, but when I got downstairs to the car, Fiona was sitting in it.

"We're going shopping," she said. "Robin likes to see us in traditional gowns. Don't worry; we'll get real clothes later. Think of this as an appetizer."

A driver chauffeured us around to traditional Malay shops, where heavily made-up women in patterned silks fussed over us, costuming us in brightly colored sarong Kebayas and sarong Baju Kurongs, complete with matching bejeweled shoes, hair pieces, and jewelry. We must have bought ten each. The driver shelled out note after note and toted all of our bags to the car.

That night, Robin had portraits of Fiona and me taken by the fountain in the entrance hallway of the palace. I stood there all wrapped up in a traditional gown of beaded pink silk, with a glittering pink fake flower adorning my hair. Most of the photos were of each of us individually, but in some of the poses Fiona and I sat next to each other and held hands like it was a wedding portrait.

Fiona was becoming more than a friend; she was an older sister of sorts, in a pervy way. I had always wanted a sister. That night I felt that my position in the hierarchy of the harem made me a participant in something ancient. Part of it was treacherous and terrible, but part of it wasn't so bad, this world of women with one enigma of a man who held sway over us all.

❀   ❀   ❀

Our next shopping trip was something else entirely.

Fiona and I sat in the back of yet another car, this time heading back to the Bandar Seri Begawan airport, where we hopped on a private plane to Singapore. The interior of the plane was all white leather and gilded hardware and walls that looked like white marble veined with gold. Chic flight attendants served us drinks and lunch, fanned out magazines for us to choose from.

"Thank you, Siti. Thank you, Jing," she said to the smiling flight attendants as we exited the plane. Fiona learned and remembered everyone's name.

Fiona walked through the airport like she had somewhere to go, but never like she was in a rush. She always wore heels and it gave her hips a slight swing—nothing too slutty, but enough to affect a gravitational pull on the attention of the men she passed. I mirrored her gait all the way to our waiting car and then out again when we reached the Hilton, where we were staying in the Prince's private suite. The suite occupied an entire floor, had its own full staff, and was more like a villa than a suite. The interior was classic Robin, with a big indoor fountain and lots of solid-gold doorknobs.

Fiona was a class act all the way, whereas I felt like Courtney Love stumbling around in Buckingham Palace. I resolved that if I was going to have flight attendants and pilots and drivers and maids waiting on me, I should at least be worthy of the part. I started by making a conscious effort not to use the words *fuck* and *like* in every sentence. Emulating Fiona's British accent was going too far, but, barring that, I forced my syllables to fall in step with her proper diction. I tried to trade whatever Jersey harshness hadn't been pounded out of me by years of acting lessons for her silky contralto.

I watched how she sat with her back like a rod at dinner and still looked relaxed. I began to keep my fork in my left hand, cutting small bites of chicken and managing to talk and still keep my mouth closed while I chewed. I studied Fiona as if doing an acting exercise. I was definitely playing a role, but it wasn't a role that was going to be so easy to step out of. When I stood on that balcony in Singapore and felt that I was on the brink of being transformed, I had been right.

We slept over that night and ate a breakfast of bacon and eggs together in the morning. Fiona ate like a lady, but she ate every bite. She wasn't a dieter.

"You'll learn that Robin never keeps skinny girls around for long," she said. "Now tell me, who can resist a man like that?"

It was true. Who doesn't like a guy who likes his girls zaftig? I skipped the bacon but giddily helped myself to more eggs. It was such a relief.

We talked about our lives at home. She had already bought herself and her parents townhouses with her earnings from acting. Then she had given her townhouse to her sister and bought a second house for herself with her earnings from Robin; rather, with her "gifts."

I tried to explain to her what experimental theater was and I could tell she thought it was the stupidest thing she had ever heard.

"How artistic," she said politely.

I could tell that she found me, if not fabulous, then at least amusing; if not an equal, than at least a worthy playmate. It dawned on me that I had not climbed the ladder so quickly because Robin had fallen head over heels, though I believe he was genuinely growing fond of me. It was because Fiona had wanted a friend. Fiona was the one who had picked me, guided his affections.

"I told Robin that you had to come along shopping with me this time," she told me, a little reminder of who was in charge.

After breakfast, we each set off separately with a driver. I had thought we should go together, but when I told Fiona this she had shrugged me off, telling me there wouldn't be room for both of us in the same store at the same time, which seemed ridiculous. Next to my driver sat a bodyguard with a Louis Vuitton sack full of cash, like a parody of a bag that robbers in a silent movie would use to heist a bank.

The bodyguard asked me where I wanted to go. He knew the location of all the stores in Singapore; I only needed to choose. I named the first designer I could think of: Dolce and Gabbana. Done.

Singapore reminded me of a silver, sci-fi utopia located under an oxygen dome. Like microcosms of Singapore itself, the malls were gleaming and modern. The first mall was shiny, white, and curled upward in a spiral, like the Guggenheim. I gingerly fingered the clothes at Dolce, staring at the multiple zeros on the price tags. A salesgirl hovered behind me and yanked each piece of clothing off the rack as soon as I touched it. When she had an armful she handed it off to another girl, who ran it to the dressing room. It was like a bucket brigade.

When I went to try on the clothes, I discovered that the salesgirls at designer shops in Singapore are slightly different from those at Urban Outfitters. Three of them piled into my dressing room and pretty much took my clothes off for me.

I started out slowly, trying on everything twice, looking at price tags, asking everyone's opinions. The salesgirls clucked and pulled at the fabric and nodded approvingly. I frowned and spun in front of the mirror until my guard got fed up with me and took me by the shoulders.

He looked at me and said, "This is just your first shop."

He picked up one dress off the bench in the dressing room and then took three others off the hanger, gave them all to the salesgirl, and spoke to her in Malay. She took them to the counter.

"Take them all. You may only shop once in your life."

He picked a purse out of the spotlight on a glass shelf and gave it to the next girl, who took it to the front of the shop.

"But how much can I spend?" I didn't want to reach my limit and wind up with a bunch of clothes I didn't really love, especially if I might only shop once in my life.

"Just get them and let's go. I'll let you know when you're close to your limit."

Chanel, Hermes, Versace, Dior, Armani, Gucci. We exhausted the first mall and went to the next and yet another until everything, even the most expensive things—especially the most expensive things—started to look cheap and nauseating. We never even took the bags with us; they were sent on ahead. It was frantic. I was like some suburban mother who wins a holiday raffle and gets ten free minutes at Toys"R"Us, running through the aisles with a shopping cart, grabbing everything she can reach.

I was aware of my rabid consumerism. What about the eight-year-old slaves in China who stitched these ridiculously priced rags together? What about hungry people? Homeless people? Entire countries besieged by poverty and famine? Entire blocks of New York where the sidewalks are lined with encampments of cardboard?

This is what I told myself: It wasn't my money to spend it was Robin's and he wasn't spending it on the homeless he was spending it on clothing for his mistress and if I didn't buy that dress right there it wouldn't help anything it wouldn't give one abused garment worker a cubic inch more of fresh air. I was being silly, entertaining the pretensions of the bourgeois bleeding heart. Not buy a dress because people were starving? Even the guilt itself was an embarrassment, kind of like experimental theater. Fiona would have scoffed. She would have deemed my foolishness unforgivable. I convinced myself that Robin was probably a really charitable guy in other ways. After all, everyone had health care in Brunei; everyone had a good education free of charge. What was the harm if he wanted his girlfriends to look nice, too?

After the shops closed at nine p.m., security guards opened the doors for us. Salesgirls stayed late in the stores and we kept shopping, my arches aching in my sandals as we power-walked the dim corridors of the closed malls. I started throwing down Chanel gowns on the counter without even trying them on. I figured I might as well go until I hit my spending limit, but I hit a wall of exhaustion first and gave up. We drove back to the hotel close to midnight. I had been shopping since eleven that morning.

"What was my limit anyway?" I asked the bodyguard when we were in the car. I couldn't believe I hadn't hit it. I had certainly tried.

"You didn't have one. No limit only for some girls. Only for very special girls."

"Well, how much did I spend, then?"

He told me a number that left me speechless. The number far exceeded the down payment on the house I live in today. I felt drunk.

Fiona and I ate in silence. I was dehydrated and the noodles seemed gummy and tasteless. We went straight to our rooms, exhausted. Fifteen identical suitcases lined the wall. My new clothes were already folded and packed inside them. I lay on the bed and tried to squeeze my knees so tightly into my chest that I would wring the disgust out of my gut.

chapter 16

The mirror in my bathroom had begun to separate
from the wall just a hair, but enough that I could
see a small red light come on from time to time in the dark
recesses behind it. I dragged the other girls into my bathroom to confirm it. This much was certain: Sometimes
there was a light.

It was not news that we were being watched, but it
could still make you feel crazy, paranoid. Who was watching? What were they watching for? Even though Taylor
had gone home and I was allowed to keep my room as a

single because I had so many new clothes that I needed the closet space, I never felt truly alone. It was like a pea under the mattress—enough to make me uncomfortable but not enough for me to peg exactly what was wrong.

I have heard that privacy is a construct of privilege. Privileged as I was growing up, I never felt I had a stitch of it. My father took the locks off our doors. My mother read my journal and said that it had fallen out of a drawer when the housekeeper was cleaning. I never took for granted the fact that in my own apartment in New York, no one would open doors without knocking or go through my drawers, and I didn't have to encode my journals so intricately that even I wouldn't understand them later. In Brunei, I was again living in a world in which not even the page was private. Anywhere I sat to write in my journal, there was a mirror behind me and behind that a camera recording every scribble.

What did the cameras see? What was my great shame? A mustache wax? Air guitar? A vibrator? I couldn't have cared less.

No, I cursed myself because they saw a girl sit on the floor of her room and stare at the suitcases for two days, unable to unpack. Because when she half-unpacked, the room looked like it had been ransacked and it stayed that way for another three days. Because the girl managed to pull an outfit out of the rubble and paste herself together for the party every night, but every morning she woke in pieces again. All she could do was read and listen to music. She stopped working out, stopped swimming, stopped hitting the tennis balls shot out at her from a machine.

It had hit me so fast. Somewhere between Singapore and Brunei, a cannonball had come sailing out of the sky, nailed me in the gut, and knocked the wind out of me. Every day I vowed to change, to be efficient and cheery like Ari, capable and witty like Madge, mercenary and glamorous like Fiona—anything but lazy and out of control and sunk. Anything but me.

I was in the grip of the tentacles of a depression that has come and gone throughout my life, at times administering only the tiniest sting and at other times immobilizing. It wasn't the first time I'd succumbed to it. When the shadows of depression darkened my field of vision in high school, I had blamed it on my father, on my school. Now that all those things were behind me I saw that I had been wrong; the blame rested squarely on me. I accused myself of being weak-willed, lazy, self-indulgent. The list of indictments goes on.

I was sure if I just tried hard enough, did enough yoga, chanted the Hare Krishna, read Freud and Jung and the Dalai Lama and Ram Dass, stopped eating chocolate, started working out more, and learned those fucking French tapes I had dragged along with me, I would heal. I was sure that if I could just scale this fortress I would reach a height with a sunny blue sky and fresh air. I would stand there and experience myself as redeemable rather than ruined. I had no idea what kind of animal I was facing.

If you had suggested to me at the time that my problems were due to some faulty wiring, some chemistry experiment gone wrong in my brain, I'd have said you were suggesting that I not take responsibility for my own choices. Now I know I was wrong. Now when I'm haunted by the specter of depression, I recognize it for what it is. I don't systematically dismantle my life every time depression pops out from behind a tree. But at that time, I was sure it was fixable if the world would just change faster, or if I would.

Part of this illusion was sustained by the fact that changing the scenery appeared to work. When the world around me altered, for a minute or two the newness, the adrenaline, the endorphins could sometimes snap me out of my sludgy funk. I was skating on those very endorphins when I sprang out of my bed and finally unpacked my suitcases from Singapore, while simultaneously packing a suitcase for a trip to Malaysia. Fiona and I were to be included in the royal entourage for a two-week diplomatic mission to Kuala Lumpur. With the typical lack of notice, I was informed I'd be leaving the next day.

I think Ari felt sorry for me because of how I was treated by the other girls, though not too sorry. She was paid handsomely enough for all her hard work, but was never showered with the kind of immediate jewels and cash with which the girlfriends were. And we didn't work very hard at all, in her opinion. It chafed her, but she kept it in perspective. Ari always bore a hint of disbelief about her job. After all, she had gone from taking care of a Bel Air estate to procuring prostitutes for a prince.

The girls Ari brought to Brunei were almost never prostitutes to begin with, but I never saw one who refused the Prince's advances once they saw the rewards.

Everyone I met in Brunei had a price and Robin met it without fail. I only once even heard an expression of remorse, and a hefty jewelry box squashed it later in the week. In fact, the girls who came from normal jobs, normal boyfriends, normal lives were the quickest to lap up the new lifestyle. I was embarrassed for them, the way they drooled all over their Rolex birthday presents. Just because you're sequestered in some parallel-universe sorority house doesn't mean you can't have a little dignity.

Ari, on the other hand, had dignity aplenty. And she seemed to retain her identity in the face of Brunei's warping influence. She also retained a fiancé named John at home. John was a successful contractor. He had one blue eye and one green eye and was ridiculously handsome, as if he had just stepped out of an aftershave commercial. All that and he volunteered teaching swimming to autistic kids once a week. He was a perfect romantic-comedy lead, if you're into that kind of thing.

Even though Ari was in no way romantically involved with anyone in Brunei, it was taboo to mention John. Women like Ari and Madge were entrusted with difficult jobs involving lots of money and sensitive information, but they weren't allowed to be married or have boyfriends. Or at least there was an agreed-upon silence around it. For Ari and Madge it was an infraction to have a boyfriend, but for Robin's girlfriends it was suicide. You'd find yourself on the next flight home if anyone found out.

Even Ari got lonely in Brunei, so she sometimes talked to me. Though I wouldn't have counted "trustwor-

thy" as one of my primary virtues right at that moment,
I was still probably her best bet. It's not that Ari trusted
me, exactly, but she counted on me being smart enough
to know that crossing her would in no way behoove me.
Ari talked to me about her wedding plans without ever
mentioning the word *marriage*. She sat cross-legged on the
bed while I packed, eating avocado out of the shell with
a spoon.

"I'm a little anxious right now because, of course,
they changed my departure date to four days sooner than
I'd planned and now I'm missing appointments with the
caterers and the planner. The president can meet with the
architect. I'm not complaining."

Ari was going to marry John in six months. She
called him "the president" in code, because his name was
John Adams. Ari was twenty-five years old and building a house in Malibu. It made sense to me that she was
anxious to hang up her traveling shoes and settle down
to have a family. Might as well—hadn't she seen enough
by twenty-five?

"Can your mother do it for you?

"Yeah, ultimately my mother's going to do the whole
thing. I know it. But you only get to do this once, so I'd
like to at least see my invitations before they get sent out,"
she said. "Did I tell you already that when you get to KL
you're not to leave the hotel room for any reason unless a
guard comes to get you? Very important."

Then, weighing in on my packing decision, she said,
"Ooh, I like that dress. What is it?"

"Dior."

"Take that one with you for sure."

I closed my suitcases and didn't even bother to take them off the bed. I knew someone would fetch them and that they'd magically appear at my destination.

Robin was looking for his fourth wife, and for a fourth wife it wasn't out of the range of possibility that he'd choose from among the girls who attended the parties. For a first or second wife, that would be unthinkable. But once the royal lineage is secure, the royal boys have more room to play. I thought sometimes about what it would be like to marry Robin. It wouldn't be so bad to have a husband who was around only once in a while, especially if you had a staff to take care of your every need and a jet to fly you to Singapore on a whim. But freedom to buy whatever you wanted wasn't the same thing as freedom. I knew that if I married the Prince, I'd never act in another play, never backpack around Europe, never go to a movie with a male friend, never even go to a mall without a bodyguard.

Sometimes I fell prey to fantasies of becoming a princess. It seemed so strange that it had entered my orbit of possibilities. What Disney-brained American girl hadn't lain in bed and known deep in her heart that she was worthy of being woken from an evil spell by the kiss of a prince? That she would open her eyes and, due to no effort of her own, find that she had been saved? Who wouldn't consider attempting to grab that gold ring, that diamond crown?

But I wasn't brainwashed beyond all reason. I knew I didn't really want to marry Robin, not even at the height of my success there. If I did, I'd never again have a date on a rooftop in the rain.

After the shopping trip to Singapore, even the few girls who had been neutral toward me before had grown bristly. So when I left for Kuala Lumpur, I happily walked out the door dressed in my most conservative Chanel suit of pink-and-gray tweed. They had pushed me so far, had been so mean that I no longer felt the need to make myself smaller so I'd be liked. Who cared if those morons weren't my friends? That's what Fiona would have said and that is what, after weeks of their cruelty, I finally truly felt. It was liberating. It was akin to my preteen discovery of the Ramones and my subsequent initiation into the world of punk music. I could create a whole other reality. I could actively choose to be different from the kids who made my life a misery. I could state once and for all that I wasn't wrong, they were.

In high school, I spent my time with the theater crowd and in the ceramics room. I made my own clothes, dyed my hair most of the primary colors in succession, and discovered a passion for punk rock. Due to the somber colors of our wardrobe choices, my friends and I were dubbed by the preppy and privileged student body the Children of Darkness, a moniker we cheerfully appropriated and wrote on the wall over our preferred table in the cafeteria.

The Children of Darkness were an oddball crew of kids who had funny haircuts and did things like write rock operas or draw their own autobiographical comics.

They opened their goth capes and tatty overcoats and en-
folded me in acceptance. I could do whatever dorky thing
I wanted for the school talent show and I would always
have a cheering section. We were a tribe. But my new-
found acceptance came with a stash of black eyeliner and
decorative safety pins. And the dorky things I did for the
talent show shifted from shuffling off to Buffalo to performing acoustic covers of Siouxsie and the Banshees.

To my father, all this had signified an egregious devi-
ation from acceptable behavior, an embarrassment to the
family, a personal insult to him. He stood poised on the
brink of an explosion at all times. So when I was at home,
I imagined myself to be a punk version of Glinda from
The Wizard of Oz, floating in a pink bubble above it all. I
was untouchable, just like I was when I raised my hand
and gave the vipers in Brunei a little wave good-bye.

"Ciao."

What would Patti Smith do? She'd say, Fuck them.
She might not be wearing a Chanel suit when she said it,
but you've got to put your own spin on things.

We flew in a royal caravan from a private airport. I saw
faces I recognized milling about—Dan and Winston and
Dr. Gordon from the parties—but no other women. I
wondered if we might actually see one of Robin's wives in
person, but there were no wives and not even any Robin
to be seen; just a handful of men in suits who ignored us.
Dan nodded and Winston smiled.

Winston had always been my favorite. He and his
girlfriend, Tootie, were sweet together and spent the

nights talking and holding hands. Sometimes I looked at them and felt a pang of envy, though it didn't last long. She surely wasn't earning one thousandth of what I was making, but her boyfriend actually seemed to like her. Still, if I'd had to choose, I would have picked the money.

Fiona and I flew in our own plane again, which is definitely the way to travel. At the airport in KL, we were hustled under intense security through a hallway and straight out into the waiting cars. There was no such thing as customs when traveling under the umbrella of diplomacy. No one questioned our presence. I had learned to let myself be guided and not ask questions. I was a leaf in a stream, I told myself. I was living in the moment. I was practically a Zen monk.

With our own personal guard, Fiona and I were driven to the hotel in KL and deposited into rooms next door to each other. Our guard instructed us not to leave unless summoned. He posted himself in between our doorways. I bid good-bye to her as we entered our neighboring luxury prison cells. Five minutes later she called to chat.

"Why can't we even hang out with each other?" I asked.

"Don't worry. He won't stand out there all day. I'll see you for dinner."

She showed up in her pajamas a couple of hours later, soon followed by a bottle of wine and room service. She prompted me to order whatever I wanted. Order a bottle of wine; order three.

"Do you have any idea how many people are here?"

she said. "Martin and Robin each have an entire floor for their entourage and a separate penthouse suite each for themselves. Do you really think anyone is looking at the bill?"

We spent most of our days hanging out in each other's rooms ordering caviar, which we ate by the spoonful out of the jar, watching movies, and drinking expensive wine. Champagne and caviar is hideously cliché but wonderful when consumed while wearing sweats and watching the *Today Show* via satellite. We ordered up massages and listened to music and did each other's hair and once we even escaped to go get a pedicure in the hotel salon. I was so nervous while we were down there that I gave myself hives.

I don't know what Fiona did with her nights; we didn't talk about it. Robin completely ignored me for six whole days. While Fiona was gone during the evenings, I read Artaud and Hesse and went stir-crazy. I read Artaud's words *I am not fully myself* and thought, That's me. I'm not fully myself. I don't even know who that self is. I told myself I had to get out of there soon—to do something real, to be free.

I called Johnny, who was home for a brief spell in between getting kicked out of one boarding school and being shipped off to another. My parents were concerned because the volume on Johnny's Obsessive Compulsive Disorder had apparently turned way up since I had seen him last. My mother had told me during our previous phone conversation that she had a hard time getting him out the door because he had to complete so many rituals just to leave the house. He lived locked in a private world of tics, outbursts, exclamations, touching doorframes, spitting in puddles, tapping spoons against the sides of bowls.

"Bro."

"Sis."

"How are you?"

"Mellow. Mellow. I'm residing at the homestead for the time being. Ralph Reuben heard from his mom that you're a slave in China."

"I'm in Malaysia, actually. And how did Ralph Reuben's mom hear that?"

"She ran into Mom at the ShopRite."

Fantastic. Apparently my mother was disclosing my whereabouts to everyone she saw at the supermarket.

"Could you please tell her to be a little more discreet?"

"Sure. I'll let her know. That should take care of it."

"What are you going to do now?" I asked him.

"Mom and Dad would very much like me to depart for yet another fine learning institution."

"Why did you leave school this time?"

"I felt like I used to feel when I went to church with Anthony Dante. I always liked it until the times in the service when the little things would drop down from the back of the pews and everyone would kneel and I'd be the only one left sitting. That's how it was at that school. I was the only Jew in church."

"I know how you feel."

Even in casual conversation, Johnny was a poet. I

worried for him. He seemed fragile, translucent. Poetry didn't get you very far and the world wasn't kind to people with obvious expressions of mental illness. But I was 30,000 miles away and couldn't do much to convince him to try to work it out at this next school. I couldn't even convince myself to stay put. How could I make a suggestion to him that sounded like a prison sentence to me?

"I love you, bro. I miss you," I said. My voice echoed back to me over the international phone lines. The words sounded insufficient. And then there was the pause that I had learned to wait through.

"I love you, too, sis."

Sitting forgotten for days, I wanted desperately to get back to New York, back into rehearsals. As Robin ignored me, his pull on me lessened. My life was disappearing, each hour dissolving while I rotted in a cage of a hotel room. When I tried to talk about Artaud to Fiona, she told me in no uncertain terms that Artaud was a maniac and I was a brat.

"Can't you just sit still for five minutes? It's not like you're being asked to dig ditches. Go ahead and write all the poetry you want right here. Learn twelve new monologues. Knock yourself out. It's not where you are that's the problem."

But Fiona was older than I was. I had no idea what a dollar meant, thought nothing of eating peanut butter straight from the jar for lunch and Pop-Tarts from the box for dinner. I hadn't really cared that I was poor, so getting rich for doing nothing didn't seem like a big deal.

This was when I still truly believed in my heart that I had a great career ahead of me on the stage.

I was restless, but I was still conflicted. I hadn't completely given up on Brunei yet, wasn't willing to concede defeat. So when I got the call that Robin had invited me upstairs, I rallied. I aimed to dazzle. I hoped to spark something that would galvanize his attentions again and that would, in turn, inspire me to stay. I dressed to accept my Oscar in a sequined Armani gown with a plunging back. Robin was an ass man; I tried to choose my attire accordingly.

Our guard escorted me upstairs to an opulent dinner party in the penthouse suite, where I, the lone woman, sat next to Robin. I recognized many of the men around the dining table, but there were new faces, men with accents that differed from Robin's and his usual entourage's. Some might have been Iranian; some were British. They seemed more jocular than usual, as if celebrating some sort of success.

It was one of those nights that flew by on a magic carpet of champagne and right moments and good timing, the kind of night in which everything clicks into place and you feel beautiful and clever. I could tell I pleased him. There was none of his usual darkness or the criticism that his phony smiles often imparted. Robin's expression remained clear of the clouds of dissatisfaction that portended punishment, banishment from his bed for days, the flaunting of a rival girl in front of you.

But, as with every night with him, the party wore on long after everyone else was exhausted. He was one of those people who didn't need sleep, who judged everyone else for sleeping through their brief hours on earth. He was the kind of insomniac who, if he was a normal person, would spend many lonely late-night hours. But because he was a filthy-rich aristocrat he could pay a party full of people to stay up round-the-clock with him if he wanted.

Robin excused the other guests at four a.m. and took me to his bedroom suite. The room had floor-to-ceiling rounded windows, as if the whole twinkling city was in our private aquarium. We fucked with the curtains open and the light off.

After we were done, I expected to be excused with the usual smack on the ass and kiss on the cheek. Instead, the incomprehensible happened. He pushed a button on a remote control that closed the curtains, curled his body around mine, draped his arm over me, and said good night.

It completely freaked me out. The intimacy was such a leap. In Robin's presence, I was always electrified with tension, posed and aimed to please, never thinking of my own needs. I was so frozen in that mode that I couldn't even kick the covers off my too-hot feet for fear of disturbing him. I lay awake, my feet sweating, heart pounding, stomach cramping. I hoped he would fall asleep first and snore or something and then I could relax. I pretended to sleep.

"You are not sleeping."

He wasn't fooled. I felt like a failure. He finally gave me a sleeping pill and took one himself.

When we woke, we ate room-service breakfast together and watched CNN while he dressed for work. For the rest of the trip, that was how we spent our evenings and mornings. It became normal. I gave only a passing thought to the fact that Fiona was now the one waiting around alone.

The first Gulf War had recently ended, but you could still see its aftermath on the news. Only months earlier I had protested the war in Tompkins Square Park, but by then, in Brunei, it seemed faraway—the war and Tompkins Square Park both. Most people who ask me about Brunei assume it is in the Middle East, maybe because of the oil and the brown skin. But Southeast Asia is far from Iraq and I didn't perceive any connection. Of course, there was a connection. Every oil-rich sultan, king, president, and prime minister is slipping around in the same oil slick.

Robin was tied into this network of oil in ways I didn't understand and could never talk to him about. That wasn't exactly what I was there for. But I wondered about it as I watched him scanning the news all the time, a constant stream of it superimposed on everything else he did. I lay in the huge hotel bed, the city of Kuala Lumpur humming forty floors below, and watched the ever-present CNN as Robin got ready for work, whatever work was. Morning after morning, I watched, among other things, the wizened face of Nelson Mandela addressing the world about the crumbling of apartheid.

As Robin became something to me that looked more and more like a lover and less like an employer, I occa-

sionally ventured to ascertain Robin's opinions about the
events we watched every day on the news. But he was
usually evasive, so I didn't ask too many questions. I
knew there was no freedom of the press in Brunei, that
the Sultan was an autocrat (if a genial one) and that it
was a serious crime to disparage him. None of these were
admirable things but I preferred to ignore them. I wasn't
there as a representative for Amnesty International. It
wasn't my country. It wasn't my concern.

All my political convictions, my years of activism,
were suddenly irrelevant. It's not that I was exactly going
all out for theocracy, polygamy, and unchecked consumerism, but it didn't really matter what I believed.

In high school, I had bussed down to Washington for
pro-choice marches, for gay-rights rallies. I wrote papers
on the Zapatistas and planned a post-graduation trip to
Chiapas. But I never did make it to Chiapas. Instead, I decided to wed my activism with my artistic ambitions and
join the illustrious history of the theater of protest, until I
discovered that it didn't pay very well and the realities of
self-sufficiency began to erode my ideals. Neither art nor
activism had any place in my Brunei world, which, as the
months wore on, was becoming my real world.

Closer to Robin's interest than the end of apartheid
was the British royal divorce. Closer still was the ticker
tape of international finance, which we watched in English but might as well have been in Malay, for all I knew
about Dows and S&Ps. My father hadn't taught me a
thing, probably because I had never asked. But I did tell
Robin my father was in finance, and this impressed him

for a minute, but he lost interest quickly. Instead, I came up with cute stunts to keep him amused.

One morning, I teased Robin because he wouldn't take a bath with me.

"I will only share a bath with a duckie," he said.

That afternoon I sent a guard out to get a rubber duckie, and I gave it to Robin as a present so he wouldn't be lonely in the tub. That day he was particularly charmed by me, more than usual. I hadn't planned to do what I did, but the seed that Taylor had planted in me had taken root.

Robin liked to throw Serena's name into conversations, particularly when things were going well between us and I was getting complacent. I don't remember how it came up. Were we talking about acting? Singing?

"Serena, I think, is a singer in a band in Los Angeles. Isn't she?" he asked.

"Yes, I remember she told me she sings in her boyfriend's band," I replied. It was so easy. He had handed it to me.

"Did she say that?" he asked sharply.

"That she's a jazz singer?" I pretended the boyfriend part had just slipped out without my even noticing. "That's what she told me."

I kissed him good-bye that morning and then went to the windows and stood there looking out over the city for a long time. I did the same every morning. I always had a couple of hours to kill before a guard came to fetch me and bring me to my room, where I'd nap, order room service, read for a while, then get dressed and do it all over again. But my favorite time of the day was when Robin left for work, the first quiet of being alone. When being alone got old, I sometimes called Fiona's room, but she was never around during the day anymore. I tried not to think of where she was.

I kissed Robin good-bye every morning and sat next to him every night at dinner. It was like having a boyfriend, except he was a dictator's brother who was married three times already and had forty other girlfriends, one of whom I was actively trying to deprive of her livelihood.

It's hard to explain why I fought so hard for Robin. Sometimes I thought he was scheming and fascinating, the sexy villain. Sometimes he made me feel impossibly lovely. Sometimes I thought he was a little prick and felt an overwhelming urge to bean him in the head with the remote control. But here's the grimy, ugly truth: I shared Robin's bed and I felt I was part of something powerful and important. Power was something I'd never experienced before. I'm not sure that I was in love with Robin as a person, exactly, but I was in love with that feeling, ecstatically in love. I may have gotten the two confused.

Power tasted like an oyster, like I'd swallowed the sea, all its memories and calm and rot and brutality. It tasted like an oyster I ate once as a kid, an oyster still flinching with life. My father's favorite food was shellfish. On a trip to Boston once when I was about seven, he took me to Faneuil Hall and set a dozen raw oysters between us and a dozen raw clams next to that. He speared his first oyster, dunked it in the cocktail sauce, and then slugged the whole thing down and dared me to do the same. We actually drew a small crowd of people who wanted to see the little girl eat oysters.

I held the creature aloft in front of me for a beat, wanting to chicken out. It was the underside of a tongue, wet and meant to be hidden. I put it in my mouth and tried to chew it and it slid to the back of my throat, making me gag. The crowd laughed. They cheered. *Come on, kiddo, you can do it!* I gagged again before figuring out how to open my throat and swallow.

It made me want to vomit, but I sucked down that oyster and then I sucked down four more. I know it made my father proud. And with each oyster, I understood a little more. They're disgusting, they're delicious, and you swallow every last one just to prove you can.

I had wanted something dazzling and I'd gotten it. I was a royal mistress, standing around in La Perla underwear and overlooking Kuala Lumpur from a penthouse suite. And if I had the feeling that the oyster was poisoning my blood, if I had an echo of a thought that something irretrievable was being traded, I nudged it aside.

chapter 17

The guard knocked in the middle of the day and informed me I was to dress in an evening gown. Previously on the Malaysia trip Robin had called for me only at night, so it seemed strange. When we got on the elevator, the guard pushed the button for the roof. My chest tightened with panic. I knew too much and they were getting rid of me. There was nothing I could do. I was trapped. I was like that guy in the gangster movie who knows he's about to get whacked for some infraction, yet has no choice but to get in the car with his soon-to-be killer. I imagined the headlines.

DESPAIRING SPURNED MISTRESS THROWS HERSELF OFF A MALAYSIAN ROOFTOP

AMERICAN PROSTITUTE DIES IN A DRUG DEAL GONE WRONG AT THE KUALA LUMPUR HILTON

JERSEY TEEN DISAPPEARS WHILE ON HOLIDAY IN SOUTHEAST ASIA

At least I'd die in an evening gown. But no one pitched me off the roof. Instead, I found a helicopter waiting for me on the helipad, kicking up a crazy wind. It was the first time I had been in a helicopter, and the headphones the pilot handed me wrecked my by-then-perfected five-minute updo. I imagined I looked like a Hitchcock heroine after having been chased over a foam studio mountain while the industrial fans blew my evening gown into a twist.

The ride seemed laughably short, barely a Spider-Man hop from one roof to another. But looking down on the gridlocked traffic creeping through the streets of KL, I was sure that what was a three-minute flight would have been a three-hour drive. That helicopter flight, the drives to and from the airport, and the view from my hotel-room window were all I would see of KL. I never smelled the food smells blown out the back of the restaurants, never tried to buy a scarf from a street vendor, never ordered my own cup of tea, never even put my shoe to the Malaysian pavement except to walk from the hotel to the car,

and that only twice. I had been to Malaysia, but I hadn't.
I had been to the island of Borneo, but not really.

I was greeted at the helipad by two mirrored-sun-
glasses-wearing guards, who ushered me into the door
of yet another hotel suite. This one stretched on forever. I
began to fix my hair, taking my time to look around and
prepare for yet another marathon wait. I turned around
and on a love seat at the far end of the room sat the Sultan.
I jumped and nearly screamed from the shock of finding
myself not alone.

"How do you like my country?" he asked, patting the
seat next to him. Robin had asked me the same question.

Of course, we weren't exactly in his country at that
particular minute, but I knew what the Sultan meant.
The world was his oyster; everywhere was his country.
And not in a John Lennon kind of way.

He seemed a football field away. In front of him, on
the coffee table, was a delicate bone-china tea set edged
in gold. The Sultan asked me to call him Martin as I sat
next to him and poured for both of us. Talking to Martin
was easier than talking to Robin. He was gracious and almost breezy, his smiling face much less imposing than the
stern countenance on the money and the billboards. We
finished one cup and even half of another before retiring
to the bedroom. The suite where I met the Sultan of Brunei was easily ten times bigger than my whole house is
now. The Pope himself couldn't have dreamed up a more
lavish spectacle.

I was being passed along after all. But I had been
in Brunei long enough to understand that it was a com-

pliment rather than an insult. I was some sort of a trib-
ute paid, part of a system of honor and respect between
brothers. I was a gift.

Just by kissing Martin I could tell how different
he was from Robin. He was less complicated, less needy,
less manipulative. The difference can best be explained
by the following: Robin demanded that you love him;
Martin just wanted you to suck his dick. He politely requested that I do exactly that, after asking me to remove
my clothes, walk back and forth, turn around, and then
do a little dance. Afterward he cheerily sent me back to
the helicopter with the pronouncement that his brother
had good taste.

I never saw the Sultan again, but after that it always
amused me to look at his face on the Bruneian dollars.
Angelique, the singer whom Prince Sufri loved, later told
me that I shouldn't feel bad that he didn't ask me back. In
fact, I should be flattered that I met him in the first place.
She told me that he almost never fucked Western girls
and when he did he never kept them.

That night Robin was eager to know if Martin had
liked me. He seemed like a little boy looking for his father's approval. Robin was always famished behind the
eyes. It was the kind of hunger you could never really
feed, the kind that keeps you up until five a.m. every
night, the kind that drives you to fuck girl after girl, to
buy Maserati after Maserati.

He looked like an alcoholic near closing time, like
someone who had gotten everything he had ever wanted
and despaired to discover that he still felt empty. It wasn't

the first time I suspected that for all his relentless pursuit of pleasure, he actually had a hard time having fun. There aren't enough girls or cars in the world to satisfy that kind of appetite.

I slept in Robin's arms and dreamed that I was the Sultan, or not exactly the Sultan but a man.

I am a man and I walk into the Kit Kat Club on Fifty-second Street, push through the curtain of thick tinsel slabs that hang in the doorway, dodge the mirrored columns, and round the corner. I sit at one of the booths along the wall and buy a lap dance from a girl whose face I can't really see, but I can feel her heat. It surprises me how profoundly naked she is in my lap. In the dream I'm awed by her softness. I think, You can buy a girl, a whole warm, velvety girl.

I never got it before. I never understood why you'd want to buy a girl, until that dream. In my dream I was so grateful to be a man.

chapter 18

I returned from Kuala Lumpur to find Serena was gone.

"Gone?"

"Gone. Closets cleared out. One-way ticket. Gone," said Ari.

Oh, happy day! Serena gone! I think I actually did the running man. Then it hit me. Had the jab at her that I had slipped into my pillow talk with Robin caused her to be sent home? If so, who cared? I should feel victorious.

She had tried to do the same to me but it hadn't worked because she was too transparent.

I flashed back to her eating that strawberry. I knew the feeling of running your tongue over the tiny beads, anticipating the taste, pretending, always pretending, that one bite is enough, that you don't ever need to feel full, to feel satisfied. I felt a pang of something. Not guilt, exactly. Disgust. At Serena and at myself. For what a vicious harpy she had been, for what I had been reduced to in the face of it. But isn't this who I wanted to be? The ruthless one, the one who fights and wins, even if I come out bloody? The opposite of fighter isn't lover, it's runner. Who do you want to be?

I asked Ari why Serena had gone home and she finally spilled all the beans about Serena. The story of Serena was that Serena had been number one before there was ever a Fiona. Serena had been number one before there were any other Western girls in Brunei. Robin had adored Serena once. But, like the wife of Bluebeard, she just couldn't resist the one thing that was forbidden her.

Back in the early days of the Brunei party girls, a whole eight months before, Ari, Serena, and Leanne had regularly been allowed out to the Hilton to have lunch and swim in the pool. They had gone shopping in Singapore and then gone out to the zoo together. They had each lived in their own guesthouse.

During this golden age, Prince Hakeem, Jefri's oldest son, whom I had yet to meet, would come to the parties every night. He had a friend named Arif, the handsome counterpart to the behemoth Hakeem. Arif began to show up at the Hilton pool on certain days, which were magically the days Serena happened to be there.

Serena used the house phone to arrange the trysts. Apparently our favorite frosty blue-eyed beauty also had a taste for talking dirty on said phone and not to the Prince. Robin rarely used the phone for social reasons. Why would he? Other people made his calls for him. If he wanted to talk to someone, he mentioned it to one of his aides and the person soon appeared in front of him.

Serena was the trailblazer in Brunei. She didn't know the phones were tapped. She never suspected that her private conversations would be played back for the Prince himself, who never confronted her directly, but rather would just drop hints by repeating, at opportune moments, choice phrases from her conversations with Arif. I imagine that he enjoyed how her body went stiff and dropped in temperature, how her eyes registered fear and guilt that not even she could conceal, how she broke a light sweat and tried ever harder to please him, feigning greater passion.

The Prince didn't summarily cut off her head. He didn't even present her with a one-way ticket home. What fun would that be? It wasn't his style. If he was the Grand Inquisitor and he had you stretched out on a rack, he'd make it last for days. He'd turn the wheel in such minuscule progressions that you might not even notice you were being tortured until you saw your intestines on the ground next to you. No, he pretended he had forgiven Serena. He invited her back and sat her in a chair and proceeded to ignore her for months while he romanced every other woman in the room, but most pointedly her rival. That rival would be me.

Ari told me all this over cheese sandwiches and watermelon spears. I felt my toes turn cold. Fiona, my best buddy Fiona, must have known this and never mentioned it to me. It wasn't like she didn't warn me. "I'm not your friend," she'd said. Another useful lesson I learned in Brunei: When someone tells you something like, "I'm not your friend," believe her.

Taylor had lain next to me in bed and urged me to avenge my mistreatment. "You're smart, too," she had whispered in my ear.

Was I? I had made a move that looked good at the time, but it turned out the other players in this game had way more information than I did. With Serena gone, would I be cast aside, no longer needed in Robin's scheme to torture her? He enjoyed the infighting among the girls. Would I be less fun for him without a rival? Would I go back to New York and wait for a phone call from Ari that never came, my hope fading as the months wore on? If I had even influenced Serena's departure at all, had I been shortsighted in my manipulations?

Had Fiona seen this far ahead? Had she used me to get rid of Serena, counting on the fact that Robin would lose interest in me once Serena was gone? Or was I just constructing an elaborate soap opera in my mind?

I should have just stuck with what I was good at: looking cute and telling funny stories and selling it. My father's words came back to me, with a twist. *You're no great international call girl, so you've got to sell it.* I knew I'd never win in a match with Fiona, but I'd learned enough from her to give her a good game. Every time I started to get batty with boredom or sick with self-hatred and ready to beg for a plane ticket home, something happened to pull me back in.

Robin got a new Lamborghini. Before I even entered the party room, a guard fetched me and brought me to the back entrance of the palace, where Robin picked me up for a spin in his car. I stepped in and the doors closed downward automatically, like the hatch of a time machine. The seats were so low I felt as if I was lying on the ground. A speed bump would have grazed my ass.

We sped along jungle-flanked roads lit only by our headlights. Riding in a car with Robin was another strange intimacy, as if we were a normal couple and could go anywhere, could go out to dinner or to the movies. Except, of course, we were going straight back to the same place we went every night. I watched Robin watch the road. Something pulsed against his skin and behind his eyes and through the veins in his neck. It was as if he was struggling to hold himself back from driving five hundred miles per hour. He seemed almost unaware of me. I wondered if he wanted just to drive and keep driving, to go somewhere where he wasn't a prince at all.

"What do you think?" he asked me, surprising me out of my reflection. *I think we should just leave and go to Thailand,* I almost said. *Bring nothing at all. Buy a new wardrobe when we get there and stay in a hut on a beach in Phuket and go cliff diving.*

"What do you think?" he repeated.

"Of what?"

"Of the car," he answered, annoyed. The car. Of course. As if there were anything else.

I searched for an adjective to describe the car, something to make him feel good. What I really thought: ugly, ridiculous, pathetic. But what I said was: "Tough."

"Tough?"

He looked unsatisfied.

"Beautiful. It's a beautiful car."

Beautiful got thrown around so recklessly in Brunei. Everything was beautiful: the jungle, the necklaces, the girls, the cars, his art, his home. He owned it all. It was all the same. *Beautiful* was always what he wanted to hear. You possess beautiful; you hold it in your palm.

Some of the faces had changed during the two weeks we were gone. Most noticeably, with the absence of Serena, Prince Hakeem had returned to the parties. He was like a blown-up baby doll, easily three times the size of his father. Robin dropped me off at the door and I walked down the stairs alone. Prince Hakeem was on the landing in front of the door to the party room playing with an electric remote-control car that was a miniature replica of the Lamborghini out of which I had just stepped. Two slim Thai girls who looked about the right age to be dressed up for their homecoming dance slouched against each other on the stairs, giggling at his antics.

I customarily bowed as I walked by him. It felt different to bow to Robin than it did to bow to a guy my own age with an oversize remote control in his hand. With Robin, the tone of the bow was submissive, sexual. With Prince Hakeem it was sarcastic.

Two new girls, Delia and Trish, had taken Serena's place. I entered to a group squeal from the Thai girls. Yoya, Tootie, and Lili smothered me with hugs. I couldn't figure out why they were so sweet to me. Maybe because I defied convention and frequently drifted toward their island in our little archipelago of girls. I perched on the edge of their crowded couch and asked them the words in Thai for *please* and *thank you*, and in return they treated me like a long-lost childhood friend. Some girls in Brunei were good girls, sweet girls.

Fiona greeted me with what I suppose was warmth, which for her looked something like nonchalance but not like disdain. Robin and his cronies entered to the strains of Angelique's passionate "How Am I Supposed to Live Without You." Eddie tapped me to leave the room about an hour after the men arrived. A guard led me to the hall of doors and opened one I hadn't been through before. Behind door number two is a lifetime supply of Turtle Wax, behind door number six is a stack of gold bricks, behind door number three is . . . a bath. A really big bath.

Some Orientalist painter should have been sitting in the corner, brush in hand. A bath the size of a small pool stood in the center, lined with tiny gold tiles that reflected shimmering rays of light around the steamy room. A platter stacked with fruit, honey cake, and chocolate was laid out beside the tub. The rubber duck I had bought for Robin in Malaysia floated in the water, sadly tilting to one side. I didn't want to get in the bath and get all sweaty before he got there, but I felt stupid in my gown, so I hung my clothes and lay naked on the divan, an odalisque plucked from one of his paintings. The only thing that ruined the absolute authenticity of the harem bath fantasy was the TV mounted in the corner of the room blasting CNN as usual. I guess his plan was to show me that he wasn't afraid to take a bath with a girl after all.

It seemed like he had set up a romantic little interlude for us, but when Robin came in, his expression was chilly and hard. He had barely said a word to me in the car earlier in the evening. Our familiarity from Malaysia was gone. I suspected that he was probably disappointed to come back and find Serena missing, even though he was the one who had made the call that exiled her. But I had left him no choice. He knew she had a boyfriend and I knew he knew, so he couldn't let her stay. It was my fault she was gone and he had no one left to punish, so the punishment fell on me.

Even if Serena hadn't been a casualty, I knew him well enough by now not to wonder why his attitude toward me had changed so rapidly. There didn't need to be a reason. It made me nervous when he turned icy, but not as nervous as when he was kind. When he was kind, you could be sure he was setting you up for a fall. Maybe my penalty would be mild.

"You look very nice."

He changed in the other room and when he came back, he hung up his robe and stepped into the bath, submerging only to the waist. I slipped in beside him and he turned me around without even kissing me. I felt myself floating up toward the ceiling as he fucked me. It was the kind of fuck that was meant to make you feel bad, but it didn't. I was less and less tethered to my body all the time. I could tumble right out of myself at will and leave behind only a hologram. Far below me the hologram grabbed the nearby leg of the divan to steady herself. But I was free. I wasn't one of his groveling subjects. I wasn't even subject to the laws of gravity.

After he was dressed, right before he left me to go back to the party, I tried out one of my memorized Malay sentences. This one I had been saving for a special occasion.

"Aku cinta padamu," I said.

Like I said before, the Sultan just wanted you to suck his dick, but Robin needed your love. People who need everyone to love them are exponentially more dangerous than people who are content merely with power and money. You have to go way further to make them happy.

"That's nice," he replied.

What I had said wasn't exactly true. What I felt for him was something like love, but not quite. It was something like love but also something like nothing at all.

When I walked back into the room, Fiona beckoned to me and I crossed the room to resume my seat at Robin's left and await my fate.

chapter 19

Prince Sufri returned to the parties after an extended stay in England. The parties changed in tenor when Sufri arrived. For starters, we began the evenings at the badminton courts. The courts were located in a cavernous, brightly lit airline hangar of a room with a spongy floor that would snag our heels and trip us unless we lifted our feet as carefully as Clydesdales.

When Robin showed up at badminton, it was with an expression of disinterested tolerance. He stood in the corner with his arms crossed over his chest and looked often toward the door. But Sufri was the older brother and Robin deferred to him. We called Prince Sufri Ben. Ben sounded gentle. When I looked at him, the Jackson 5 song we had listened to in summer camp ran through my head. I had always thought the song was about someone's ugly friend, until my friend Liz told me it was actually about a rat.

The real-life Ben was disfigured by a skin condition that caused boils the size of marbles. Ari said they were a result of his cancer treatment, though I've seen a lot of cancer patients and have never seen anything quite like Ben's affliction. My new roommate, Delia, with whom I'd become close, speculated it was wicked royal inbreeding.

Ben's throat cancer had resulted in a laryngectomy and he spoke through a cell-phone-size machine that he held to a voice box in his neck. This, combined with the skin condition, made him look and sound like a warty, flesh-toned toad. The boils distorted his face, making him bug-eyed. His sandy-colored hair was thin and stood up from his head in reedy spikes.

Most of the American girls were freaked out by his appearance and kept their distance, fearing that it was somehow catching or that he would take a shine to them and they'd wind up obligated to stroke the moonscape of his skin. I thought they were stupid. If there is a choice between a monster and a playboy, always choose the monster. Monsters treat you better. And though I already had my assigned stall in the playboy's stable, I befriended Ben. It was refreshing to converse with someone less cruel, less manipulative, more impressed by me than Robin had ever been. I looked at Ben and saw myself turned inside out.

Yoya and Tootie also snuggled up to Ben, and the three of us girls grew closer as the weeks wore on. They let me in on their opinion of American girls. We were spoiled, ungrateful whiners. We spoke our own language terribly.

Yoya mocked the California vernacular: "But, um, but, like, totally, ummmmm."

They didn't exempt me from their judgments. They thought I was a spoiled whiner, too.

"You also whine. Whine, whine," Tootie told me cheerfully.

"I do?"

"But we like you anyway," she reassured me. "You our friend anyway. "

Ben had a few favorites among the Filipino and Indonesian girls, but I don't think he took it much further than requesting that they play doubles on the court in front of him. Hookers in bare feet and evening gowns playing badminton is a sight to see. While we witnessed the spectacle, Ben told me that he was hopelessly in love with Angelique, but she refused his advances, returned his gifts.

Returned his gifts? I was floored. No one returned these types of gifts. That was purely the stuff of movies. It spoke either of Angelique's exceptional virtue or of Ben's exceptional repulsiveness. I hoped that it was a stand made on principle. I liked Angelique, and I wanted to believe that there was a woman who could not be bought, period, not just a woman who couldn't be bought by a toad.

Ben's routine was to watch the girls play terrible badminton, then to herd the whole caravan into the party room to watch Angelique sing. When Ben was in the room, the singers didn't trade off. It was the Angelique Show. After a while, Ben would walk out, demonstratively brokenhearted, with his hands in his pockets and his head inclined. After he left, things would return to the way they had gone before Ben got back from England.

I watched him go and thought that Ben, perhaps alone among the brothers, was getting to have the human experience of having his heart broken. Unlike Robin, Ben didn't have to get everything he ever asked for and wonder why he was still dissatisfied. Maybe it is easier in some ways for the ugly and the outcast, the men disfigured by boils and the preteen girls who eat lunch in a bathroom stall to avoid the cafeteria. We don't have the same expectation of happiness.

A few things changed after Serena left. The first was my new roommate, who was a righteous and down-to-earth chick. Delia was a bathing-suit model with an impossible body who had nevertheless passed her prime, knew it, and, miraculously, wasn't in deep denial. Rather than pursuing radical cosmetic surgeries in an attempt to match her appearance to the age on her résumé, she was building a legit business as a wedding and headshot photographer. With her only-semi-ironic cheerleader attitude and her ass-length blond hair, she managed to keep a steady gait in Brunei that few could maintain.

When Robin called Delia once and never again, which was his standard protocol for all but a few, she never made a big deal about it. Rather, she ingratiated herself with Ari and Eddie, initiated conga lines during the disco portion of the evening, and occasionally got a little drunk on the dance floor and spun around so her skirt flew up. Delia probably did better in Brunei than most of us, while paying a smaller price to the devil, or whoever exacts these things.

The visiting dignitaries loved to invent ways to look at surfer-girl Delia, and usually requested that I accompany her. We sometimes got called to sit and sunbathe for hours out at the upper pool, long after anyone would want to be outside in that heavy, sweaty air. We brought along books, a boom box, and tons of sunblock, lest we fry. We never actually saw anyone, but Madge clued us in that there were conference rooms and dining rooms behind the opaque tint of the palace windows that overlooked the pool deck, so I guess we were meant to be the scenic view. Beyond the view of Delia and me in our bathing suits, all that was visible from the windows of the palace were the guesthouses down the hill and then the miles upon miles of rainforest surrounding the walls of the enclosure.

Delia and I were called upon to perform other random party tricks as well. One day a guard showed up in our room with tennis whites and took us to the squash court, where we received a condescending lesson from some asshole from Dubai. What he didn't know was that my father had put a racket in my hand when I was about four. I had quit when I was a teenager, but I could still smack a ball around. And it turned out that Delia was exactly as athletic as she looked. Even though we lost, we impressed the ambassadors from Dubai, and when word got around, we became an amusing anomaly, often called out of the party to play doubles with yet more drooling dignitaries. Imagine, girls who could do something well— more to the point, girls like us who could do something well.

In spite of these improvements—the absence of my rival, a new friend, momentary whirlwinds of attention— the monotonous grind of the days was beginning to wear me down. Robin often ignored me, not saying more than a few words to me for days at a time. I spent many nights sitting next to an empty chair while Fiona and I made small talk. We volleyed gossip back and forth in a man- nered way, like we were sitting on the sidelines of a cro- quet game.

One night, Fiona and I were gossiping about Yoya and Lili.

"I think Robin calls them together most of the time," she told me.

"Really? Scandalous."

"Indeed. Would you like more scandal?"

"Of course."

"How old would you guess Yoya is?"

"I don't know. Young. A baby. Seventeen?"

"Is seventeen a baby? Lower."

"Sixteen."

"Lower."

"What? That's terrible."

"Oh, don't be dramatic. She's lucky to have a job. And Lili, too. But Lili's got a scandal worse than Yoya's."

"Tell."

"Lili is a couple of years older than Yoya, but when she was Yoya's age she had a baby. Couldn't leave it with her parents because they didn't know. She had to leave her baby at an orphanage to come here."

"How do you know all this?"

"I know everything."

I wanted to find out more of the story. Was it true or was it invented? But Robin came by and held out his hand to Fiona without even a glance in my direction. They walked together to the back elevator and left the party early. Fiona was the only girl who left the parties with him. I never asked her where they went.

With all we talked about, we never talked about our respective time with Robin. I followed Fiona's lead and in this, as in most things, she was smart. I never knew what Robin did with Fiona, so I never got a chance to compare it with the things he did with me. That way we never really knew where in Robin's favor we were in relation to each other. This elected ignorance made it possible for us to be friends.

I sat alone as the lights turned on and the rest of the party guests waited by the door to make a break for it when they got the all clear. I watched Lili, studied her. For what? For some previously unnoticed haze of grief that would confirm Fiona's story? For a corner where her sweet and smiley mask had peeled back and I could see underneath that she was disfigured, broken by what she'd done?

I imagined what Lili's choices might have been when she'd been offered the job in Brunei. You can become a whore and pay whatever other whore is the least popular to hold your baby while you work because crying babies are bad for business or you can not be a whore and tell your family the truth and be considered a whore anyway. You can starve in Thailand with your baby or you can leave your baby behind to go have threesomes with a prince and make more money than you ever thought you'd see.

If the baby story was in fact true about Lili, did she sit there every night and watch the bubbles rise to the top of her champagne and wonder where she could have chosen a different road, or did she thank her lucky stars that her ass was on that couch and not being pounded into a dirty mattress in a Bangkok brothel?

The thought occurred to me that maybe my birth mother hadn't been a ballerina at all. Maybe my music-box fantasy was exactly that. Maybe my parents had only told me she was a ballerina because it seemed like a fairy tale and fairy tales have better endings than true stories. Maybe my birth mother's choices, too, had been between ugly and uglier.

That night I had the recurring dream I hadn't had in years. I am a child on the beach in Beach Haven. I play with my sand toys by the shoreline. Farther up on the sand my mother and Johnny lie sunbathing on our blanket. In the distance, walking toward me along the water's edge, is my birth mother. I can't see her face because she's far away and the sun is in my eyes, but I know who she is. Then I look toward the sea and I see what has been rising behind me while my back has been turned. It's a tsunami, churning with swirls of blue and white like in a Japanese painting. It's as tall as a mountain and still gaining height and power.

I want to run and warn my mother and brother. I also want to run in the direction of my birth mother to finally find out the answer to the mystery of where I came from—quick, before the wave comes and washes us all out to sea. And as I kneel there frozen by indecision in the shadow of the wave, it crashes down on me. I tumble in the surf. I try to grab hold of the ground but you can't hold on to sand. I feel the sand rush through my fingers and my hair as everything is swept away all at once.

I am no wiser and no one is saved.

Night after boring night, I sat anchored to my chair on the neglected sidelines and tried not to panic. I watched as some of the other girls began to unspool in the face of Robin's subtle and sadistic games. Leanne, for instance, was rumored to have once rivaled Fiona for number one. Robin generally kept Leanne hovering at around number three or four, but hadn't called for her in months. I wasn't the only one around there being ignored. I watched Leanne get drunker, thinner, louder. She spent all day on the couch in her bathrobe smoking and watching *Pretty*

Woman and all night pulling stunts to try to get Robin's attention.

One night, as Robin was leaving the party, Leanne cracked. She hurled herself to the floor, lay prostrate on the ground in front of him, and grabbed his leg. She sobbed real tears.

"I love you. I love you. Why can't you see that I love you more?"

I thought about my final exchange with Sean. *I love you. Don't leave me.* So unoriginal.

Leanne's outburst might have been the only time I witnessed genuine surprise on Robin's face. He froze. Everyone froze. Eddie finally remembered himself and dragged Leanne off Robin's leg, but Leanne was stronger than he'd expected. She shook Eddie off and nearly tackled Robin, falling to her knees and wrapping her arms around his waist. Robin didn't lift a finger either to move her or to comfort her. It was Madge who finally pried Leanne away and subdued her.

Robin didn't kick Leanne out for this infraction. I think he enjoyed it, in fact. Nothing like a little bit of real pain to liven up an evening. But Leanne was spent. She stayed a few more weeks and left on her own. If it had been an acting job, it was an award winner. But I think it hadn't been. I vowed not to become that girl. He wouldn't break me down that far.

After Leanne left, I began to notice that Brittany was often the girl gone from the room during disco, the girl who returned to the guesthouse after lunch. I took the opposite tack Serena had taken. First of all, Serena's method hadn't worked, and second of all, it wasn't in my nature to ostracize and torture other people. Instead, I sidled up to Brittany and made her my friend. Wasn't that what Fiona had done with me? But I flattered myself. I was no Fiona. Fiona had done more than just kiss my ass for information. She had done more than my unoriginal attempt to keep my enemy closer. Fiona had created me.

Brittany had a lot to say about the shabby-chic couch and love seat she was going to buy. White, white, white— she'd always wanted a white couch. She wanted white couches flanked by wrought-iron candlesticks and a matching wrought-iron canopy bed surrounded with the most transparent white silk curtains, blowing in the breeze from the open French windows, no doubt. I was convinced she was styling her own music video starring her and Vince Neil.

"Have you spoken to Vince?" I prompted her. She never tired of the question.

"Well, he's on the road. It's hard. We keep missing each other. But I believe in us."

"You're a girl of great faith."

"Vince told me that if I ever have doubts, I should just sit very still and close my eyes and think of his face. He said that I'll be able to feel what he's doing and then I'll know in my heart he's being faithful. Also, if I concentrate hard enough, he'll feel it too and he'll know I'm thinking of him. And do you know what? It works."

If in fact she was telling the truth about her conversations with Vince, I hoped for her sake that Vince wasn't employing the same psychic technique on Brittany.

My new friend was as stimulating as an instruction manual for a dishwasher, but she did have her usefulness. For instance, she revealed to me her dieting secret. Dr. Gordon, the Prince's doctor and a regular fixture at the parties, was giving her diet pills. I'm pretty sure Robin didn't know about it, because he wouldn't have approved of his girls starving themselves.

Now, I'm a person who never turns down pills. And if you are the kind of person who never turns down pills, you must always, always turn down pills. I hadn't figured that out yet.

"Can I have one?"

"Of course. This will be great. We can be diet buddies. We can work out together. We can support each other."

Brittany pulled out a white plastic bottle that rattled with half-clear, half-blue capsules, the kind with a billion little beads inside each one. I put one in the palm of my hand and popped it into my mouth, because that's what some girls do. Hand some girls a pill from a bottle labeled in a foreign language and they'll put it right on their tongues without a second thought.

"Super," said Brittany. "Start out with one and work your way up to two a day."

I had begun about fifteen thousand diets in my eighteen years on earth. I had started my first diet when I was nine. But I wasn't done yet, not even close. I'd diet until I liked myself, goddammit. I was convinced it was possible, even though all of the evidence showed that it didn't work. Not the diet part; that usually worked just fine. It was the liking-myself part that never happened.

The landscape of my body over the years, the deposits and erosions, the seasons of it seen next to each other would look like a time-lapse movie that spans thousands of years in a few minutes. I am a curvy, sturdy lass by nature, with thick peasant hands and hips to balance a laundry basket on. I generally lean toward the fecundity of spring but occasionally tilt madly toward winter. I like to, when I can, shed my leaves so that the branches are bare, brittle. I like my blood to run cold as the snow—no fuel to feed the fire that warms it.

Basically, I am a chubby girl with fits of anorexia and bulimia. And nothing makes me feel better than to have that delicious sensation of control when the numbers start peeling off the scale. In high school, I imagined I could subsist on the minerals from the air, like an orchid. I tried to grow thin, thin, thin, no longer bound to the earth, to my family and its landslide of pain.

It worked. I did it. I was finally light as a ballerina, my arms lovely ribbons, my ribs a keyboard. My skin was blue pale, my body so immaterial that it seemed to me the light of inspiration, the light of God himself, could shine through me. Touch my bony chest and you could feel my heart so close to the surface that it thumped like a funk bass line through a subwoofer. Except nobody touched me. People turned their eyes away. I noticed, but no longer cared. I was impeccable. I had never felt so clean.

My lips turned purple. I wore layers of sweaters

and filled my pockets with quarters in anticipation of the surprise attacks of the school nurse, who would pop out of doorways and drag me onto a scale, looking for a number low enough to warrant hospitalization. Even as the spring sun revived the muddy winter lawns, I stayed cold. I wrapped my body in boots and long skirts and petticoats. I braided my hair and imagined myself a tragic consumptive character out of a Jane Austen novel.

In a condo in Roseland, a few miles down a stretch of Route 10, my grandmother grew thinner and thinner too, as her cancer gained strength and mass. She had mesothelioma, cancer of the lining of the internal organs. She got it from breathing in the asbestos fibers that had permeated the air inside the Newark schools where she had worked for so many years as a librarian. There are so many ways poison can take hold.

She told me one day, as I massaged the chain of knots that her spine had become, that she didn't want to have to watch me die, that her dying was hard enough as it was. She asked me to eat.

Her request was enough to inspire my eating a carefully measured quantity of brown rice, seaweed, and vegetables each day. I gave the eulogy at her funeral and then got out of New Jersey about five minutes after they lowered her coffin into the ground. My grandmother had been my best friend and I spent her last year so hungry that I couldn't pay attention, so self-obsessed that I forgot to ask her about her life, even though I knew she'd be dead before the year was out. If I didn't ask, who would?

She never kept a journal, so her memories are gone now, a treasure buried without a map.

When I got to NYU I started drinking and the drinking led me back to eating and within six months I had gained the fifty pounds back and more. I had lost all that time, starving and distracted and unable to think clearly enough to ask her even what Vienna had been like before the war, for nothing.

And not only did I commit that crime, but I didn't learn from it. Because still, I thought this time would be different. The little pill went down with a swig of iced tea and I imagined I was swallowing not speed, not poison, but hope, help.

I took the phentermine pills and started quietly obsessing about losing weight again. I wasn't alone. Most of the girls in Brunei took pills. We drank laxative teas. Even though we could have ordered any food we wanted, we ordered plain chicken and steamed veggies and tried to fill up on lettuce sprinkled with lemon juice and balsamic vinegar. This is the Faustian bargain for many women who make their bodies their livelihood. Your body will be worshipped by others but hated by you. It will give others pleasure but it will give you only pain. In the mirrors at the gym, we watched for the appearance of every new hollow and cut as we did the Cindy Crawford workout on a screen the size of a whole wall, Cindy's mole the size of a tennis ball. I tirelessly admired my own clavicle.

Before I left for Brunei, Penny had given me Jeanette Winterson's *Sexing the Cherry* to bring along with me.

I read it while, pills or no, hunger gnawed at my stomach. The heroine in the book had a giant hiding inside her, a monster. That was me. Except inside me wasn't a giant. Inside me was a skeleton. Lurking inside me was the anorexic girl whose elbow circumference had exceeded that of her forearm. I was that kind of monster. But that monster was the real me, I thought. When I starved myself, I was becoming that real me. To reduce yourself to only the very essential elements, that was poetry. Maybe Robin wouldn't notice. Or maybe, conversely, it would make him finally notice me again.

I lost fourteen pounds in only a few weeks, and at the party one night Robin told me I was getting too thin. The tricky thing about starving yourself is that it starts out feeling terrible and then it feels great until you realize you can't stop. By the time Robin mentioned it, I had already crossed that line. I knew I was hurting my chances with Robin but I was past logic. I wouldn't—I couldn't—start eating.

Fueled by ephedrine and willpower, I spent my late afternoons on the tennis courts, hitting ball after ball fired at me from the machines. I remember one particular day that when I finished, it was dusty pink twilight. I was steaming and drenched from the weather and the exertion. I walked over to the lower pool, shed my clothes, and slipped into the water. When I had cooled down, I pulled myself onto the pool deck and lay on my back, looking up at the crescent moon that was rising above the palace. At night, Brunei was breathtaking.

I lay in the shadow of a fairy-tale palace, breathing

air so heavy with the smell of flowers it should have been bottled. I'm happy, I thought. Right now. Alone. In between the ground and the stars, in between the empty afternoon and the torturous evening. No mirrors. No party dresses. No one asking me for anything and nothing I want. And then the moment was over and it was time for the mirrors and the party dresses again.

A month came and went without my cycle. Was it possible that I was pregnant? A royal pregnancy was what all the girls hoped for because if you had the Prince's baby, you would be taken care of for the rest of your life. Of course, you would be taken care of under armed guard. You would be installed in a luxury apartment in Singapore and would never have another boyfriend, never even be able to go out to dinner again without being watched. At first I was scared; then I began scheming.

There was no question that I would have the baby, but I would have to get out of Brunei first. I would have to do it without anyone knowing. It would be our secret, the baby's and mine. One day I would tell her that her daddy was a fabulously wealthy, devilishly handsome Southeast Asian prince, and that I had loved him very much, but that I'd had to spirit her away to a life in which we could both be free. Maybe we would struggle, but it would be a life of such overwhelming love.

The thought of pregnancy gave me new hope, a new reason to stick it out in Brunei for a little while longer. I figured that my life with Robin was now a finite thing and that I would need all the money I could get. I hugged my chest and poked my fingertips into the sides of my breasts. They ached. They were definitely bigger. I strayed from my diet and snuck down to the dimly lit kitchen at five a.m. to stuff my face with cream puffs from the pastry tray. I didn't sweat it too much; I told myself I was just having cravings.

But there was no pregnancy; I was just starving. And when I started eating for my imagined two, I got my period. I sat on the toilet and lay my chest on my knees. I saw that my secret baby fantasy was at best laughable, at worst delusional. For months I had been teetering on the edge of a depressive episode, and the day I saw blood the scales tipped. Of course I hadn't been pregnant. I was all torn and sick inside. Nothing could live in me. I was toxic straight through.

The depression always crept back in, like carbon monoxide slipping under the crack in the door: colorless, odorless, sure to rob you of your oxygen and kill you silently if undetected. I barely bothered getting out of bed until it was time to go to the parties. I spent hours at a time in the bathtub. The volume on my self-loathing turned way up. I got obsessed with the cameras everywhere, the surveillance. I imagined the men watching me and laughing at my every flaw. I began to think of these invisible watchers as ghosts, spirits, creatures from another world who lived in the house with us even though we couldn't see them.

I wasn't the only one who was haunted. Rumor was that the guesthouses had resident ghosts. There was even a night when mass hysteria had sent four of the girls in house six running out the front door in the wee hours, insisting that they each had been visited by a weight, a presence, something or someone who had crawled into bed with them.

I had thought, with not a small measure of misogyny, Why, when a bunch of girls get together, does it inevitably turn into *The Crucible*? Now I wasn't so sure they'd been wrong. I kept seeing shadows flicker in the corners of the room, kept looking over my shoulder in the dark hallways. On top of this, Robin had put me in cold storage. I sat there every night maintaining my perfect posture and my strained smile as he ignored me.

When I couldn't take it anymore, I begged to leave. I told Ari that my father was having surgery and I needed to be there. My father's surgery was long over, but it's always good to couch a lie in the truth. That way you're less likely to forget what you said. Ari was sympathetic and arranged for me to go home, insisting that I promise to return in three weeks.

Maybe if I hadn't been so restless I could have stuck it out for longer and stockpiled a greater fortune. But I had no idea what it meant to be patient. I had no idea what kind of windfall I had stumbled into. I thought diamond Bulgari sets and money in $100,000 increments fell from the sky every once in a while. I told myself that maybe I'd come back and maybe I wouldn't.

Some girls in Brunei came and went like weekend guests, and some became the lady of the manor for a time. I started out the belle of the ball, but I became the crazy lady in the attic. I was more fragile than I ever would have thought. Delia, older, wiser, more mentally stable, tried to talk me out of leaving, but I was determined. The truth was, windfall or no windfall, I needed to go home to guard what was left of my sanity.

Robin was in London on business when I left. I didn't even get to say good-bye.

chapter 20

As I packed my bags, something alternately rose and sank in me, like a tide. I'd be going home—home to New York and my real life and my real friends and family, where I could remember who I really was. Would I turn right back around?

At the party the night before I left, my friends among the Asian girls buzzed around me. They never got to go home until they were going home for good, so they wanted to hear all about what I was going to do and whom I was going to see and where I lived and what my family was like.

Winston, with his kind eyes behind wire-rimmed glasses, asked me, "What are you going to do when you get back to reality?"

I answered coyly, carefully. This was my default mode in Brunei, even with Winston. "This isn't reality?"

"No," he said, with rare clarity. Everyone in Brunei usually acted like the parties would go on and on. "This isn't reality for any of us. It's a dream and someday we'll all wake up."

Eddie took me out into the hallway and sat down with me on the staircase, where the peach-colored carpeting shone with threads of real gold. He handed me a fat stack of notes each worth 10,000 Singapore dollars and then he put a wide, square box in my lap. I opened it to find a gold Tiffany set that belonged on Cleopatra— a basket-weave choker and a matching bracelet and earrings. The jewelry no longer shocked me. I would have been crestfallen if, after all that time, I hadn't received an outrageous gift. I had Eddie help me with the clasp.

When I returned to the party, Fiona said, "I hope your father feels better."

She looked at me like she was on to me.

"I know you'll be back soon. I'll say bon voyage, not good-bye."

I added my new Tiffany set to the heart necklace, the Cartier watch, and the diamond-face Rolex that Robin had given me already, threw my jewels and my money into my carry-on to Singapore, and managed to cram the rest of my clothes into four suitcases. Ari gave me a lecture on how to get my loot and myself back into the country safely. Then she gave me a hug, my passport, a ticket home, and a ticket to return again in three weeks. My housemates all stood behind the porch's marble banister and waved good-bye as the car pulled away.

In Singapore, I carried myself confidently, like I knew what I was doing. I pretended it wasn't my first time try-ing to negotiate the streets of a foreign country alone. I was a CIA operative, fluent in seven languages and highly trained for covert ops. If I faltered, if I showed a soft spot, it was all part of my cover.

Ari had instructed me to change my money at a bank in Singapore in order to avoid the IRS inquiry that would result if I changed it over in the United States. In line at the bank in Singapore, everyone stood about three centimeters from the person in front of them. I breathed in the earwax smell of the pomade in the hair of the man in front of me, could smell the bubble-gum breath of the woman behind me.

I was no longer a leaf in a stream. I was halfway home in my mind and I had a duffel bag to fill with cash and shit to do and I wanted those people out of my face. A belt of panic tightened around my chest and I swayed, unsteady on my feet. I felt the temptation to surrender to it, to black out, to fall into velvet darkness and wake with my skull on the granite floor. I tried to breathe. I closed my eyes. There is something about being almost to the finish line that makes me start to unravel. My mantra went from "You are a leaf in a stream" to "Don't blow it now." Do. Not. Blow. This.

What would Patti Smith do? She wouldn't be there in the first place. Really, she wouldn't. I was far out on the water without my fairy godmother to guide the needle of my compass. When had that happened?

But I didn't blow it. I collected my cash and loaded it, stack by bound stack, into the duffel bag. I walked out the door with piles of hundreds. I could have bathed in it. I was back in my personal spy movie, walking down the streets of Singapore with a duffel bag full of cash, checking the reflections in store windows to see if anyone was behind me. I hailed a cab back to the hotel, where I'd make the drop to a bartender with a yellow rose on his lapel. *Cut.*

Next shot: morning of my departure. Whatever cash didn't fit into my two money belts I stuffed inside my stockings. I got rid of the jewelry boxes and wore the jewelry.

I threw a loose sweat suit over the top of the jewelry and became a nervous-eyed, thick-waisted girl with big gold earrings on. I sweated the whole flight to Frankfurt and then scarfed Chinese food and drank Jack Daniel's at the airport. I got back on the interminable flight feeling sick to my stomach and not nearly drunk enough.

Many hours later the spiny peaks, right-angled valleys, and soaring bridges, the floating Marvel comic metropolis that is New York seen from high above, brought tears to my eyes.

chapter 21

I returned to a breezy, budding New York April. I dragged my suitcases one at a time up the two flights of stairs and dropped them in the middle of the hovel I would now be sharing with not only Penny but also a director friend of ours named Sam. Penny and Sam had hooked up while I was gone and Sam had as good as moved in to our one-bedroom, bringing his waffle maker with him and little else. The two of them welcomed me back with a waffle dinner and a new cat they had found at the local bodega, whom they named Nada after the underground theater across the street, where Penny worked the box office.

I unpacked my designer clothes into my miniature closet with the paint peeling in tongues from the door-jamb. My only possessions until then had been a futon on the floor, a scavenged desk, and a bunch of clothes and records stacked in a wall unit fashioned from crates. Hippie tapestries were tacked over the windows as curtains. Dusty votive candles covered every available surface. A palace it was not. I put the rest of my jewelry, worth well over a hundred thousand dollars, in a shoebox in my closet. I wondered if rats were attracted to shiny things or if that was just magpies. Would the tenement rats, fat and self-assured, sneak in, gnaw their way through the cardboard, and make off with my Tiffany set?

I put the clothes that wouldn't fit in the closet into two suitcases and later that week I took them with me in a cab to Jersey, figuring I could store them in the closet in my parents' garage. I dumped the suitcases as I came in and even from the downstairs I could smell onions and roasting chicken. It was the first time I'd smelled any kind of food actually being cooked in months.

My mother called out from the kitchen to my father in the backyard, "Jill's home!" As if I'd been away at camp; as if it was still my home.

I was coming up the stairs as she came down; we met in the middle with hugs and uneasy smiles. It didn't seem to be getting any easier to hug her. It was always uncomfortable, like hugging a distant relative who had known you when you were a kid but whom you can't remember at all. And this made me feel like shit, because my mother was a kind lady who cooked me chickens. I kept waiting for the discomfort to disappear as time passed, as I put more distance between my parents and me, but I hugged her and there it still was.

My father looked like he'd gained half his weight back already, and he vibrated with the same manic, distracted energy as ever. In his excitement to see me, he put me in a half headlock and rocked me back and forth. He'd been outside planting flowers and his shirt smelled like potting soil and grass.

Twenty minutes later I sat on the gray couch in the gray living room and looked out at their newly landscaped front yard through the gray stripes of the vertical blinds. They had asked me about the trip, of course, but had settled for my vague answers and had moved on to other things. I think they were relieved to let the subject drop.

"Did you move the fence in the front yard?" I asked.

"What fence in the front yard?" my mother responded.

"Wasn't there a fence there before?"

"No," said my mother.

How strange. I knew every corner of the house: every china pattern, every book spine in the study, every Hanukah-present hiding place, every piece of jewelry in my mother's drawers, every bottle of liquor in the liquor cabinet. I knew where my father hid his small gun, an heirloom from his father. But I still remembered things wrong sometimes, weird things like a phantom fence in the yard. I felt like the girl who had lived in that house wasn't me, but a person I'd read about in a story. A story I couldn't quite recall.

"How long did you live here for, moron?" added my dad, though he said it affably. He was fond of using words like *moron* and *schmuck* in an affectionate way.

Weeks before I had been a beautiful femme fatale, sipping champagne and overlooking a foreign city and waiting for the Prince to return home from his princely duties. Now I was a moron, with a wicked zit growing on my chin and at least two hours left before I could make a polite exit and haul ass back to the city. I felt the migraine coming, as if someone had thrown a fishhook into my eye from behind and started to yank.

After dinner my mother, as always, brought out the gifts. She gave me a hand-knit beret from a crafts fair, a feminist-slogan T-shirt from her trip to Washington, D.C., with her women's organization, and a jade necklace that had been my grandmother's. I gave her the Cartier watch that wasn't my favorite. I thought she'd get more use out of it than I would. I wanted to give her something nice.

I would have just left the stacks of hundreds split between my underwear drawer and my filing cabinet, but Sam marched me down to the bank on Canal Street to get a safe-deposit box. I refused to put my Rolex in it. I wanted to wear it.

"Why don't you just throw it in the East River?" he said. "Quit that soul-sucking job. Stay here with us. Come on, let's do it. Let's go throw that thing in the river."

Sam was a theater director, given to sweeping gestures.

"No way."

Sweeping gestures were the same thing as getting mad and throwing a plate at the wall. Sweeping gestures felt dramatic and significant, but afterward you were left looking foolish because afterward nothing had changed. Things don't explode and disappear; they explode and leave a mess all over the floor. There are always ceramic shards that escape the bristles of the broom and embed themselves in your bare feet for weeks afterward. The watch stayed.

Three weeks dissolved the way weeks will if you let New York have its way. I enjoyed my little life with Penny and Sam, reading the *Times* together in the morning while drinking espresso from the new machine I had bought. I wandered New York shopping and picking up the tab for lunches with friends.

When the date on my ticket rolled around, I called Ari and told her I needed to change it. I told her my father needed me there to care for him for a few more weeks. Truthfully, I couldn't bear the thought of packing up and leaving again. I told myself I just needed a break, that I'd feel differently soon. I bought a pair of cowboy boots with real silver details. I bought a platform bed.

I was struck by mad inspiration. I decided that I was going to write a one-woman show based on my experiences in the sex industry. Not terribly original, but it seemed like a good idea at the time. By day, I sat in cafés and wrote my performance-art masterpiece. I bought a video camera. I bought a microwave oven.

After the theater closed for the night, Sam, Penny, and I would drink Baileys on our fire escape and talk about memes and the viral transmission of ideas. Across the country, Southern California was in flames with the Los Angeles riots. We talked about the impossibility of outright revolution given the brainwashing effects of consumerism. Revolution would have to happen with a collective shift of consciousness. If what we were doing didn't in some way precipitate that shift, we deemed it worthless. Being home and among my real friends was such a relief. I could talk again. I could breathe again. Another three weeks passed this way and I pushed my departure date again as Ari's voice grew impatient on the other end of the line.

I bought a pair of Chanel sunglasses that made me look like a fly. I bought a stun gun because you never know.

Sean returned my phone calls but squashed any hope I'd had of reconciliation. To get my mind off Sean, Sam took me one night to meet an old Princeton buddy of his named Andy. Sam knocked on the doorjamb next to where the curtain hung that separated my room from the rest of the apartment. He told me that Andy had called from the late-night club held at Windows on the World. Andy was there hanging out with Moby and he wanted to know if we'd join him. Sam had told me about Andy, the former child-prodigy composer who had never lost his Texas-bred predilections for six-packs and football games. I agreed to go; I wasn't doing anything else.

Yet another of the valuable skills I picked up in Brunei was the ability to get ready for almost any occasion in ten minutes. I had recently dyed my hair platinum blond and had discovered that blond privilege wasn't an invention of my low self-esteem; it was a genuine fact. And though the bleach had burned my scalp and broke the ends of my hair clean off so I had to cut it into a bob, I was enjoying the extra attention. I was the Marilyn now. I styled it in pin curls in five minutes flat.

I was used to dressing for clubs frequented by drag queens, so I glued on false eyelashes and sported a bustier, knee-high platforms, and zebra leggings. But when we arrived, the scene was more about techno music and oversize pants. I felt out of place among the girls who slouched around Moby, starved vegans wearing pacifiers and funny hats.

Andy was an electronica composer, as well as a computer programmer—and he looked like one. He had long, stringy hair, terrible fucked-up teeth, and smart, blue-gray eyes. With his old classmate Tom, he had recently started a company called Tomandandy. Tomandandy had created a buzz. They had composed a popular dance hit. They had scored the exploding-head scene in Oliver Stone's *JFK*. Andy was goofy and unassuming, but every time I got off the dance floor, he was waiting for me with a drink in his hand, the ensuing conversation hollered over the music with his lips occasionally brushing my ear. This, I thought, is why we like our music so loud at clubs. I couldn't understand the words. His voice was part of the music itself.

"What?" I yelled.

And he leaned in again to repeat himself.

At the end of the night the crowded elevator, the one that made your ears pop as it whizzed downward from the one-hundredth floor, got stuck. It stopped quietly, without a lurch or a screech. It took us all a few minutes to figure out we weren't moving. A woman in a yellow dress stood rigidly and stared at the unmoving numbers. Her boyfriend, who had too much gel in his hair, scratched his neck and shuffled his feet. One of the other guys began to argue with the over-gelled guy. As the minutes went by, the elevator started to smell like panic and sweat.

Andy and I were both calm. We sat down on the floor and talked, as if we were alone.

"Sam told me you just came back from Singapore."

"Brunei. I was actually in a country called Brunei."

"The Sultan of Brunei."

"Exactly."

I tried to describe my job in a truthful but not overly truthful way. I told him that I had been a royal guest, a couch decoration at nightly parties. I waited for the fallout but as far as I could tell there was none. He acted as if I was describing my job volunteering at the children's hospital. He listened with interest, without judgment. This guy was unicorn rare, because all men react one way or another to the revelation that you're a sex worker.

"If we were caught in this elevator for the next three days and the elevator-music channel was stuck, what would you want it to be playing?" I asked him, right before the cables came to life and the suspended box in which we sat resumed its journey down.

"Bruckner," he said. "I would want to sit here with you and listen to Bruckner."

He had one up on me because he had heard of the Sultan of Brunei, but I hadn't heard of Bruckner. When we reached the bottom floor, we walked out into the night, spent and bonded by the fact that we had averted disaster. The financial district, emptied of its bankers and executives, looked like the proud ruins of a lost civilization.

"I want to show you something," he said.

He took my hand, led me to a spot dead-center between the towers, and lay down on the ground without an explanation. I lay next to him. We looked up at the identical monoliths rising to touch the low night clouds, watched as they swayed slightly in the wind. I thought it was an optical illusion.

"No," he said. "They're actually moving. Architecturally a building is much stronger if it gives a little bit."

Years later, I would remember that night. I would remember how New York had sparkled outside the wall of windows. How the whole city had seemed to breathe to the rhythm of the dance beat that throbbed through the club, which only hours before had been an elegant restaurant. How I had remembered sitting at that same restaurant with my parents when I was a little girl. We had gone for dinner there after the ballet one night. Maybe it had been *Swan Lake*.

And I would remember that while the other people in the elevator had begun to get agro and fight with each other, Andy and I had sat down in the midst of it and talked about Bruckner. As I watched the towers fall almost ten years later, I thought of the night I got stuck in the elevator of the World Trade Center. I thought of the night I met Andy.

The next night, Andy invited me over to the Tomandandy studio—an überhip SoHo loft still under renovation. I stepped out of a cab and navigated the cobblestones in my heels. His studio took up the entire floor of an old building on the corner of Spring and Greene.

When the elevator doors opened, the starved vegans from the other night reappeared, smoking and leaning on the window ledges along the corridor. The lights were out for some reason, something about replacing the wiring. The hipsters in the hallway were lit only by the streetlights outside and by the glowing cigarette cherries next to their faces. I walked past them to a cavernous room that reeked of fresh paint. Piled in the center of the room was a disjointed city of computer and music equipment that remained lit due to the presence of a noisy generator. Snarled piles of cords were everywhere.

In the corner of the room, washed in the blue of a computer screen, was Andy. He turned to me and smiled his wolf smile, his upper canines so crowded and pointy that it looked like he had a whole second set of teeth growing above the first ones. I knew that I was looking at a piece of my future.

As I moved around the darkened loft that night, drifting from one cluster of bored New Yorkers to another, I noticed a trend. I fell into conversation with a Brooklyn filmmaker and his Norwegian-model import girlfriend. The filmmaker said Andy was his best friend. I met a club promoter who said the same thing. So did a Unix programmer and so did practically everyone else I talked to. I would later discover that people often said Andy was their best friend when he barely knew their name, because Andy was the world's greatest listener. He inspired an easy intimacy that compelled strangers at bars to tell him their secrets and often spawned rivalries for his attention. The people around Andy were close with him but antagonistic toward each other.

Andy and I snuck away from the party and went for a walk. We made out in a TriBeCa alley under a cupola of scaffolding. I recognized that Andy was a rare find. He was in need of a de-geeking makeover, but that was an easy fix. After a few more dates, I wedged myself into his life, becoming a regular installation at the studio and a source of untold drama between Andy and his business partner, Tom. I fit seamlessly into the pattern of everyone loving Andy and hating each other.

I was in love, real love with a real boyfriend. I thought about Robin often, but didn't miss him at all. When the date on my ticket came around again, I didn't show up at the airport. I didn't call Ari to cancel. I threw the ticket in the trash and walked forward into my new life as if the old one had never existed.

Andy was infinitely fascinating and made lots of money and pretty much did whatever I said, which made him the perfect boyfriend in my eyes. Within a month we had moved in together. My realtor cousin found us an apartment on the corner of Mott and Houston. It might have been the ugliest apartment building in all of New York, one of those brick boxes with cheap brass fixtures and polished granite lobbies. Our building was the kind of eyesore that was the precursor to the glass-block monstrosities now blanketing downtown, encroaching farther and farther east toward the river until soon the whole Lower East Side will be a mass of cheaply built condos with the Gap or Jamba Juice in their bottom-floor retail spaces.

But apartment hunting in New York was a horror that I didn't feel like facing; I was characteristically impatient and took the first thing that came along. Our apartment was a one-bedroom comprising two minuscule white boxes, with an Easy-Bake-size kitchen along the wall of the living room.

I packed up and moved my entire room at Penny's in about five hours. I gave Andy a makeover and a home and he paid our rent and gave me someone to love. We got a python. I bought us a bed, a dresser, and a couch at a cheap furniture store on Sixth Avenue. My parents came into the city to have lunch with me on weekends and my mother constantly restocked our freezer with lasagna and chicken soup. I reheated her food for our dinners and called it cooking. We were practically all grown up.

It was my fantasy in many ways, having this normal life but still being complete freaks. An arty hooker (or a hooker-y artist, depending on the day) and a genius

computer hacker, taking over the world by day while enjoying quiet nights at home watching classic films and
eating Chunky Monkey. On odd nights, when the stars
aligned, this is what our life looked like. But truthfully, I
spent many of those nights alone. Andy was a workaholic
and was almost never home. I told myself that it was ideal
because I was a girl who needed her space. Andy wasn't
the only one with a career. I had my own career to think
about.

I went on auditions and went back to working at
the Wooster Group a few hours a week. I filled note-
books with my scribbles of script ideas. Most afternoons
I walked to Andy's studio, sat on the long orange cus-
tom-made leather couch, and ate sushi while I watched
Andy work, composing music on his elaborate computer
console. He was so talented, so unassuming, so fucking
smart. I envied him. He didn't have to audition for anyone
or fuck anyone or pretend to be something he wasn't or
kiss anyone's ass or beg for a role, a job, a chance. He just
had to be Andy. That's what you get from the world for
being exceptional. The rest of us have to work harder. If I
were just me, just Jill, I'd be nowhere.

Andy and I never used birth control. My little hysterical
pregnancy in Brunei aside, I didn't really think I could get
pregnant. As a result of starving myself in high school, I
didn't get my period for a year straight. And I had never
been regular after that. I thought I had turned my own
insides to stone.

So it wasn't my lack of a period that alerted me to

something being wrong; I just knew. But I peed on the stick and it came up negative. I peed on sticks again and again and my doctor insisted the sticks didn't lie. When I finally demanded a blood test, I was almost three months pregnant. Andy was strangely unfazed when I showed up at his work with the news of a pregnancy. He consoled me with a brief hug before going back to work, leaving me frozen in front of the orange elevator doors with the receptionist staring at me.

She and I must have had warring astrological signs or something, because our interactions were always bristly. She was the one who screened my calls when Andy didn't want to be disturbed. He denied it, but I knew it was true. I stuffed any display of weakness or emotion and planned to have my feelings when I got somewhere private. But when I got home, I couldn't find the feelings I'd put aside for later. That's the danger of pretending. You can forget what you were pretending not to be in the first place.

Andy assumed that I'd have an abortion, because there was no other option in his universe. When he came home later that night, he started talking details, like when he would have to take off work to take me to the clinic and whether he'd have to take a whole day or a half day. I made him a BLT and served it to him on our crappy sleeper couch. I had picked out the couch while trying to be thrifty, and it was terrible. It was made of black canvas and was tilted and lumpy, and the cushions were always sliding out. We had to put them back in place ten times a day. That albatross of a couch dominated the living room. It was an indictment of me, a visual reminder that I couldn't do anything right. I wasn't even woman enough to pick out a good couch.

"I'm not sure I want to get rid of it," I said.

Andy generally complied with my wishes without protest. It was a good trick he had. He made people feel like they were in control, but actually he was getting them to take care of everything for him. Sure, I could decorate the place any way I wanted, but the catch was I had to do it all myself. That way when things went wrong, like with the couch, it was never Andy's fault.

In this instance, however, I saw a side of Andy that I hadn't before. He was quietly decided and direct. It seemed that he was capable of having an opinion after all. He may have had opinions all along and just hadn't been letting on.

"If you want to have a baby," he said, "you'll be doing it alone."

In high school, I had bussed down to Washington to march with pro-choice advocacy groups. When the militant antichoice organization Operation Rescue attacked New York in force during the Democratic National Convention, I volunteered with the National Abortion Rights Action League doing clinic defense. We gathered at various clinics at six a.m., locked our arms, and protected the entering women from screeching picketers with gory, unforgivable signs. I had rarely felt such a clear sense of being a participant in the fight of right against wrong. We were right; they were wrong.

I didn't really tell Andy or anyone else how badly I wanted to keep the baby, how my heart twisted in protest against the decision my head had made. I was nineteen and my boyfriend didn't want a baby. I would rather have chewed tacks than asked my parents for help. My friends were career-minded artists. My choice was spelled out.

I hung out in Penny's kitchen, my old kitchen, and drank tea.

"It's a loss," she said. She'd had an abortion a few years before. "I don't regret it, but it still haunts me."

"Nineteen years ago my birth mother had this same conversation with her best friend. She came up with a different solution."

"She was a different girl in a different time. This is your life, not hers."

But I thought about my birth mother probably more than I ever had as I made my decision. And in my thoughts she wasn't a long-limbed ballerina in a spotlight; she was a girl like me, imperfect and feeling totally screwed. I wondered if, like me, some part of her had believed that her boyfriend was going to turn around and tell her that she wasn't alone. His eyes would have the tilt, the gleam of a man who had changed his mind. He would offer her a family, a little bohemian tribe. And she would offer him one right back. And her life would change in dazzling and unexpected ways.

When I had thought I was pregnant in Brunei, the choice to keep the baby against all odds had seemed so simple, so noble. Maybe deep down I'd known all along that I never was pregnant.

I thought of my adoptive mother newly married and vacuuming the brown rug in her New Jersey apartment as again a month came and went without anything taking root inside her, her insides slippery and hollow and out of her control. I thought of her ticking off each interminable minute of each month until doctors became lawyers and creating a family became a project of proportions neither she nor my father had ever dreamed of.

But then there was the baby, the perfect and whole baby in her arms, wrapped in a pink blanket and sleeping through the flight from Chicago to New York, breathing in and out and smelling like sweet, powdery newness. My mother's life changed in dazzling and unexpected ways. And for a moment, she was happy.

It was the end of summer, the beginning of September—usually my favorite month in New York.

But this was what savvy girls did, postfeminist girls, girls with futures, right? They tried hard not to get knocked up in the first place, but if the unfortunate accident happened they grimly proceeded to Planned Parenthood and exercised the choice their mothers had fought so hard to guarantee them. They did it and maybe went to some therapy. They did it and acknowledged the scar tissue, but they did it.

A baby was an unthinkable encumbrance. Having a baby at nineteen was something only girls in urban projects and Midwestern trailers did, girls who knew that it was unlikely that their future would differ from their mother's life anyway. But my mother had raised me to believe that without question my life would differ from hers.

My body, my choice, I had shouted on the steps of the United States Capitol building. And so it was. It was my choice alone and it was alone that I sat, in an office on the second floor of a building somewhere in Midtown.

I waited in a cold hallway, wearing a gown and paper slippers, craning my neck to watch *Batman* on the television. The women who waited with me talked to each other with the candor that women have, the ease we often share at nail salons, at the gym, in doctor's offices. The woman across from me was Latina, with green eyes and cocoa skin. She was wide around the belly but had slim and shapely legs crossed at the knee and covered with goose bumps. She told her neighbor that she had three kids already and had been on the pill when she got pregnant.

"Ninety-nine percent effective my ass," she snorted.

Every plastic bucket of a seat was filled. My arms brushed the arms of the women on either side of me. I spoke to no one.

Andy's genes, I thought. Andy's wonderful, brilliant, musical genes. I recognized that I was on the precipice of something irreversible, far more so than any choice I'd made before that. A piece of me was turning cold, dying. Maybe it was the piece that believed so strongly in my own rightness, in my own goodness, in the fact that I would do better than my mother, my mothers, that I'd outshine them both by immeasurable wattage. I'd outrun them both by a thousand miles.

Instead I shuffled down the hallway, no better than they. Worse. Worse.

One thing they often tell adopted children is, Your birth mother loved you so very much that she gave you away so you could have a better life. That may be true. It may also be true that if she had loved you just a little bit more, she would have kept you.

I didn't love my baby enough. But I did love her in those last moments. I could feel her with me. And in my head floated the "stages-of-development" fetuses, the plaster casts on display in the Museum of Natural History, the exhibit my father had taken me to see as a child, the miracle of life.

What did she look like? Her eyelids. Her ears. Her hands folded over her tiny, beating heart.

I lay on the table in the small procedure room with my legs strapped into stirrups, my gown hiked up to my waist, and a three-inch square of paper towel draped across the top of my thighs. I've always had difficult veins. The anesthesiologist sighed impatiently and stuck me several times.

"If you would just stop shaking, I could get this needle in."

Silent tears streamed across my temples and into my hairline. Finally, I felt the sting in the crook of my elbow and then the swell at the back of my throat and then the sleepy warmth.

In the moment before the twilight sleep took me into nothingness, I dreamed of the hospital, of my father. You don't see a vein; you feel a vein. It was a recurring dream, grounded at least partly in memory.

❅ ❅ ❅

At age twelve I had ovarian cysts so painful that the doctors almost removed my appendix. As a result, I was in and out of the hospital, but I didn't mind. I liked the hospital better than school. People took care of me and brought me chocolate bars and I ate floppy string beans and white bread with butter packets and watched TV all day in my pajamas. My dad took off work to stay there with me. He also liked hospitals. Medicine was his true love. He would have been a doctor but for his inability to concentrate, his lack of patience, his poor bedside manner. He says it's why he wound up in finance instead.

An inept medical tech stabbed at my arm with a needle. This was my least favorite part about the hospital. I looked in the other direction, the same silent tears running down my face. My father watched from the other side of the room until his rage overtook his sense of decorum and he lifted the tech off his seat by the collar of his lab coat and threw him up against the wall. He held the man there by his throat and pointed an emphatic finger a centimeter away from the tech's nose.

"You don't see a vein, you fucking moron. You feel a vein."

He dropped the man and sat beside me, gently and capably feeling for the vein in the hollow of my elbow before inserting the IV catheter in one try.

I don't know if this occurrence was a hallucination or the real thing, but I know that in my dream replay of that moment, I love my dad so much.

❅ ❅ ❅

Andy picked me up at the clinic. He cried in the elevator when he saw my face, but he dropped me at home and went back to work. When he came back later that night, he brought me Ben & Jerry's and moved the television into the bedroom, breaking my adamant no-television-in-the-bedroom rule. It hurt. It did not feel like cramps, as they had said it would. It didn't feel like cramps at all. It felt like something was clawing its way out of me.

I bled through pad after pad. Andy found a friend who had some Vicodin. I took one. Then I took another, and was magically enveloped in a soft cloud of okay that floated me into a mercifully dreamless sleep.

When I woke, a brick-red stain, brown at the dried edges, was spread out on the sheet beneath me. Something was wrong. I took two more Vicodin and thought, If I just had a Vicodin tree, a never-ending supply, my problems would all be solved, would melt into the ground like butter into toast.

When by the afternoon the bleeding hadn't stopped, I called my doctor and left a message. I considered a trip to the emergency room, but the thought of a New York emergency room on a Saturday afternoon drove me back to the Vicodin bottle and back into bed, towels folded underneath me. It took a few days before the bleeding finally eased. The doctor told me it was caused by something called "retained products," pieces of tissue that hadn't been properly removed. Retained products. You try to scoop out the consequences of your actions but the residue hangs on. She called it harmless—painful and disturbing, but ultimately harmless. I wonder sometimes now—after injecting countless syringes full of powerful hormones into my stomach, after going to clinic after clinic for a series of fertility procedures straight out of the movie *Species*, all of them failing—if she was wrong.

I curled around a heating pad and watched *Law & Order*. I watched it and then I just kept watching. The doctor at the clinic had said that I would be up and around in a day or two, so Andy couldn't really understand why I stayed in bed for two weeks watching television. It wasn't the pain. That went away after a few days. And the Vicodin went away a few days after that and in place of warm nothingness I found a pit, a crater, a black hole, the sides of it lined with retained products.

I wanted to fall into that black hole and become so small that the force of the compression itself would send me exploding into a billion pieces, would explode my arrogance and my careless decisions, explode the unshakable sadness, the heavy stone tied around my throat from the inside. I wanted to give up and just explode the self I couldn't quite find, flailing and unwise. My own big bang. Please, I begged whomever, whatever, let me just fall apart and start over.

chapter 22

Her name was Carrie Gardner. It sounded perky and Midwestern and plain, the name of an airline ticket-counter worker, a waitress at Outback Steakhouse, a kindergarten teacher.

Slowly and on shaky legs, I'd been emerging from my funk for a few weeks. At Penny's behest, I had begun seeing a therapist named Paul Pavel. I rode the A train every day to his uptown apartment. He was a man of uncommon hope, a man who rescued half-frozen animals from Central Park in the wintertime, a man who had himself been rescued half-frozen in the snow by American soldiers after the liberation of Auschwitz. Paul reached his hand, his tattooed arm, out to me and defrosted me as well. He led me out of the darkest part of the depression that had come hard on the heels of my abortion.

Paul was convinced, among other things, that my biological origins were of far greater significance to me than I was willing to admit. He made a connection between the loss of my birth mother and my crippling guilt over my abortion. And just as my therapy was excavating all this, Johnny called me with my birth mother's name.

Johnny was home for the High Holidays from yet another boarding school. As usual, I wouldn't be observing the holidays except to call my parents and wish them *l'shanah tovah*: for a good year. And while I didn't miss the hypocrisy, the moneyed religion, the rigidity of the doctrine, I felt a sadness I couldn't put my finger on. Maybe the holidays made me yearn for a time when I had believed in something as unlikely as God, or a time when I had believed that I was a part of something.

There had once been High Holidays when distant cousins swarmed me in the temple lobby with open arms and lipsticked smiles, smelling of Chanel No. 5. I remember pressing my face into new wool suits that were too warm for a sunny September New Jersey day. I remember sneaking out of the children's service downstairs and walking around the temple grounds while the sun shone through the turning leaves, colorful and translucent as stained glass. I remember cut apples dipped in honey, so sweet they hurt your teeth.

Johnny, who ten years later would be so religious he would have all these things and more, was at the time a rather gifted criminal. Our parents had always told us that they had no information about our biological parents. The only birth certificates we ever saw listed our adoptive parents as our parents. Period. Any previous records had been sealed permanently. The pieces of paper were insistent and so were my parents. Johnny called that day to tell me that he had uncovered evidence discrediting my parents' story.

My parents did, in fact, have information about our birth parents. Johnny had found it by breaking into a lock box. He uncovered detailed information about himself, as he was younger and benefited from more relaxed adoption laws. But for me, Johnny had found a name—a name and a brief story pieced together from an attorney's correspondence, and an old address.

Everything I know about what Johnny found I know from my memory of our conversation. I have never seen the papers with my own eyes. I'm sure my parents would show them to me now, but I can't bring myself to ask. It is still a sore spot for them and a source of guilt for me. I'm guilty that we snooped, that we cared in the first place. I am ashamed, illogically, to have discovered that they lied to us.

I vaguely remember Johnny telling me that there were some newspaper clippings about a birth father who tried later to regain custody. But maybe this was a conflation of my life with an episode of *Law & Order* or a CNN sound bite. It was such a strange moment that I can't remember exactly what he said. But I do remember that there was confirmation of a story my parents had always told me. I expected to discover that this story had been a lie, too, but it wasn't. My parents had been telling the truth when they told me that my birth mother had been a ballerina. I realized how much I had clung to this one little thing only when its confirmation flooded me with a sense of profound relief.

A young ballet dancer in Chicago is pregnant with a baby she is unable to care for. . . .

I wrote the name and the Highland Park, Illinois, address on a piece of paper and put it in a drawer. Somewhere there was a woman to whom this name belonged, who had once written this address on the official forms she had signed when she gave her baby away. My music-box mother, locked up safely with satin lining and a perpetual soundtrack, a princess transmuted by a spell into the body of a swan. Carrie Gardner. An airline ticket-counter worker, a waitress at Outback Steakhouse, a kindergarten teacher. A name that wasn't an answer, it was a question, a question to which I decided to seek the answer; I just wasn't sure how yet.

I had a habit during that time of browsing one of New York's many international-magazine stands, buying a few beautiful and unfamiliar glossies and reading them at a café, frequently Café Orlin, on Eighth Street. Before there were Ed Hardy T-shirts (and bottled water and office supplies and motorcycles and shower curtains), Don Ed Hardy was an artist who published a beautiful art

magazine called *Tattootime*. Once I picked up the magazine, I was hooked. Each *Tattootime* had a theme: New
Tribalism, Life and Death Tattoos, Art from the Heart,
Music and Sea Tattoos. As it does with most people who
are drawn to tattoos, the imagery and the history of tattooing struck a chord in my soul. The San Francisco tattoo artist who has done most of my work says that the
tattoo gods announce themselves to you when it's time.

I looked at the people in the pages of *Tattootime* and
felt an instant camaraderie. I, too, was a pirate, a sailor, a
prostitute, a gangster, a sideshow attraction, but nobody
knew it. Nobody saw it. It occurred to me that I'd have to
achieve a deeper level of authenticity in how I was living
or wind up a shapeshifter—will do whatever—for the rest
of my life.

The tattoo gods announced themselves to me. It was
nothing less dramatic than that. No sooner had I begun
to seek my first tattoo than I had a plan for what I wanted
my whole body to look like. With my story writ large on
the surface of my skin, I would no longer be tempted to
fool people into thinking that I was normal. Tattooing
was going to be my own radical statement about perma-
nence and impermanence. It was the scarlet letter that I
would proudly embroider across my chest.

Reading *Tattootime*, I learned that across the island
of Borneo, in the rainforest of the Sarawak, not far at all
from the royal yachts and palaces and car collections of
Brunei, live the Maori tribesmen, who tattoo their bodies from head to toe using a bone chisel. The spiraling,
swirling, black-ink tattoos have a sacred significance.

The Maori warriors emblazon their ferocity on their skin. Their tribal designs have migrated to the West and shown up on the arms of weightlifters in Venice Beach and street punks in Tompkins Square Park. While I had sat in the palace in Brunei and spun stories for Robin that evaporated into the air, miles away tribesmen were embedding their stories into their skin.

These were the pieces of my story that I decided were missing: I needed to find my birth mother and I needed to get a tattoo. I wanted to find myself and at the same time I wanted to create myself. The two things converged in an unexpected way. I studied the magazines and found the perfect artist. His name was Guy Aitchison and he lived in Chicago. The great thing about a tattoo is that you have no room for the luxury of doubt. You have to stand behind your decisions

A young ballet dancer in Chicago is pregnant with a baby she is unable to care for. . . .

chapter 23

On the plane to Chicago for my twofold mission, I dozed and in my half sleep I thought of Robin. I was supposed to be on a plane back to him and his world. Who was there now? Was someone else already in my chair and, if so, had he forgotten me completely?

I couldn't say I missed him, couldn't say I missed that whole warped world, but part of me, and not just the Patty Hearst part, had cared for him. Part of me remembered his face at odd times, remembered eating peaches off the hotel breakfast tray, the morning light cutting

across the sheets in hot, white stripes while he dressed
for work.

The girls in Brunei weren't the only ones with a role
to play. Robin, too, had a life in which he was called upon
to play role after role. Even princes tire of being princes
sometimes. There were moments late at night when he was
sick of the party, moments in the morning when he lingered an extra ten minutes in bed before complying with
his rigid schedule, moments when he drove his car too
fast on curvy country roads and I wondered if he wanted
to just keep driving. These were the moments that crept
into my unguarded consciousness when I was sleepy or
spacing out on a walk through the park or staring out the
window of a plane.

I thought, too, of Andy at home. He hadn't seen me
off at the airport. He had been working, of course. He
barely came home when I was awake anymore. I placed
my bets on all the wrong horses. I loved only the ones
who left me with a belly full of longing. At love, I was a
jackass. But they say the ultimate tattoo is the one that
changes the jackass into a zebra. I hoped for nothing
less. My first tattoo is a big tattoo, a life-changing tattoo. It's a purple snake spine that spirals out from my
navel and across my whole stomach, blossoming into a
garden of flowers that crawls down my left thigh and
decorates my entire pussy with thorny monster teeth.
You can now find photographs of my tattoo in a bunch
of tattoo books.

Before we started, Guy sagely tried to steer me away
from the idea of a pussy tattoo.

"Maybe you want to get something on a different part of your body until you know what it feels like."

I told him that I was quite sure of myself, that I wanted to be transformed.

He shrugged. It wasn't the province of tattoo artists to stop people from being stupid and melodramatic. Guy was famous for his ectomorphic sci-fi landscapes and exquisitely detailed poisonous gardens. Even if my first tattoo isn't in the wisest location, at least it's a beautiful tattoo.

One of the many unoriginal questions heavily tattooed people get asked when walking down the street is, "Does it hurt?" My friend in San Francisco wears a T-shirt that reads, FUCK YES IT HURTS. My whole nervous system misfired. When Guy tattooed my ribs, it felt like he was working on my neck. I twitched and broke a sweat and eventually I settled into some kind of accord with the pain. They tell you to lean into it. When your insides have been all twisted, the pain of a tattoo becomes a metaphor: This is unbearable and yet this I can live through.

The next day I felt like I had a terrible road rash on my stomach, and I also had a slight fever, but I was elated. I had my membership card to a new club. Guy, his girl-friend, and I took a day off. The three of us ate a handful of psychedelic mushrooms and went to the science museum to see an exhibit of giant insects. We walked under a cerulean Chicago sky and the wind came off the lake and blew through the too-thin dress I wore, helping to numb my burning skin.

When we entered the museum, the woman in the

ticket booth asked Guy how much his tattoos cost. This is the second most popular question after "Did that hurt?" That day with Guy, I learned my first lesson in having tattoos: When confronted by oglers, you need to have your routine down, whatever it's going to be. They treat you like a freak. So what? So what are you gonna do about it? What would Patti Smith do about it?

Guy looked like Al Jourgensen, but with violet-blue eyes. He responded to the woman with a growl and a milk-turning, I-will-sacrifice-your-baby-to-Satan glare. I had spent two days with Guy and found him equal parts sweet science nerd and acid-dropping hippie. He was the nicest guy. Satan would have turned him away at the gate. The scariness was completely an act, but it shut her right up.

Inside, the insects were colorful and alien and phosphorescent. I had stepped into an alternate universe. I stared at my reflection in the luminous shell of a purple scarab twice my size. Maybe it was the hallucinogenics or the fever or the fairy dust of the tattoo gods, but I swayed with a vertiginous sensation similar to the one I'd had on the balcony my first night in Singapore: There she is, the girl I want to be, real and unashamed and rendered in bold Technicolor strokes—just out of reach, but closer.

With the tattoo, I felt something essential about myself had fallen into place. The following day I hopped a train to Highland Park in search of another missing piece. I'm not sure what I had expected, but the Highland Park train station was a platform in the middle of a suburb. It was the kind of place where businesspeople parked their cars and commuted by train to the city for work. I hadn't thought to rent a car. I carried a driver's license as ID, but I hadn't driven since I left home at sixteen, and that poorly and very little. I was used to subways dropping you practically at the front door of anywhere you wanted to go.

I crossed the parking lot to the shoulder of a road where I saw a fair flow of traffic and threw out my thumb, another first. There was no other option, unless I turned around and went back. I always made up for in willingness what I lacked in forethought. A black Cadillac with a mercifully non-creepy driver took me to the entrance of Highland Park Hospital, a brick structure landscaped with long beds of pink impatiens. I wandered the hallways looking for the records department, where I was met with blank stares.

"We've got nothing for you here," said a woman with pearlescent green talons.

"You're strange and extraordinary," I said in response to her nails, a reference to my all-time favorite movie, *Cabaret*. She looked at me even more blankly, if that was possible.

"You know. Sally Bowles. Green nails. Strange and extraordinary."

She didn't know.

"You could try the County Clerk. For your birth certificate," she said.

Of course there was nothing for me there. And I already had my official birth certificate. It told me nothing. It wiped out my history as if it had never existed.

I went to the maternity ward, because I couldn't think of anything else to do and I would feel defeated walking out so quickly. When I looked through the glass at the babies squirming in the nursery, I felt the cold adrenaline of a shoplifter. Why did I feel like I was doing something wrong? I left with the beginning flickers of a migraine and an emotional flatline.

I had only one more lead. I considered myself an old pro at hitchhiking by that time and I hitched another ride to the address I had scrawled on a piece of loose-leaf paper. The lawns of Highland Park looked like those of the affluent suburban town in which I had grown up and they inspired the same reaction: terror. The trees were just starting to turn, their leaves edged with hints of the gaudy colors to come.

I looked at the pretty houses and stores and a sense of hopelessness overwhelmed me. I got claustrophobic and my right eye began to swim with white spots. It felt like half my brain was being probed by alien electrodes. I thought for a minute I might also be getting ready to have an asthma attack, but it was just hypochondria. Trips to the deep suburbs give me asthma and migraines and rare diseases.

The aging Jewish trophy-wife-type woman in the driver's seat scolded me for hitchhiking and then cross-examined me about my sojourn to Highland Park. She tapped her French-tip acrylics against the steering wheel. I thought of my mother—my real mother, my adoptive mother—the thousands of carpools, the air-conditioning on high. I thought of her big black glasses with the purplish tint, her fingers, swollen with early arthritis but still shapely and perfectly manicured, wrapped around the wheel.

"I'm looking for an old friend."

"What's the name? I've lived here a hundred years. Maybe I know her. Him?"

"Her. Her name is Carrie Gardner."

"Gardner. Maybe there was a Gardner ahead of my daughter in junior high, but I didn't know the parents."

I got the feeling that she was making this up. She seemed like the kind of woman who couldn't stand to be caught without the answer.

"I never pick up hitchhikers, you know, but I could tell you were a nice girl. My daughter was at school in Michigan before she dropped out. Now she follows the Grateful Dead around. Thinks she's an activist. Ridiculous. So smart, that kid. I figured you could have been my daughter standing there. I'd want someone safe to stop for her."

What would my mother say? *My daughter was at NYU before she dropped out. Now she flits back and forth from New York to Southeast Asia. Thinks she's an actress. Ridiculous. So smart, that kid.*

The woman consulted my creased piece of paper and dropped me off at a ranch-style suburban house, plain and assuredly middle class.

"You sure you'll be okay?" she asked me.

"I'm fine. I've got a ride from here. Thanks a lot."

I considered asking if she would wait for a minute and then drive me back to the train station. She didn't seem like she had much to do. But I decided not to. I was pretty sure she would have said yes, but I didn't want to talk to her anymore, didn't want the reminder of my own mother, of the betrayal I was committing by standing on that particular square of yard.

A moonfaced woman opened the door and squinted at me, brushing a lock of hair out of her face. She told me that she had moved in only a year ago and had no information. Before she moved in, there was a family who was there three years, but she couldn't remember their names. Maybe Carrie had stayed with the family who was there before them. Maybe the family before that. She was just guessing. Nineteen years was a long time, after all. Nineteen years of waves rolling over any sandcastles Carrie might have built there.

"Is there anyone on this block who lived here nineteen years ago?"

"Not that I know of. It's a young block. It's a family neighborhood," she said. "Now, who are you, again?"

In ghost stories, it's always some terrible tragedy that leaves a mark behind, an assault so grievous that time itself steps aside to allow for a spirit to hang around and decry the injustice. But what about our mundane personal tragedies, the prosaic injustices perpetrated without a police file, without an audience? These slip away, washed from the counters before the next family moves in their boxes of dishware. I suppose I could have stayed in the neighborhood and been a better investigative journalist, but I was suddenly nauseated, my headache growing progressively debilitating.

Hitching a ride from there to the train station proved to be harder than I had anticipated. I walked for about an hour down a long stretch of road, feeling stupid and stopping once to throw up behind a bush, before anyone stopped. Otherwise, it was uneventful. I don't know what I had expected. Somehow it had seemed important for me to smell the smells and see the colors of that town, but all I had smelled was the same autumn, the same trees, the same hospital trays that were everywhere else. I was embarrassed by the visit to the nursery, by my own sentimentality.

On the train home, I laid my head against the window and thought of Joni Mitchell. In high school I had decided that I looked like Joni Mitchell, in spite of her delicate, elfish features. I didn't look like her in obvious ways, but in ways only I, intimately acquainted with my own bone structure, could see. I even sang like her when I sang alone. On stage in musical-theater productions I was a classic belter, but in my secret moments, I sang just like Joni, my voice high and breathy and folksy.

I had read in *Rolling Stone* that Joni Mitchell gave a baby up for adoption. This baby was the child born with the moon in Cancer that she sings about in the song "Little Green." I was certain that this baby was me. Never mind the fact that I was a Leo. Never mind the fact that the 1971 *Blue* album with "Little Green" on it came out two years before I was born. Never mind that I was hardly the blond and blue-eyed sprite Joni Mitchell was.

I filtered out the contradictory evidence and knew, beyond all reason, that my birth mother was Joni Mitchell. Because her spirit was the spirit I had inside me. And what I needed was not a mother who had carried me in her body. That I could live without. But I needed to find the place my heart came from. My heart refused to be an orphan forever.

I got my tattoo not to say "I wuz here," a tag on a freeway overpass, but rather to say "Here wuz me." Here they are, the landscapes inscribed behind my eyes. Because even when your dream slips away, your mother slips away, your baby slips away, your lover slips away— even then, you have your story. With my tattoos, I serve as witness and documentarian to myself.

After the first tattoo, I got many more. Now people often run their hands over my tattoos as if they're braille. All this touching gets on my nerves sometimes. People who don't know me at all will reach out and grab my arm, will run their palms over my forearms. But I get it. My tattoos are pulsing with stories. Hold your ear close to them and you'll hear the ocean at Beach Haven, you'll hear an insistent knocking on a door in Brunei, you'll hear the train pulling out of the Highland Park station.

I let Highland Park disappear behind me. That town held nothing, not the smallest clue that there once had been a girl somewhere in that house pregnant with me, feeding me her thoughts, feeding me her fears, staying maybe with the last nameless family or maybe with the family before that; no one can remember.

My mission in Highland Park had been unsuccessful, but I had figured out something, at least. The air there weighed a million pounds, but riding the train out of town I felt so light. I recognized time's shifting weight—the heaviness of the past, the lightness of the moment.

What I was looking for wasn't in Highland Park, wasn't in any one place. Sometimes all you need is a Joni Mitchell song to know who you are. Sometimes you find it by accident on a foreign balcony at dawn. And sometimes your story looks like the purple spine of a snake spiraling outward across your belly, etched forever under your skin.

chapter 24

A snake tattoo is preferable to a live snake. I drank an espresso and stared into the cage of my vicious Burmese python, Varla. Only our extremely strange cleaning woman, Shakti, potentially part reptile herself, could handle Varla without elbow-length gloves. I had wanted a pet and anything cute with fur was forbidden in our apartment, so I had walked into a Lower East Side pet store one day and walked out with Varla. I had always liked snakes and thought it would be fun to have one. I was wrong.

I hadn't realized how traumatic it was going to be to feed the snake live mice. Even more traumatic was when I sought advice for dealing with Varla's bad temper and the man at the pet store told me to stun the mice first. He said it would help her lose her lunging instinct. I was mortified. I was the little girl who, inspired by the Met's Temple of Dendur, had buried my hamster in a shoebox painted to look like a pharaoh's sarcophagus, had wept for weeks over his garden grave. But I had bought the snake and she was my responsibility. I put the girl who had lovingly constructed Habitrail castles behind me.

After that, every time Varla needed to eat, I would cry and put a mouse in a paper bag. Then I would profusely apologize to the mouse as I smashed the bag against the wall. I would drop the mouse into the terrarium and it would twitch while Varla ignored it for hours before eating it and I drowned in guilt. It was gruesome.

Andy refused to feed her.

"You wanted her, you feed her."

It was the couch debacle multiplied by a thousand. Varla was every bad decision I'd ever made coiled tightly and hissing out at me from a smelly cage. That morning, I was contemplating how the fuck I was going to move that huge terrarium and whom I could get to adopt a mean snake, when the phone rang.

It was legendary downtown theater director Richard Foreman calling to tell me that I had been cast in his upcoming play, *Samuel's Major Problems*. When I hung up the phone, I screamed and danced around like a housewife who had just gotten a visit from Ed McMahon.

I wanted to call Andy and tell him, but his assistant screened me out. I decided to walk over to his studio and tell him in person. He could tell his assistant to hold his calls, but he couldn't exactly turn his girlfriend away at the door. Living with a workaholic, even one who paid the bills, wasn't all I had hoped it would be. I picked up my script at Richard's Wooster Street loft on my way to tell Andy the news.

I starred in the show with Steven Ratazzi and Thomas Jay Ryan, both fabulously gifted actors. I played Maria Helena, sort of a ghost/devil/succubus/nurse/Marilyn Monroe figure. My time in New York didn't get any better than walking from my Mott Street apartment to St. Mark's Church for the first day of rehearsals.

It was the beginning of December and my body buzzed with warmth under my overcoat, my nose frozen at the tip from the wind cutting a swath down Second Avenue. "On the Street Where You Live" played in my head—*I have often walked down this street before, but the pavement always stayed beneath my feet before*—my dorky musical-theater background impinging on my rebirth into the avant-garde. I entered the wrought-iron gates and cut past the dilapidated front doors and along the paving stones of the church, through the graveyard and back to the theater.

Richard stages plays that aren't plays, exactly. They're more like three-dimensional poems or philosophical treatises told as a nursery rhyme. Being cast in one of his shows means that you'll be standing in for any number of the shadowy figures in his subconscious and that essentially you'll be moving around inside his head for a few months. This was alternately sublime and maddening.

Richard was a nebbish, genius sweetheart and he was also a maniacal, condescending tyrant. He completely changed the set around every few days, adding obstacles, such as three waist-high black poles that blended into the rest of the scenery and caused painful accidents. During one lunch break he took away all our props and added a Plexiglas wall between the actors and the audience. During another he added body microphones and directed that all the dialogue be delivered in a whisper. During yet another he added all the props back in and changed the shape of the stage.

It was a blast. Every person on the crew was fascinating and we all tended to get drunk and make out with each other at parties. We had a costume designer named Lindsay Davis, a leather queen with an infectious laugh and a closet full of sharp little hats. Lindsay and I fast discovered that we were soul mates. I went to his loft on Thirty-eighth Street for fittings and wound up staying the whole afternoon, smoking pot and then going for pancakes at the diner downstairs. He made me a beautiful black dress that looked like a perfect 1950s cocktail number except it was completely see-through.

On my legs, Richard instructed me to put stripes of black electrical tape that were visible through the sheer fabric. They echoed a diagonal of stripes on the stage, which looked like a very narrow crosswalk. The electrical tape, reapplied each night, left red welts on my legs that didn't go away for the whole run of the show. I felt proud of them; they were my battle scars.

We rehearsed for the month of December and the play ran for the first three months of 1993. I took a handful of hundreds out of my safe-deposit box and bought a dress to wear to dinner after opening night. It was made of burgundy crushed velvet, with a cluster of silk roses at the small of the back. True, I had a closet full of fancy dresses I never wore, but I wanted something bought by my own dollars at a store I had wandered into off a SoHo street, not a dress purchased in a frenzy by a royal guard with a sackful of Monopoly money. I wanted a dress to celebrate nothing less than a dream come true, because that's what it was, the whole thing, from the grind of the rehearsals to the nauseating anxiety of opening night.

My parents, supportive to a fault, drove into the city and watched me perform at least once a week. Even near the end of the three-month run, my father still insisted he had no idea what the show meant and my mother still insisted on bringing the crew loaves of banana bread and trays of rugelach. My father enjoyed harassing whomever was in the seat next to him (it would inevitably be Wallace Shawn or John Malkovich or someone), demanding that the startled soul explain to him what the hell was going on up there. I might have been able to explain it, but he never asked me. I think my father much preferred frightening the glitterati.

There was a windfall of perks that came with acting in *Samuel's Major Problems*. We got great reviews in *The New York Times* and *The Village Voice*. Before the run was over, I already had calls for other auditions. I had a lunch date with Don DeLillo the day after he came to see the show (during which I acted like a complete dipshit, but really, sue me, I was struck dumb).

Andy came on opening night and I believe he was proud of me. On one or two other nights, he left work and snuck in after the show had started. On some nights he'd come out after the show and drink with the cast and crew at Mona's or 7A. He was a hard-drinking Texan and he could stay lucid and charming while everyone else got plastered. Everyone adored him and no one could understand it when we broke up. It was a weird thing how it happened. Andy and I never even talked about breaking up before the day I left.

The idea of Andy, the life I had imagined for us, had disintegrated before Mark showed up. But before Mark, I didn't see it was gone. I didn't notice. I was busy. It was a full-time job just being me, trying to stamp myself onto the face of New York, as if the heels of my shoes held a red-hot branding iron.

One night when the theater was dark, Andy asked me to come with him to meet an old Texas friend of his for drinks at Mona's. This friend of his was visiting town from Los Angeles. He was an art director who was having a hard time holding a job in film because of his cocaine problem. I didn't connect the dots until after two drinks. This Texas friend was the older man with whom Andy had had a "relationship" when Andy was twelve years old, a two-year relationship that had ended with an arrest in the back of a station wagon. I knew that Andy still talked to the guy, but I never expected to find myself sitting across a table from him.

They prey on the sensitive ones, the smart ones, the lonely ones. Before I left for camp the summer I would turn thirteen, I saw the movie *Marjorie Morningstar* and I figured that I was just like Natalie Wood. I was that fresh and daring inside. And I would rewrite the ending. I would never wind up a mediocre, lost housewife on a porch.

I favored white Keds and headbands. In the first week of camp I bleached orangey highlights into my hair with Sun-In and I tanned my skin with baby oil. I imagined I looked like a girl on the beach in *Blue Hawaii*, except I didn't need a bra. Though I did steal a pink disposable razor from Erica's shower caddy to shave off my leg hair for the first time.

Nathan was the archery guy. Everybody liked him when they didn't kind of hate him because he was much too glamorous for that run-down camp. He was twenty-one and from New York City and rumor had it that he was a model for United Colors of Benetton. You could just picture him in one of those ads, slouched against some global-y model with an Afro and a striped scarf. Nathan had bleached blond hair that he wore parted and hanging over one eye. His khaki shorts were slung so low that you could see the waistband of his boxers. He gave me stomachaches and asthma attacks. He was more handsome than John Travolta in *Grease* and sometimes *Welcome Back, Kotter*. Cooler, even, than Elvis in *Jailhouse Rock* and *Viva Las Vegas*.

The archery range was located down a grassy slope near the girls' side of camp, between the nature hut and the pottery shack. Free play was the time before dinner when we could pretty much run wild and do whatever we wanted. I decided I wanted more than anything to learn how to shoot an arrow. But I never picked up a bow. Instead I hung out by the archery range, sitting on the nearby hill with my knees tucked under my chin.

One evening, I noted that it was too chilly for Nathan to be wearing just his T-shirt, so I ran back to my bunk and got him an oversize fuzzy pink Benetton sweater with a big white *B* on the front of it. When he put it on, I knew that it meant we had a secret, but I wasn't sure yet what it was.

I sat quietly and watched him shoot, too far away to really talk. He was all height and angles, perfect stance, casual and confident, with the arrow placed neatly in the bow, pulled back taut.

Sometimes we girls snuck across camp to raid the boys' side in the middle of the night. The counselors normally pretended to sleep through the nighttime shaving-cream shenanigans and panty raids. The night after I gave Nathan my sweater, I put my small travel alarm, set for three a.m., under my pillow. I kept gum by my bedside and slept carefully on my hair. But that night was different than usual, because I wasn't waking any of my friends. I was embarking on a solo mission.

I traveled across the familiar path with tense steps, the darkness outside the beam of my flashlight dancing with disorienting shadows, saturated by the characters from every camp ghost story I had ever dismissed with a

snort. I was madly inspired and frightened. The adrenaline emboldened me. It sailed me across the camp until
finally the wet rubber of my sneakers tapped up the green
steps to his door, which creaked as I opened it. I walked
through the rows of sleeping boys in their army cots, suck-
ing on my spearmint gum, wondering if I should swallow
it. Saliva traveled down my throat like cold acid. I shook.
Nathan made me ill. He had poisoned me.

I touched his shoulder blade to wake him and it was
bare and sharp. When he sat up, he was a full head taller
than I. I had never been that close to him before. I could
barely make out his expression in the dark, but he didn't
seem surprised. He put out his hand in front of him and
whispered to me, "Give me your gum."

And when he kissed me, I thought, Tongues are like
velvet shellfish. And men are easier than I ever thought.
I was surprised that I had gotten what I wanted. I had
gotten him to break the rules. I thought it was quite a
coup. And if I often wished that I had never gotten involved with Nathan, if I felt hopelessly and immediately
in over my head even though our early morning make-out
sessions never really went very far, I didn't admit it. Not
even to myself, most of the time.

Later, when Nathan got fired and I was humiliated,
my father had said, "What did you think was going to happen? That's what you get for always breaking the rules."

I drank too much that night. I was short-tempered and
sarcastic and finally had to excuse myself. I walked home
alone and passed out.

Later that night, Andy came back and sat on the edge of the bed. I squinted at his silhouette in the blue darkness and hazily came to the realization that the person who was stroking my calf, more like petting it, wasn't Andy.

I sat up like a shot, immediately awake and terrified.

"I lost my job."

It was Mark, of course. I had been having nightmares about Nathan and I woke looking at Mark.

Do you know what you do to me? I have to watch you run around in your shorts all day long. It makes me crazy. And I can't do anything about it, and I can't tell anyone.

"Andy?" I called out.

"He had to stop at work and get something," Mark slurred.

Why did he have a key? He wasn't staying with us. Andy told me he had a hotel room.

"No one will hire me."

Maybe this guy was a psycho. Maybe he resented me for living with Andy and was going to kill me. Or maybe he was just a sad-sack, alcoholic, run-of-the-mill pedophile. I figured in his current state I could probably take him. My fear was suddenly steamrolled by a surge of fury that rose to the back of my throat, threatening to spew out like vomit.

"Really? Why is that, Mark?"

"Because I like boys."

Is this okay, honey? You are so pretty and soft. Is this okay, sweetheart? You are so beautiful.

"Because I like little boys," he repeated.

I'm going to pick you up from school and take you into New York and we're going to see bands and movies and do things, okay? I'm going to take care of you. Isn't that what you want?

I looked around for a weapon of some kind. Where was that fucking stun gun? What's the point of a stun gun if you can't remember where you put it? Maybe he wasn't the danger here. Maybe I was. Maybe I was going to kill him.

But I didn't. Instead I yelled at him to get the fuck out of my apartment. When he sat there dazed, I yelled it again. I yelled it after he was long out the door.

Go on back to your bunk now, honey. Come again tomorrow. Promise?

Later, when Andy came home, I yelled at him, too. Tall, broad-shouldered Andy sobbed in a ball, hugging the edge of the bed. It never occurred to me to protect Andy, that we should have protected each other. I only expected him to protect me.

I broke up with Andy because he gave a predator a key to my home and I felt unsafe, but that was only part of it. I broke up with him because he was never around and I was lonely, because he screened my phone calls and I felt foolish and unloved.

The day after Mark surprised me in my bed, I went to Lindsay's loft to smoke pot and cry. Lindsay needed a shoulder, too, due to a recent heartbreak of his own. His boyfriend of ten years had just moved out and Lindsay talked about the sad quiet in the morning, the neatness of the bathroom, smoking an extra joint to make it easier to fall asleep alone. I realized I had all those things and I was still living with my boyfriend, my maybe-gay and definitely very dysfunctional and confused boyfriend. It seemed there was an obvious solution—I should move out of my unsatisfying relationship with Andy and be Lindsay's new roommate.

When I left, I wasn't kind. I couldn't wait to get out of that white box of an apartment that I couldn't figure out how to decorate anyway. Who wanted to see their mistakes, their inadequacies, their attempts at a tile mosaic on the bathroom walls staring them in the face every time they pee? Two roads diverged, and I took the one that looked like freedom. Andy came home one day and I was already packing my boxes.

He sat on the couch and held his head. I was so surprised. I thought he would pop the top off a Budweiser and go off to play *Sonic the Hedgehog*. That is how far I had drifted from knowing him. In my mind, our distance was entirely his fault. He was the one who was absent. My own absence hadn't occurred to me.

The thing I miss most now about doing theater isn't the applause. It's the experience I have onstage of being completely present. For me, something about the limited world, the adrenaline, and the lights banishes any sense of self-consciousness. My mind empties out, my body grows balanced, and my heart opens. I've never been a big method actor, thinking of starving children or bleeding baby seals or my dead grandmother in order to make myself cry. What I love about performing is that when I'm doing it well, I don't think at all.

It's true that you never leave the theater entirely. In *Samuel's Major Problems*, the whole stage was a spiderweb of string, tied from the edge of a bookshelf to the leg of a chair, from the edge of a candlestick to a chalkboard on a high shelf. In real life the string is there, but it's invisible. Your body may exit gracefully (or ungracefully) stage left, but you leave with that string tied to your heart. All your life, when you turn the wrong way, when you least expect it, you will feel the tug.

It's not just the theater. I imagine my heart sticky and throbbing at the center of a spiderweb with its network of silky strands radiating outward, attached to every thing I ever loved, every thing I thought I walked away from clean.

chapter 25

*A*fter attending her amazing one-woman show *Post Porn Modernist*, I met performance artist and former porn star Annie Sprinkle. I was taken with her bindi-wearing, speculum-toting, vagina-baring antics and we soon became friends. Annie is a true revolutionary. She introduced me to a new option—being unashamed. She does the same for many people.

I went to brunches with Annie and met other people whose work straddled the worlds of art and sex work. Most of them were more famous than I was (they were the kind of people who traded memories of Robert Mapplethorpe), but I had a few unique jewels in my tiara. I was the nineteen-year-old girl with the tattoo on her pussy. I was the girl who had just returned from the harem of the Prince of Brunei. That was how Annie always introduced me.

I modeled for Annie's Post Modern Pin-Up Pleasure Activist Playing Cards and this catapulted me into fetish modeling, sometimes for well-known artists. Some of the modeling experiences were great and made me feel empowered and others were exploitative and made me feel something akin to when a high school teacher of mine began rubbing my shoulders and I couldn't find it in me to tell him to stop because I was too embarrassed. Some of the photos make me cringe now, but most of them are beautiful and I'm glad that I have them. I recommend that everyone find a way to get naked in front of a camera when they're nineteen. Do it. Even if you think you're ugly. Because fifteen years later you'll look at them and realize you never were ugly at all.

I constructed an identity for myself by wedding performance art, activism, and sex work. When people asked, I said I was a feminist sex activist. I was a porn performance artist. I even went on a couple of dates with Camille Paglia because she supposedly championed the sacred whore, the sex worker as sex goddess. But I couldn't seal the deal because she was just so short and bitchy.

She stormed off in a huff and later did an interview with *Playboy*, in which she described a date almost identical to ours and said that if she had been a man, she might have stabbed a woman for teasing her like that. Camille used the treatment to which this tease subjected her as an example of how some men are provoked into justifiable violence against women. And I thought it was just a lousy date.

The performance piece I was writing kept growing and I did actually complete a few video segments of it. But, all told, the experience reminded me of a time I had helped a stripper friend of mine move a futon. As soon as I held up one corner of the futon, the other sagged to the ground. When we thought we had a good grip on it we'd walk a few steps and it would start to unravel. It took us about three hours to drag that thing ten blocks and up a flight of stairs. My theater piece was exactly like that. Every time I supported one end of it the other fell down. I knew it was no good but I had no idea how to fix it.

Penn Jillette, the taller half of the magician duo Penn & Teller, lived in the loft below Lindsay and me. Long before I ever moved in with Lindsay, Penn and I had been friends. My moving into his building was one of those small-world moments. Penn's computer-genius friend, Colin, made frequent trips up the stairs to hang out. Colin and I became, and remain, close friends. It was like living in a dorm. I'd ride the elevator down with computer problems or tuna sandwiches and then back up again to push the rug aside and get two-stepping lessons from Lindsay on the living-room floor.

"Relax that arm, princess," Lindsay would say. "Don't make me feel like I'm wrestlin' a gator."

Lindsay was like a surrogate father. He not only taught me to dance; he applied first aid to my garish fashion sense. He called my closet Victoria's Slut Closet, and routinely pointed out to me that Jackie Kennedy wouldn't be caught dead in the shoes I was wearing. I reminded him that my clothes had been bought for my career as a hooker and not as a first lady. He said that those kinds of rigid distinctions were only a failure of my imagination. I still occasionally wore trashy shoes, but Lindsay's tutelage did bring my game up dramatically. He also got me to keep the house tidy, dragged me to the gym, and encouraged me to cook meals once in a while.

Even a porn performance artist, a feminist sex activist, has to look at the facts eventually. It had been a year since I left Brunei—a year of changing my hair every month and buying sixteen pairs of boots at Barneys and a complete luggage set at Louis Vuitton (maybe not the Patti Smith–est of moves). It had been a year of cycling through designer jeans and picking up lunch tabs all over town, a year of sleeping in Pratesi sheets and cruising the flea markets for antique furniture I didn't need.

I wasn't alone in my excess. That was what all the Brunei girls did. I told myself I was practically Warren Buffet–frugal compared with them. From the occasional phone calls I got from Delia, I knew that the minute the feet of the L.A. girls hit the L.A. soil, to a man they marched to Mercedes-Benz of Beverly Hills and bought the most expensive model on the showroom floor, usually in cream with a tan interior. They all bought L.V. luggage so why shouldn't I? It was a staple, a loaf of bread, a quart of milk, right? After a year of this stupidity, the well wasn't dry yet, but I could definitely see the bottom.

The Foreman show had opened up doors for me and, if I seized my moment, there was a real chance that my acting career could take off. What would Patti Smith do? Patti Smith would step up and take what she deserved and knock everybody on their ass. They would hate her; they would love her. But they would all see her and no one would forget her.

But every time I sat down to consider my options, I was distracted and fidgety. I wasn't in the mood for seizing. I got tired and took a nap. Where had my old sense of relentless ambition gone? It had ebbed somewhere along the way. I tried to pinpoint the exact place where it had leaked out, figuring I could patch it and I'd immediately fill back up with the same drive that had kept me taking the bus into New York every Saturday all through high school in order to take acting and dance classes. When I looked, I saw there were so many holes I didn't know where to start spackling.

I was failing as an auteur. I watched hours of Amy Fisher on Court TV and took long walks up to Columbus Circle. On one of my less slothful days, I visited the Empire State Building. I could see it from my window and one morning I threw on my vintage leather coat and went to see what it looked like from the inside.

On my way to the Empire State Building, I passed by Macy's and took a sharp right turn on impulse. I went to the men's department and walked to one of the cologne counters, where I sought out a bottle of Egoiste, Robin's cologne. I picked up the bottle and sprayed it on the pulse point of each wrist, then waited until the alcohol evaporated before holding my wrist up to my nose. I felt a twinge, small but unmistakable.

At the top of the Empire State Building, I looked down through the netting meant to catch pennies and whatever else people throw. The city looked like a diabolical rat maze, covered in soot and pockmarked with potholes. I put my wrist to my nose again and thought for some reason of Robin's habit of saying "good girl" to me. It was demeaning that he'd talked to me like a five-year-old or a terrier but I had still kind of liked it. It had still felt like approval, almost like love. It had felt like a victory.

The girl I was in New York might be closer to the real me, but the girl I'd been in Brunei had been purposeful, at least. I had felt powerful. I hadn't been confronted with things like the prospect that the show I was writing was a failure. I hadn't done things like getting an abortion, like hurting someone recklessly. I hadn't succeeded at getting a good acting job and then still felt aimless. In Brunei, even if the course was hazardous, the rules were so simple, the goal so obvious.

I had also spent a big chunk of my money in the year I'd been home, and somewhere along the way, I had gotten used to that money. I had built up a world that required it, even. Sex work has many pitfalls, and this is one of them. It's the reason that the stripper putting herself through school so often turns out to be a myth.

Sure, a lot of strippers start out putting themselves through school, but school starts to lose its appeal pretty quickly. Your sociology degree doesn't qualify you for an entry-level job that can even come close to making you the kind of immediate cash with which you walk out of a club.

But it's more than the money. There's a persona you create to fill in for you on strangers' laps all day, or to lie forgotten between black silk sheets in a prince's office bedroom. This persona is sexier, bolder, wilder, and inevitably feels less pain than the real you. If she doesn't, you haven't done a very good job inventing her. So maybe you start to visit that persona once in a while when you're not at work. On weekends, you know, just when you're being socially awkward at a party, or when a friend hurts your feelings or you're out on a date and feeling vulnerable. And you find out that she helps you, that brazen stripper, that sophisticated call girl. So maybe you start to bring her out a little more often.

Sex work is dangerous work. Yes, it's dangerous for the obvious reasons. It exposes women to all kinds of exploitation by pimps and by glorified pimps dressed in suits and calling themselves club owners. It makes us an easy target for violence. It can put us at risk for contracting sexually transmitted diseases. But the subtler and more ubiquitous danger is that you won't be able to tell the difference anymore between your work persona and yourself. And that girl who wears the thong so effortlessly in public might not be the one you want making major life decisions for you. But give her an inch and you know how the rest goes. She's a stripper, after all. She'll take all she can get. It's her job.

I didn't tell myself that at the time. When I made my decision to go back to Brunei, I told myself I had spent nearly all my money and had forgotten to go to Paris. Just one more time back to Brunei and I'd do it right this time. I'd go to Paris and then I'd return and find a proper agent and in no time I'd be splashed across a marquis; I'd be a name rolling up the screen, the very top of a list of credits. I told myself, too, that I missed Robin, that I had never said a proper good-bye. In retrospect, I realize that I didn't miss Robin so much as I missed her, the girl in the penthouse suite, overlooking all of Kuala Lumpur, already a success, with nothing to do all day but dream.

Colin came upstairs from Penn's and did some last-minute tinkering on my computer as I packed. Months before, he had convinced me to get this wacky new thing called a laptop. Colin was doing his best to set up my computer so I could send e-mail from Brunei. I figured they'd probably confiscate the whole thing, but it wouldn't hurt to try.

"Do you think I'm making a mistake?" I asked Colin.

Ever the pragmatist, he replied, "No. No way. Plenty of women suffer in the suburbs their whole life for some jerkoff's money. You're just taking your punishment up front. Then you can take the money and do whatever you want. This time just figure out what that is exactly and you'll be golden."

In between our exchanges, Colin typed incredibly fast and talked on the phone to various clients at the same time.

"You know," he said. "The thing that kills me is that the Prince is purchasing so little of what he could have with you. I mean, he could say, 'Write a play by Tuesday and stage a performance of it by Friday.'"

"Not everyone wants to see my plays."

"But still, it's all that money. It makes you boring."

"That's true. It's definitely boring."

"Can you write novels in your head while you're sitting at the parties?"

I thought about it. It hadn't even occurred to me to write novels. But something about it appealed to me. It was kind of a good idea.

"I don't know. I could try. I could start with a short story."

"Try it. Write it in your head while you're at the party, then write it down and e-mail it to me when you get back to the house at night. Don't let the bastards make you boring."

The plane ascended and I watched the shining towers of my Emerald City turn into spindly toys. I set my watch ahead to Singapore time. It helps you to adjust on long plane rides if you set your watch ahead right at the beginning. All I had ever wanted my whole life was to move to New York and be an actor. And there was New York below me, growing smaller and smaller, along with my family and the friendships I had forged and the offers of real acting jobs. And somehow, I couldn't wait until it was out of sight and there was nothing but twenty hours of blue.

chapter 26

I sleepwalked through the routine: New York to Frankfurt to Singapore to the Westin Stamford and a flight into Bandar Seri Begawan the next day. Ari told me I was to meet three newbies at the Westin and we'd have an extra day to adjust in Singapore before the final leg of the trip. Because Ari couldn't come until a week later, I was meant to show them the ropes. She asked me to do her the favor of getting everyone through the airport in Bandar Seri Begawan and making sure they were all okay. She still trusted me. That was good.

Last time, I had passed out as soon as I got to the Westin. This time, I decided to be social as part of my penance for staying away so long. I went to the hotel restaurant to meet the new girls: Gina, someone forgettable, and Sheila. I watched them tally up the value of my outfit as I approached the table. The only obvious high-ticket item I wore was my handbag. I had drawers full of Chanel and Hermes bags by this point. I could have worn a new one every day of the month. But otherwise I traveled in jeans and no makeup. The girls' faces fell in disappointment when they saw me. All of them wore dresses and had faces pounded with eyeliner and lip gloss.

When I hugged them hello, I began to get a sense of what Ari had meant about things changing in Brunei. These girls were savvier than the last crop; it hung about them like a perfume cloud. They looked like they had walked out of a Rampage dressing room and they smelled like the cosmetics department at Bloomie's.

They asked about the money right away. We had barely introduced ourselves and they were falling all over each other asking how much. How much do you make a week? How much do you get altogether? Do you get jewelry? I told them what people had told me: Don't worry, you won't be disappointed.

Sheila was the most colorful of the bunch. She had a raspy voice and a ratty handbag. When she pulled out pictures of her one-year-old son, part of her purse's torn lining flapped out over the side.

"This is my son," she told us over the omnipresent plates of satay and peanut sauce. As far as I'm concerned

peanut sauce is one of Southeast Asia's great contribu-
tions to the world.

"Are you single?" she asked me, while they served
our third round of drinks.

"Yes."

"I don't know if they already told you this, but I was
a *Penthouse* Pet of the Year. I lived with the Gucciones.
The Gucciones are like my family. So I'm no stranger to
this kind of life."

"Do the Gucciones own a country?"

"I get it. You're funny. You'd love Bob junior. I'm
gonna set you up with Bob junior when you get home.
He lives in New York. You're smart like Bob junior. He'd
love you."

She regaled us with stories of the goings-on at the
Guccione indoor pool until we all called it a night.

The next day we did some bleary-eyed sightseeing.
We went to the Singapore Zoo because it's supposed to be
so humane and gorgeous and all that. We dragged around
in the steamy heat and petted baby elephants. Singapor-
eans and doughy Western tourists alike stared at Sheila's
cropped shirt and tight shorts. The other girls enjoyed the
zoo, but I couldn't; I never can. The gorillas make me so
sad, with their human hands.

When the four of us boarded Royal Brunei Airlines
the next day, I told myself that the nauseous, sinking feeling I had was the jet lag.

When we arrived at our guesthouse, I saw that Sheila,
Gina, and what's-her-name comprised only a small frac-

tion of the new bevy of beauties. Of the last crew, only Delia was still there a year later, cheerful as ever and holding tight as she quietly built her bank account and planned for the future.

Gone were the days of single rooms and unlimited phone time. There were two full houses of American girls, and Sheila and I were assigned to be roommates. In my first hour there, I already sensed the atmosphere was rowdier, more crowded, less tightly managed. I soon learned Sheila wasn't the only girl with *Penthouse* bragging rights. Playmates and pageant queens and bathing-suit models abounded. When we crowded around the marble table for lunch, I looked around and thought, Is this it? This is a big bunch of Pets and Bunnies and calendar girls, an adolescent-male fantasy come to life, and this is all there is?

They were just girls, real and flawed girls whose images had been smeared across the pages of magazines and airbrushed to look impossibly smooth and luscious. Maybe Robin thought the same thing. Maybe that's why he kept ordering up more and summarily discarding them.

This surge in the American population of the harem was the first in a series of steps indicating Robin's progressive greed and decadence. I was witnessing the very first snow flurry of the avalanche that, years later, would roll right over Robin. By the time it did, I would be long gone and reading about it in the papers. I would be sitting on a friend's couch in Los Angeles with my jaw in my lap as I watched Sheila blab to tabloid news reporters while topless pictures of me flashed across the screen, a digital smudge blurring my eyes and my boobs—an ineffective gesture toward concealing my identity.

But that day I had only an inkling of the transformation that was happening to the world inside the palace gates. It threw me off. It was a world that had seemed so tightly regimented that I had thought it would never change.

Some things did remain the same. I had been there for exactly one hour and was lying on the couch looking up at a lizard with his belly flattened against the skylight, when a guard showed up and told Delia and me to put on bikinis and go sunbathe by the upper pool. I slathered sunblock on my New York–pale skin and grabbed a towel. We zoomed up the familiar hill in the golf cart. I practically glowed purple in the afternoon glare. I looked like I was under black light.

"Where's Fiona?"

"Oh, sister. You've been gone a long time."

The story of Fiona went like this: After nearly a year of residence there, Fiona owned countless closets full of designer clothing, houses for herself and all her family back in the Philippines, and jewels to rival the Queen of England's. On Christmas, Prince Jefri gave her a present of a million dollars cash and an engagement ring. This was supposedly the brass ring for which we were all reaching. All of us but Fiona, apparently.

Fiona refused Robin's proposal and took the first plane home with her clothes, her money, and her freedom. Her betrayal had beaten Serena's by a mile. No one knew where Fiona lived or how to get in touch with her. I never saw her again, but I think of her sometimes. I think of her whenever I remember how I learned to really walk.

I chose an ivory silk minidress to wear to the party that night. Through the silk, you could see the faint outline of my nude Cosabella thong, along with the outline of my tattoo. I studied myself in the mirror and questioned my judgment for the first time since I had gotten it. I had no idea what Robin would think of it. A pussy tattoo, for God's sake—who gets one of those? What was I thinking? Would he be disgusted?

In the party room, our little dominion had become so crowded that we were forced to shove our asses together on the ottomans. We balanced on the arms of the chairs. The really petite girls could fit two to an armchair by positioning themselves on the very edge of the cushions. Our section of the room had once looked like the first-class section of a plane compared to everyone else's coach. Now we were all the same.

The new girls were curious about me for about three seconds. I had been here a whole year ago? But their attention faltered. The topic each girl seemed most interested in was herself. I couldn't figure out exactly what they were talking about at any given moment, but it was usually lively at least. Each girl generally interrupted the last by elaborating on how the previous comment applied to her.

"I had a cousin who went to a holistic nutritionist who said that carbonation causes cellulite because the air bubbles get caught in your fat cells. I wonder if this champagne counts?"

"I don't think so. Models all drink champagne and don't have cellulite."

"One time I was with Dave Navarro at the Sunset Marquis at like six in the morning and there were like four of us in his room watching like *The Doors* or something and we got baked and drank this like six-hundred-dollar bottle of Cristal and it was like so delicious."

"Did you know there was this French girl who brought pot into Singapore in her suitcase lining and she got the death penalty and all the governments tried to stop them, y'know? But they didn't care and they beheaded her anyway."

"Yeah. That's true. They're total fascists. You can't chew gum in the Singapore Airport even."

Something in me had changed. Listening to their conversation, I didn't want to strangle them. I didn't even want to strangle myself with my own purse strap. I had opted, among plenty of other choices, to come back and sit in this chair again. I was more comfortable in my cage here at the zoo than I had been in the concrete jungle. It was sobering. But it also made me more serene while the hours of my life ticked away in that room. I didn't suffer under the illusion that I had some big life to which to return. The dream of stardom that had lit my way until then was dimming, even smoldering. You could almost smell the smoke.

The hour of Robin's arrival at the party approached. I was nervous. I noticed I was hunching my shoulders, curling in around my chest as if to quiet the flutter inside. I had to consciously pull my shoulders back, cross my legs at an attractive angle, and act like I was having a good time.

The Asian girls also showed a turnover, but it wasn't as drastic as the Americans'. I was happy to see my friends Yoya, Tootie, and Lili, but even they were slightly reserved toward me. Tootie looked as ageless and wholesome as ever. Yoya had put on a few pounds around the hips but her face was more drawn, the weight redistributed from her round cheeks. I guess she was getting older. She must have been sixteen or so. She wore an orange Chanel suit, and her horsetail of a braid seemed to have stretched even longer.

When Robin did walk in, he looked exactly the same. He had those same tennis shorts, the same thick hair fussily feathered back. He strode in and said a few hellos, pointedly not looking in the direction of America-land. Behind him were Winston, Dan, Dr. Gordon, and the rest of the crew. I knew they wouldn't acknowledge me until he did. When he did look over, he caught my eye and made that exaggerated fake-surprise look.

"You're here," he said, as he took my hand and leaned to kiss me hello. The girls squashed together to make a place for him, but there was no need. He didn't sit down. The surprise act gave me a chill. It always contained a veiled implication that you had done something you weren't meant to do. I noticed that when Robin took his seat, he didn't have a girl on either his right or his left side. He briefly sat with two of his male friends before traveling around from table to table.

Eddie gave me a big hug and a hello before pulling me out of the party and leading me to a dining room where a table was set for a casual dinner, with heaping platters of food in the center and twelve place settings around the edge. Robin's friends soon came to join me, followed lastly by Robin. I sat on Robin's right while we ate and watched a big-screen TV in the corner that played a Bollywood movie with Malay subtitles. The rest of the men acted like high school boys, mercilessly teasing Dan about one of the actresses in the movie.

"He is in love with her," Robin told me.

Anyplace else, a crush on a movie star stayed in the realm of fantasy. In Brunei, I fully expected to see that actress appear a few days later, looking dazed, as if she had walked through a door in the back of a wardrobe in Mumbai and come out the other side in Brunei.

Over dinner, Robin asked me a few questions about my time at home. I emphasized how boring it had been and how much I had missed him. I said my father had been sick, which was why I'd stayed away. He made a fake sound of sympathy and then moved on. Either he was incapable of sympathy or he knew I was lying.

I don't believe in hell or punishing gods or retribution or even really in karma. But when I lie about my parents being sick, I think that some terrible judgment will probably be visited upon me. Maybe the judgment lies in the lying itself. There doesn't need to be any extra punishment beyond knowing that you're the kind of person who would lie about one of your parents having a life-threatening illness.

Without warning, Robin got up in the middle of the

weird dinner and a movie scenario and took my hand. Everybody stood as we left.

With the tattoo, I had a new shyness when I took my clothes off. Should I explain it? Should I say nothing? The biggest problem that I could see with the tattoo is that it contradicted my schoolgirl act, in which I played like I was amazed at every little thing he said. He sat on the edge of the bed in the old familiar palace bedroom while I came out of the bathroom.

"I have a little surprise."

I pulled the silky slip dress over my head.

"Very pretty," he said, and pulled me down on the bed on top of him. He hadn't batted an eyelash and I wondered why. Was it the tattooed tribes just a stone's throw away? Or was it the millions of porn films he had watched or the thousands of women he had fucked? Maybe it was just that nothing at all impressed him anymore. Maybe it was that he couldn't even see anymore because he wasn't looking. His eyes were even hungrier than when I'd last seen him.

I was literally shocked by his touch on my skin. It was as if he had been shuffling around on the carpet in his socks for an hour. I was so raw, so unpracticed. It felt like real sex with a real guy, affecting and uncomfortable. I felt my insides, my very organs curl further up inside of me for protection. It took a minute for me to remember myself, to catch myself. I had to grope around for my internal off switch. And when I found it, I was almost sad to flick it. I felt tempted for a minute to leave it on, but I imagined what Robin would do if I allowed him to see me. I had no doubt that he'd lose respect for me entirely. I'd no longer be a worthy opponent. I'd rot in a corner for the rest of my stay.

When I returned to the party, I hovered in the doorway to talk to Madge, who seemed genuinely glad to see me again, though she always maintained a perfectly cool British demeanor. She acted as if I had gone only for the weekend. When Madge was stressed, her face was like that of the Buddha himself, but her hand kept a white-knuckle grip on the walkie at her hip. She wasn't in full stress mode, but seemed to be somewhat on the alert. I asked her what was up.

"Oh, you know. Busy day, with King Hussein in town and all. Heard you met him today."

"I did?"

"Didn't you? When he was here for lunch?"

She had made the rare slip. Not that it was any big thing, but she had just let me know who had been on the other side of the window looking out at the scenery by the pool.

"Oh well," she said. "Lovely guy, that."

Welcome back to a world where there is a camera behind every mirror and a king around every corner.

chapter 27

The royal family had started using the play palace for lunches and sometimes even as guest quarters for visitors other than the Prince's girls, so there were days on end that we were told to stay inside and out of sight. Don't walk out the doors, don't go out on the balconies, and don't use the gym or the pools during the day. It was a kind of house arrest, with lots of laser discs and bubble baths and exercise videos.

My French tapes had stayed at home. It was too disheartening to stare at them on the shelf here. But I did stare at what I had brought instead—my laptop. I wasn't sure yet what kind of writing I wanted to do. Stories? Poetry? A play? I had long given up on my own performance project, so the field was wide open.

The e-mail system that Colin had set up worked perfectly. I plugged the phone line into my laptop every morning and sent the letters I had written the night before. I think I got away with it because it was so new that no one could really figure out what I was doing. If they had, I'm sure they would have stopped me.

The house arrest ruled out tennis, and the living room was crowded with yapping girls all day, so I started to hide in my bedroom, parking it on the bed and writing with my computer in my lap. I had kept journals since I was a little girl, sometimes with diligence and sometimes writing only scraps and dreams, but there was always a journal on my bedside table. In all of my big plans, I had overlooked the one thing I'd been doing consistently all along.

I decided to try journaling on the computer instead and it was my salvation. I lost myself in it. I had nowhere to go and nothing to do, so I banged out page after page of what it was like to be in Brunei. I copied my writing into e-mails that I sent to Colin. He began to do the same, writing pages describing his family's summerhouse in Canada, updating me on the family gossip, singing his girlfriend woes. These e-mails gave me something to look forward to.

I began to record conversations, details, observations. The writing gave me a reason to look hard at the world around me and suddenly I wasn't so bored. Suddenly I had a reason to be in Brunei that went beyond my distorted self-concept, my unhealthy attachment to a depraved prince, and my more easily understandable attachment to said prince's bank account.

Robin still called a girl out of the party every night and occasionally he called me, acting like everything was the same as it had been between us. I received only one daytime call. He gave me enough attention to let me know he still liked me, but not enough to put my ass back in the chair I used to sit in.

I had expected as much and it didn't really get under my skin until Gina started getting the morning knocks on her door. Gina had a plain, pretty face, like that of a homecoming runner-up from some town in Indiana. She made a point to tell me that she didn't show her titties in glossy centerfolds, but rather was a legit actress/model. Her skin wasn't great and she always either had a ton of base makeup on or was walking around the house in a mud mask. She was short, with a tiny waist and big boobs, which I guess goes a long way. Her style was appalling, sort of Talbots goes naughty. She wore things like taupe shoes that would have been good for a PTA meeting paired with a nauseating boatneck flower-print dress two sizes too tight.

I was reading at the kitchen table when she walked back in the door after having been called by Robin for the first time. She sat down next to me and I put down my book.

"Can I talk to you?" she whispered.

"Sure."

"I just went to see Robin." Her eyes glazed with tears.

Oh, please, spare me. I rubbed her back soothingly. What else are you supposed to do when a girl starts to cry? She sucked in irregular breaths.

"I didn't know where I was going and I was really surprised and. And. I know you were. Um. His girlfriend. So. I. Don't want you to get mad at me. I. Didn't know how to say. No. Are you mad?"

I assured her that I wasn't. I told her that she'd be okay and he was really cute, wasn't he? And she had probably done the same thing at home plenty of times and it hadn't even been with a prince, right? And then I heard coming out of my mouth the exact same thing Serena had said to me.

"Don't worry. He probably won't call you again."

I was wrong. He did call her again. And again and again. And there were no more tearful heart-to-hearts. She developed an all-knowing attitude with a generous helping of false modesty that really made me want to barf. It occurred to me that I was now Serena and Gina was me. I retroactively developed a new sympathy for what Serena had gone through, watching me come home every day, freshly fucked, newly wardrobed and bejeweled. It stung; there was no question. I just wasn't quite such a twat about it.

I had seen enough to know that just as surely as I had once landed on the space with the long, long ladder, I had now landed on the space with the equally long chute. I resolved to take my slide as gracefully as I could.

Everything was put on hold when Robin went on his hajj to Mecca. His hajj was big news. Each day the front page of *The Brunei Times* had a new photo of Robin in his white robes. A few of his closest friends went with him.

Pilgrimage sounded crazy holy to me; I thought Robin was many things, but holy wasn't one of them. It intrigued me. I had been in Brunei during Ramadan and I knew that the men fasted during the day, so their religious beliefs weren't a complete ruse. Was this pilgrimage just something Robin had to do for his public image or did it hold real meaning for him? I wondered what Robin prayed for. I wondered what he really believed in. Did he believe in Allah? Did he believe in anything?

He and I had actually talked pretty freely and to that end I had kept myself conversant in politics and finance and British royal gossip, but faith had never come up. Did he pray for a good night's sleep? Did he pray for a real friend, a friend he didn't have to pay for? And me, what did I pray for?

While he was gone the parties still went on, but they were shorter. Prince Sufri had fallen in love with a Malaysian girl who was a student in London. He told me he was going to propose to her and he seemed delighted about the whole thing. He made a few attempts to get interested in badminton again, but his heart wasn't in it and we all got to go home early.

Before I returned to Brunei, I had made repeated

vows to stay sober. I had vowed to quit alcohol and everything else that was bad for me, including sugar and caffeine. I wrote out a long contract with myself to that effect. But once I got there, one by one the bricks that made up my wall of resolve tumbled. In a matter of weeks I was drinking every night and back on the diet pills. That contract was the first of my many failed attempts to control my substance abuse. I told myself it was the fault of my circumstances. If I was going to quit anything, it wasn't going to be in Brunei.

Robin was on his hajj and I was on the anti-hajj. Delia and I danced together every night, acting totally stupid and laughing like crazy, jitterbugging and salsa-dancing to hip-hop with our Thai friends. Delia's favorite song was "Just Wanna Be Your Friend." Anthony played it at least twice a night and it became a kind of informal "Time Warp" or something, with everyone acting out the words and joining in, shouting certain lines, like *I'm so HORNY*.

Delia's and my inebriation often led to one of us practically carrying the other home. One night, a misstep at the top of the stairs sent us tumbling end over end all the way to the bottom. Luckily, the staircases in the palace were all covered in plush carpeting and had a shallow incline. We both landed with our dresses over our heads The entire party nearly died with laughter.

Every night I drank and drove. Thankfully it was only a golf cart. One night I stomped on the accelerator rather than the brake and slammed the cart into the back wall of the garage. I pitched forward and smacked my nose into the rear-view mirror. My nose wasn't broken, but it was swollen and cut and looked terrible. I was grateful that Robin was out of town while it healed.

My perpetual intoxication did have one positive result. One drunken night, I broke down and sobbed on the shoulder of a *Penthouse* Pet, a big-assed blonde with dusty green eyes, named Melody. This particular Pet also wore a promise ring supposedly from Vince Neil (same Vince Neil as Brittany, different promise ring) and talked constantly into a micro-cassette recorder because she was working on a book titled *The Way I See It*, meant to share her wisdom about life, both humorous and otherwise. She never wrote it. I've heard that instead she wound up devoting her life to Jesus.

It was the week before my birthday. Birthdays have never been my favorite thing. I hear it's a common experience among adopted children. All the party girls tried to plan it so they'd be in Brunei for their birthday because birthdays meant jewelry, but the prospect of jewelry wasn't enough to keep me from heading for a birthday meltdown. Between the Prince's rejection and the drinking, I wasn't doing so well. I wasn't taking my slide gracefully, as I had vowed to do. I had become that girl who gets drunk and cries at parties.

"I'm not going to be a teenager anymore. And what have I accomplished? I don't want to live my whole life drinking diet shakes and quitting everything I start."

The girls who were approaching thirty rolled their eyes as I gave Melody the rundown on all the travails of the past year. I don't remember what was said exactly, but

I do know that during the conversation, I must have mentioned my unfruitful search for my birth mother, because Melody shared her wisdom with me (both humorous and otherwise) and it included the name and phone number of a private investigator in Denver.

I woke with the information on my nightstand. I was mortified that I had poured my heart out to Melody, far more so than I had been of winding up at the bottom of a staircase with my skirt over my head. Even so, I took that slip of paper and stuck it in a book for later. You never know when you're going to need the name of a private investigator in Denver, written in bubbly handwriting with hearts dotting the *i*'s.

chapter 28

While Robin was gone, the sky cracked open and rained down storm after storm, wild and biblical, reminding me that beyond those palace walls was Borneo, an island of rainforests and underground rivers and famous caves. The monsoons beat at the bedroom windows, insisting that there was a world beyond our jewelry box rooms. It was during the start of the rainy season that I decided to try my hand at writing more than a journal entry.

Rain pounded the skylights above me as I finished

my first, terrible short story and sent it to Colin. He responded in kind and we began to send stories back and forth. At first, I sent them with a prologue of apologies for the horrors contained within, until Colin wrote that he refused to accept any stories that I prefaced with self-deprecating remarks. He told me that even when I did things poorly, I should do them without apology.

The first story was about a girl who had to go with her mother to pack up the china in her dead grandmother's house. The story was based on the time I went with my mother to pack up the china in my dead grandmother's house. The second story was about a stripper who sold her soul to Satan to have her own show in Las Vegas. It was a metaphor for something but I can't remember what.

While I was busy writing and the Prince was busy on his hajj in Mecca, a new lounge singer, named Iyen, showed up. She was a pretty Filipino girl with a fondness for *I Dream of Jeannie* ponytail falls and gauzy harem pants. When Robin returned, he fell in love with her at first sight. By the end of two weeks, she wore a ring on her finger the size of Brunei itself. I've tried to find out if they ever tied the knot, and if so, if they are still together, but there is a shroud of mystery around how many wives the Prince actually has, and which of them are "official." According to one former *Washington Post* reporter I talked to, the number appears to far exceed the permitted four.

Robin was pleasant to me and when he sat to talk to me there was no buried ire left in his manner. I no longer feared his retribution. I had gone from being spoiled to

being punished to being common. That was when I knew
I had landed at the bottom of the chute with a thud.

Robin did sleep with me a few more times, fiancé
or no, and he even took me for a spin in his new Aston
Martin one night, but the charge between us was gone. A
feeling of resignation hung around the girls. The Prince
was in love. There was a change in him. He rarely even
came inside the parties other than to hear Iyen sing. The
two of them sat out on the stairs talking all night while
inside we would make fun of her outfits, imagining our
taste incredibly sophisticated due to our hours and hours
of watching *Style with Elsa Klensch*. And we would wonder
how, when we were so stylish, so expensively attired, so
coiffed, so fucking slim, the Prince had chosen a chubby,
fashion-challenged lounge singer over us.

I spent my twentieth birthday in Brunei and I got
not one but two more incredible watches dropped in my
lap by Eddie. After my official birthday party, my housemates and I hung around in our nighties and had a little
birthday party of our own back at the guesthouse, with a
cake and champagne brought over from the main palace
by a small parade of smiling servants. I was no longer an
anathema, because I no longer mattered. At least I got to
have friends. But in truth, I preferred having power.

My friend Donna, a gorgeous Filipino-American
kickboxer and model, held up her champagne flute and
did her best Ricardo Montalban accent: "Welcome to
Fantasy Island," she said, "where all your dreams come
true. Kind of."

❖   ❖   ❖

I had a hard time sleeping. I started writing every night from the end of the parties until sunrise, when the first light touches that part of the world in a hundred shades of luminous blue and purple, clear and full of hope.

I wrote to Colin that I just wanted to want something. I had stopped wanting anything and I felt a terrible hole where I had once had purpose. He responded in an e-mail:

> When I climbed into an inflatable kayak at the beginning of some rapids up in Canada, I turned to my brother and asked, "Does it look like I'm going to die?" He said, "No, it looks like it's going to be fun. From here, it doesn't even look all that scary."
>
> Well, from here it looks like you're going to want something real soon. Send another story.

Four months and five stories later, I left for New York again. I left with a fatter envelope than I had before and with the kind of jewels that should come with their own bodyguard. There is something about that kind of hard, cold, sparkling sign language for power that even I, quasi-socialist sometime-vegetarian artist—even I wanted to hold up and shout, *"Look motherfuckers: I have treasure from a prince. I am beautiful."* But treasure loses its power as an ego boost pretty quickly and becomes just another watch, another pair of earrings, jewelry so gaudy it looks like you probably bought it at Patricia Field.

Eventually the jewels lose their sentimental value entirely and you wind up selling them to an estate-jewelry buyer in a second-floor office in the diamond district. As you sit across the small table and watch the little old man who sounds like your Uncle Leon examine your jewelry with a tiny telescope, you think of what your grandmother used to say to you when you waited until the last minute to write your English paper: *Pressure makes diamonds*.

I didn't exactly know that it was going to be my last time in Brunei. But I had an intuitive flicker of resolution as I said good-bye to Robin. I looked at him hard, memorizing his face. What if I never saw him again?

I had made the most un-Patti of choices. Even with the freest, most punk fairy godmother of them all, I had wound up a well-paid piece of property—only a rental property, but still, I had severed the connection between my soul and my body so profoundly that I could barely feel my own skin anymore. If I never saw Robin again, maybe I'd be free to return to myself. I knew I was facing a long road back.

chapter 29

I t took the investigator about two weeks to locate my birth mother. In Carrie's first letter to me, she sent pictures of her family. In their holiday photo, her husband is a tall, balding, kind-eyed man in thick glasses. You can see that the older, teenage daughter has special needs. The younger one, probably around six years old, is a round-faced, pretty Latina girl. The letter told me that they were both adopted.

Carrie looks intrepid and sturdy, with no lipstick on her no-nonsense smile. The four of them stand in matching Christmas sweaters in front of an aluminum-sided house, hardened patches of gray snow scattered around the dead lawn behind them. They are one of those Midwestern families you'd pass right by at Disney World.

I inserted myself into the picture. Who would I have been if I had returned from high school every day to that little house? I imagined it like a high school movie, in which the main character has pictures of pop stars tacked to her wall and blue ribbons pinned around the edge of her vanity mirror. She lies on the bed talking to her best friend on the phone while her feet rest up on the headboard. The whole scene is washed in buttery sunshine. I knew it was ridiculous, embarrassing, but I indulged myself with imagining for a moment a world in which there could have been a possibility for me other than the one I was living, a world in which maybe I'd have been equipped to make some better choices.

Carrie sent other pictures also, color photocopies with her own captions penciled in below them. Most of them were from *The Cross and the Sword*, performed at a regional theater in Jacksonville in 1972, which is where she met my birth father, Jim.

I did find some pictures of your birth father. I always thought you'd be lucky if you got his looks—not that I'm complaining about mine.

In my favorite photo, Jim is at center stage in a heroic stance. He has long, wavy seventies hair tucked behind his ears and he wears a Renaissance Faire–looking outfit. Carrie is on one end of the line of dancers behind him. She has a wreath of flowers in her hair and is wearing a wide skirt and a peasant blouse. She is down on one knee, holding a tambourine in the air, and looking up at him.

They are both so pretty, but he is even prettier than she is. In her letter, Carrie tells me that Jim was a talented actor and a poet. To me, he looks like a shifty hustler. I can see it in the eyes. I look a lot like Carrie around the nose and mouth, but my eyes are strictly Jim.

Heritage? I guess primarily white Anglo-Saxon Protestant. I believe Jim was of English heritage. My mother's maiden name was MacDowell—Scotch. I'm a mixture of Scotch, German, and I think Irish.

I've always thought I look Jewish—New York Jewish, Russian Jewish. That is what I say when people ask me my ethnicity. I'm a Russian Polish Jew. When I recently told this to my Russian manicurist, she nodded her head and said, "I knew it."

I was extremely independent and found it easier to deal with things myself. As a young adult, I was not easily fulfilled with what I was doing and kept looking for more out of life. I guess that wasn't too unusual in the sixties and seventies . . . I guess a lot of the old ideas are still somewhere within me. You've reminded me of a lot of the old feelings and ideals as I've been digging through old pictures and papers.

In this, it seemed, I resembled Carrie far more than I did my adoptive parents, who had closed the shutters and sat out the sixties as if it were a hurricane.

Carrie's letters were written on six-by-nine white, lined paper, with a slightly serrated edge at the top—practical, not a theatrical flourish to be detected. She wrote her letters to her long-lost biological daughter on a kitchen notepad.

Of course I've thought about you often. I had wondered lately what contacts I could make to make finding me easier if that's what you wanted to do. I hope I can give you whatever you want or need. I hate the stories of adopted people who are so desperately in search of their birth mother. I always hoped you would have a happy, fulfilled life without me.

Was I desperately in search of her? Not exactly. But something. I was desperately in search of something and she was a part of that something.

Carrie's letters recounted a young woman's wanderings from a middle-class childhood in Bellevue, Nebraska, to a short stint at the University of Utah to a dance career in Chicago to a show in Florida, then back to Chicago, where she got into some trouble with the wrong guy at the wrong time, then back to Nebraska, where she got married and finished college, and finally to the suburbs of Boise, Idaho, where she worked as a medical technician and a dance teacher and eventually adopted two daughters of her own.

She seemed intelligent and sane. Not trashy, not crazy, just a woman who had once been restless, had once been confused.

Did you plant your garden? I asked in my letters to her. *Did you ever wind up getting the kite with two strings up in the air?*

Lindsay and Colin sat by my side on the black leather couch in our loft when I called Carrie to ask her to come visit me in New York. I figured I was ready to put one chapter of this story to bed and to open another one. What would Patti Smith do? She would look the truth in the eye and never once would she blink.

I have stood at the arrival gate at Newark International Airport maybe a hundred times in my life, but picking up Carrie is the most memorable.

Seared into my brain is the image of her as she moved toward me down that long hallway with her matter-of-fact walk. She was sweet-faced and big-hipped like me, wearing high-waisted jeans and a plaid flannel. We greeted each other with tight smiles. I believe that both our faces were laced with some regret that we had ever made those plans to meet. It had seemed like a good idea at the time, but the execution of it was suddenly too sharp, too bright, like walking out of a dark room into the sunshine.

It was an awkward and tense reunion, but my birth mother is a tough woman. She shed exactly one tear, apologizing as she wiped it away. I am taller than Carrie. As we waited at baggage claim, she told me that I had my birth father's eyes. I already knew this from the pictures she had sent. I kept those eyes trained on the baggage carousel, pretending to be searching hard for her luggage even though I didn't know what it looked like.

Later she told me more about Jim, about the two of them, as we sat on high stools eating Chinese food in the kitchen that doubled as Lindsay's sewing room. I felt strange and out of proportion. I was tiny in the tall-ceilinged room; I was huge next to my petite mother. My hands looked embarrassingly big and masculine to me, wrapped around the chopsticks. My eyes felt swollen and tired and were suddenly sinking shut.

"We were in love. He followed me back to Chicago after the show," she said.

She lit up when she talked about him, even after all the years in between, all the pain he had caused her.

"He was very good-looking, very charismatic. He was trying to act in Chicago and we lived in a studio apartment. We struggled. I remember that Jim broke his leg and he had this huge cast on it and we got in a fight. It was snowing out, a blizzard, and he dragged himself down the street through the snow. I got in the car and skidded along behind him, hollering at him to get in."

I laughed.

"I lodged the car in a snowbank and we both had to walk home."

Then she got vague. I wasn't sure if I was disappointed or relieved that she traded her frankness for fog. Hearing her talk about my birth father and their time together had the uncomfortable scrape of talking to your parents about sex. You want to be one of those cool mom/daughter teams that talk freely about everything— best friends. But you're not. In this case we weren't even talking about sex. And this wasn't even my mother, really. But I still had an instinctive aversion to the subject matter.

"There's a lot I don't remember. I'm sorry. I think I blocked it. I had fantasies of raising you but trust me, a long-term relationship with Jim would have been a disaster. Anyway, he left. He left before you were born."

The story she told lasted through dinner and fortune cookies. It was a good story, but it felt unrelated to me. At the same time, I recognized it was the story I had been waiting to hear all my life. Here it was. I was finally hearing it. I was finally looking at another person in the world who looked like me. It was odd, off. Something in me blanched. I couldn't relax around Carrie.

I don't remember much of what we did that week, except that we hung out a lot with Lindsay and Colin. Carrie met the various friends who cycled through our loft. She was interested in everyone to whom she was introduced and she seemed comfortable with herself, even in a world of theater hipsters and art queens. I was so relieved. I guess I had been worried about what I'd find, worried that in her I'd discover some deep indictment of my character.

We went to Central Park and to the Met. We met Carrie's Rockette friend, a lithe blond woman in her early forties. I learned that the Rockettes is where ballerinas go to die. Apparently, aging dancers from all over the country travel to New York to do the Christmas show. It's run like a military operation, and being a Rockette is practically a nationality all its own. Carrie's friend was in town to weigh in, brush up, and take some classes.

Like nearly every child within driving distance of Manhattan, I had seen the Rockettes many times. I mostly remember their furry hats and their long, long legs moving as one lovely machine. It was so satisfying to the human eye, the homogeneous herd of women and the kaleidoscopic patterns their bodies sketched in space. It was glamorous to meet a Rockette wearing sweatpants in the park. We had tea—black, no sugar—and watched the remote-control boats zoom around Conservatory Water.

Planning to join Carrie for dinner after a dance class that she had decided to drop in on, I walked to Columbus Circle and met her at Steps. Steps is where all the kids from the Broadway shows take their classes. I'm an okay dancer and can usually hold my own, but the Steps dancers are vicious. I have sat in the back stairwell of the school numerous times and wept into my sweaty jazz shoes, thinking: I'm too fat; I'm too slow with choreography; I lose count. And, most damning: I'm too lazy. I could have been so much better if I had just tried harder, if I had just paid more attention in class when I was young, if I didn't always quit the minute things got hard.

"Ballerinas have long, thin necks like swans," my father had often said. He didn't need to complete the thought. Ballerinas were born swans. I could see as well as anyone that I was a duck. I would have to learn to take solace in the fact that water ran off my back.

I arrived at Steps early and tried to stay out of sight while I watched Carrie's class through the window that overlooked the studio. She was in an advanced-level jazz class, one I would never even attempt. In spite of her age, her now-un-dancerly physique, and her one leg perpetually swollen due to a bout with skin cancer that had necessitated the removal of her lymph node—in spite of all this, she was stunning out there. She had that special thing.

When her group took the floor, I saw the normally snotty dancers on the sidelines, all of them twenty years younger than she, watching her with respect. The teacher flashed her a smile. She was alive, electric. She was better than all of them. When class ended, a small cluster of dancers gathered around her. They lingered, talking while the people taking the next class trickled in.

I, of all people, who had always found a home in my group of outlandish and uncompromising friends, knew that there were many ways to make a family. And I knew that my parents, my real parents, lived in New Jersey and loved me like crazy, if poorly at times. But standing behind the glass at Steps was the first time I felt a flash of anger. I wished for a moment that Carrie had been a little less selfish, a little more together, had loved me just a little more. If she had stuck around, I might have danced like that. Or that is what I wanted to think. But I didn't dance like that. And frankly I was sick of wishing that I did.

I sat at the Newark airport for a long time after Carrie left. I parked myself in front of the wide panes of glass and watched the planes take off and land and take off again. I was only twenty, the age Carrie had been when she put me up for adoption. And when I chronicled my list of outrageous fuckups in the preceding couple of years, when I visited my dismal graveyard of buried aspirations, when I looked at all I had trampled, I was forced to forgive her.

❖   ❖   ❖

Fifteen years later I lay on the couch of a beachfront apartment with the windows open and the sea breeze blowing through. My husband and I sat there in the darkening room, watching the sea suck up the last of the pale sunlight. Patti Smith was performing on the Santa Monica pier, seven stories below, but we couldn't go to the show because I was on bed rest after my in-vitro procedure that day. I had my doubts that it would work and I was right. But I never doubted that we would have a child somehow, a child who would break our hearts wide open, who would help us to grow in compassion.

Patti's voice was unshakable after all those years. The music was muted by the space between us, by the wind, but I could still make out the words.

I have the answer now, I believe. What would Patti Smith do? She would sing to me. She would forgive me for losing myself.

epilogue

It's been seventeen years since I first stepped onto the plane headed for Singapore.

I left New York for San Francisco soon after I returned from Brunei, and I never did make it back. Leave New York and it leaves you behind so quickly. New York is like the lover you leave, the one who still somehow retains the upper hand for the rest of your life. When you pass him on the street, you will recognize him before he recognizes you. You will have to decide whether or not to call out, It's me. It's Jill. You will read his name in the paper and your body will remember.

You will watch on television as thick pillars of black smoke rise into the air and you will remember New York, like someone just ran a plane into your heart. But New York, even at its moment of greatest pain, will not remember you. And though I like my view so much better since I left, it sometimes still smarts when I realize I've been forgotten.

I am married now, entrenched in a three-bedroom life, my mornings spent drinking green tea and looking out my picture window at the lush camphor trees and the purple-frosted jacarandas that line my suburban California street. When I pause, I sometimes feel an unfamiliar emotion flickering somewhere in the periphery of my consciousness. It's there for a moment and then it's gone. It takes a moment for me to locate a name for it. I believe it may be happiness.

As I wind further into this forest of domesticity, the dense sleeves of tattoos on my arms hint at another life to my neighbors. They look at me strangely when I stop by with homemade Christmas cookies, knowing somehow that the picture is skewed. And when, at cocktail parties, I drop hints of my former sordid self, they look at me and laugh, unsure if I'm joking.

I'm sure Robin is also leading a life he never expected. In 1997, a former Miss USA filed a ninety-million-dollar lawsuit against him claiming he drugged and raped her and held her as a sex slave against her will. The charges were dismissed based on his diplomatic immunity, but it was an international embarrassment. Not long after, Prince Jefri and the Sultan parted ways after Jefri was accused of embezzling about thirty billion dollars.

The case has been in and out of court and many of Prince Jefri's holdings have been seized and sold at auction. Most recently, he failed to appear to answer contempt charges at the High Court of England; there is currently a warrant out for his arrest. I follow his travails with some interest, wondering what he'll do now and what's going to happen to his wives and children.

As for me, I'm about to take another long plane ride. A few days ago I received a call from our adoption agency saying that our son had made it through court in Ethiopia and that our travel date had been confirmed. I have a ten-month-old son whom I'll meet for the first time in two weeks. I have seen pictures of him, so I know that he has huge chocolate eyes and is beautiful beyond measure.

Though he isn't here yet, I still open his green gingham curtains every morning. I stand looking out the window, imagining what it will look like to my son, whose landscape now is so different. My son, who is about to travel so far for such a little boy. We'll both have traveled so far to find each other.

The story of Scheherazade is the story of the storyteller. We hope the story we tell will be the story that saves our lives.

My son's name is Tariku. In Amharic it means "his story," or "you are my story."